SOUTH WEST BRITAIN

Already Published

VIKING AGE SCULPTURE in Northern England   Richard N. Bailey
MATHEMATICS IN ARCHAEOLOGY   Clive R. Orton
THE ARCHAEOLOGY OF THE WELSH MARCHES   S. C. Stanford
GLASS   Ruth Hurst Vose

Some Forthcoming Titles

THE HISTORIC ENVIRONMENT   David Baker
HOUSES   R. W. Brunskill
CHURCH ARCHAEOLOGY   Ann Hamlin
THE FLOATING FRONTIER   Mark Hassall
PREHISTORIC AND ROMAN AGRICULTURE   Peter Reynolds
SETTLEMENT IN BRITAIN   Christopher Taylor

COLLINS ARCHAEOLOGY

THE ARCHAEOLOGY OF
SOUTH WEST BRITAIN

SUSAN M. PEARCE

COLLINS
St James's Place, London
1981

William Collins Sons & Co. Ltd
London · Glasgow · Sydney · Auckland
Toronto · Johannesburg

First published 1981
© Susan M. Pearce 1981
ISBN 0 00 216219 9
Phototypeset in Linotron 202 Bembo by
Western Printing Services Ltd, Bristol
Made and Printed in Great Britain by
William Collins Sons & Co. Ltd Glasgow
Distributed in the United States,
Canada and Mexico by
Humanities Press Inc.

CONTENTS

PLATES

FIGURES

INTRODUCTION

The past is closer to us than we sometimes think. Given that three human generations flourish within each hundred-year span, only fifty-eight forefathers need separate us from the Roman army of invasion. Only ninety may separate us from the farmers of the Bronze Age, and even the last Palaeolithic hunters are only four hundred or so generations behind us.

This book tries to tell the story of the people who have lived in the changing landscape of the south-western peninsula. I have defined the peninsula as the region lying west of a line drawn from Brean Down along the western rim of the Mendips, and continuing to the south coast at the mouth of the River Brit. This area is bounded by the sea on three sides, and to its east lie the great belts of limestones and chalk. A small part of western Dorset falls within the boundary, but in the main I have omitted this, because it belongs with the story of Wessex.

Archaeology has taken immense strides since Hencken[1] and Fox[2] published their classic works on the south west. The results of environmental studies are now giving us, for the first time, a hope of understanding ancient landscapes. Most excavations now include a programme of pollen analysis since surviving ancient pollen can tell us a great deal about early environments. Similar studies can be carried out with land snail and insect remains, as the various species of these creatures have distinct environmental preferences. Work on animal bones from human settlements can provide fascinating information on the management of flocks and herds, the changes brought about by human breeding control and the age of slaughter; human remains can tell us about disease, life expectancy and population levels. The techniques of petrological analysis have opened whole vistas of human trade and exchange. Insights from the disciplines of anthropology and geography are aiding our evaluation of ancient societies. Radio carbon dating has given us, again for the first time, the chance of building up an independent chronology.★

In addition to this new knowledge, the tremendous acceleration of field work and data collection has shown us a land much more densely and elaborately settled, especially in the period after 2000 BC, than most archaeologists contemplated ten years ago. Interpretations of the past in the light of a few classic excavations, like that at Hembury in east Devon, no longer seem adequate in the face of this rich variety, but new classification has not always proved easy.

Fashions in archaeological interpretation constantly come and go. Changes in human society used to be attributed to invaders or immigrants who brought new technology and new ideas and who often established themselves as a 'ruling class'. Since the publication of an influential paper by Clark in 1966,[3] British archaeologists have tended to relate change to economic and other factors within the body of the native society, without reference to outside stimulation. Our understanding of the 'Beaker People', and of the course of later prehistory, has been most profoundly affected; nevertheless there remain some problems, and perhaps, as so often happens, a compromise may eventually emerge as the most workable view. One result of all this archaeological effort is the recurrent need to gather together every decade or so the main features of each region's history.

In this account of the archaeology of south west Britain I have adopted a broadly chronological approach because I believe that a general narrative works best in this form, even though it runs the risk of suggesting that the continuous past can be crudely divided into separate sections. Sadly, much interesting material has had to be omitted. In many cases the distribution maps do not pretend to be complete, although I think that they give a fair indication of broad trends. I have simplified complicated issues to the best of my ability, without, I hope, unduly distorting them. The tedious repetition of qualifying words and phrases has been kept to a minimum but the reader is advised to keep them constantly in mind.

A book like this owes an enormous debt to the published work, and to the kindness, of friends and colleagues. I am especially grateful to Paul Bidwell who commented on an early draft of Chapter 4, to Tom Greeves who did the same for Chapter 7, and to Tim Padley who

★ The problems of radio carbon dating are discussed in a later section. In this book, I have cited radio carbon dates with the conventional signs bc and ad, and real year dates with BC and AD. In many places I have attempted to give an estimated real date in the belief that this is helpful, but I must stress that these dates are to be taken only as broad indications.

read the whole text. Help with photographs was generously given by Mrs P. Christie, Professor Charles Thomas, Mr S. Timms, Dr G. Wainwright, Mr L. Douch, Dr E. Maltby, Miss F. Griffith, Mr J. Bosanko, Mr D. Austin, Mr P. Beecham, Mr N. Johnson, Mr R. Silvester, Mr B. Cooper, Mr S. Minnett, Mr R. Penhallurick, and all those acknowledged separately. Above all, my thanks go to Belinda McCarter, who prepared the typescript, to Jeff Bennett, who prepared the drawings, to Cherry Lavell and Eric Wood for their helpful comments, to my Director, Stephen Locke, for his encouragement, and to my husband for his unflagging support.

Susan M. Pearce

1. *Hencken 1932*
2. *Fox 1964*, second edition 1973
3. *Clark 1966*

CHAPTER ONE

Figures in a Landscape

The peninsula

The south-western peninsula is a long crooked finger of land bounded by the sea on all sides save the east, stretching some 257 km (160 miles) into the Atlantic. A further 42 km (26 miles) beyond Land's End lie the Isles of Scilly, now an archipelago but probably, until the early medieval period, one large island embracing most of the present islands.[1] Although remote from most of Britain, the peninsula is uniquely centred in the sea routes which run between Ireland, south Wales, Brittany, and the Channel coasts.

The backbone of the peninsula is a major granite formation which emerges as six massifs, the mainland areas of Dartmoor, Bodmin Moor, the Hensbarrow or St Austell Moors, Carnmenellis, and Penwith, and Scilly offshore (*fig 1·1*). At its highest point, High Willhayes on northern Dartmoor, the granite rises to 622 m, and Brown Willy on Bodmin Moor reaches 421 m. Dartmoor and Bodmin Moor constitute expanses of true upland, a character shared to a certain extent by the other granite regions. Today they are all heathery moorland with wide horizons in fair weather, harsh alike in summer heat and winter mist. Above all, these same uplands and their fringes carry a concentration of mineral wealth, of tin, copper, and granite-derived clays, which is unrivalled in north-western Europe and which has left an unmistakable stamp upon the rhythm of life in the peninsula.

In contrast, Exmoor, which rises to 520 m at Dunkery Beacon, is based on sandstones, slates and limestones. Between the uplands the countryside is softer. Rich, deep grass grows from the famous Devon soil, red always and almost purple after rain. Sizeable hilly areas make up the Haldon and Raddon Hills near the Exe Valley, the Blackdowns in east Devon, the Quantocks east of Exmoor, and the Mendips beyond the Somerset Levels. There are high gorse-covered plateaux

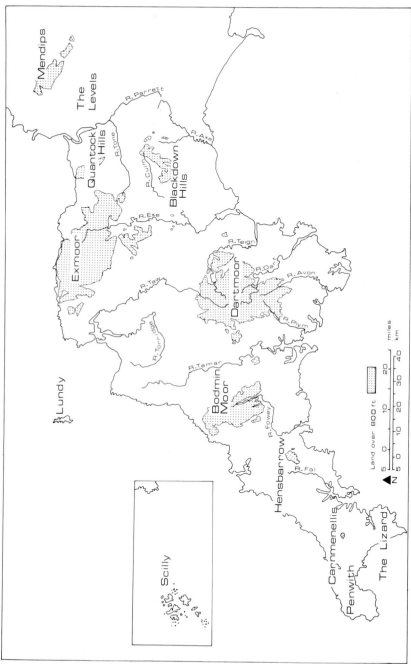

Fig. 1·1 Physical features of the region.

Approx dates B.C.	British sequence	Alpine Glacials
8,300	Flandrian–'postglacial'	
70,000	Devensian–glaciation	Würm
125,000	Ipswichian–interglacial	
c. 200,000	Wolstonian–glaciation	Riss
c. 250,000	Hoxnian–interglacial	
c. 350,000	Anglian–glaciation	Mindel
?	Cromerian–interglacial	
	Beestonian–glaciation	Günz

Fig 1·2 Sequence of British glacial and interglacial periods with possible Alpine equivalents. The dates given earlier than the Devensian should be regarded as highly tentative (*source: Mellars 1974, Table 2*).

on the Lizard peninsula, behind Hartland Head, and around Woodbury Common in east Devon, where the chalk makes its westernmost appearance at Beer Head. In the main the peninsula is composed of ancient rocks, and the younger chalk of east Dorset and the limestone of the Mendips form its natural eastern rim.

Although its fabric is geologically ancient, however, the present shape of the peninsula with its indented coastline, deep short river valleys, and superficial cover of soils, together with the extreme contrasts it shows within relatively small areas, has been formed during the last 700,000 years. Analysis of long core sequences taken from the sea bed suggests that a series of eight glaciations when the northern polar ice cap advanced, and eight interglacials when the climate grew warmer, took place during the Pleistocene or earlier part of this period (*fig 1·2*). Each glaciation itself involved more severe periods and warmer periods, known as stadials and interstadials. By about 8500 bc★ the ice retreated, and the climate quickly became much milder, although subject, during the following post-glacial period and the period in which we now live, to various oscillations of great importance to man.

The south-western peninsula seems to have been just south of the permanent ice sheets, except perhaps during the penultimate glaciation peaking around 200,000 bc when the north coastal area may have been under ice. However, throughout the whole sequence of glaciations the West Country constituted a fringe, or periglacial, zone. The

★ See footnote on page xiv.

19

land was subject to freeze/thaw processes which left boulder clay deposits, splintered the rocks, and created the weathered clitter fields and denuded tors so characteristic of the granite uplands. Ancient beaches now well away from the sea like that at Penhill, north Devon, the 'submerged forests' of preserved tree fragments now below the tide line at Westward Ho!, and marine flooding in the Somerset Levels, all result from variations in sea levels caused by the freezing or freeing of large bodies of water. The sudden and dramatic rise in sea level which occurred about 5500 bc drowned the land bridge to the continent, and the previously extensive coastal flats in the Bristol Channel and North Sea regions. This is of crucial importance in our understanding of the movement and social organization of early human groups.

Lower Palaeolithic hunters

The earliest flint tools so far to appear in Britain are those from the recently discovered bone cave above Westbury-sub-Mendip in Somerset,[2] which, judging by the accompanying fauna, belong within hitherto unrecognized warm and cold stages around the end of an early glaciation which peaked about 400,000 bc. Old tool finds from the lowest levels in Kent's Cavern, Torquay, may belong to the same horizon. However, abundant evidence of hominids does not appear until the Great or Hoxnian interglacial, around 250,000 bc, when a forest rich in lime trees was browsed by varieties of elephant, rhinoceros and deer.

The evidence is not easy to interpret for reasons which are well illustrated at the important east Devon site of Broom. Broom is a series of gravel deposits, developed as quarries during the nineteenth century, which accumulated during the glacial period by the activities of the local water flow now represented by the River Axe. This site has produced several thousand tools of the local toffee-coloured chert, including pear-shaped hand axes, narrow cleavers, and oval forms sometimes worked with a 'twist' along their length (fig 1·3). Unfortunately, in most cases the record is insufficient to establish which tools came from which deposit. Equally, no scientific excavation has been possible at sites now largely destroyed, and valuable information about the contexts of the tools has been lost. The surviving tools were gathered selectively by collectors who wanted fine cabinet specimens rather than a representative assemblage, and therefore the original balance of implement types and waste material is uncertain.

Similar hand axes have also been found in the lowest deposits at

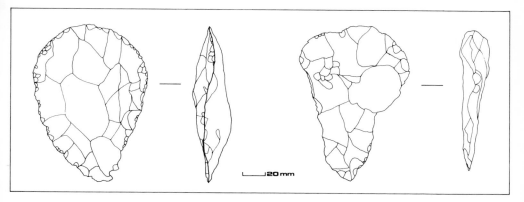

Fig 1·3 Hand axes from Broom, east Devon. The profile of the axe shows the oval twist (*Exeter City Museum*).

Kent's Cavern and nearby in Brixham Cave. The finds are concentrated in the lower valleys of the Axe, the Otter, and the Exe. As the climate deteriorated again with the renewed advance of the ice, new improved tool types appear, in the form of flakes which were struck from the parent stone and then re-touched. This development must have been stimulated by the demands of an increasingly difficult environment. More than a thousand tools of this type have been found in Kent's Cavern.

The Lower (Early) Palaeolithic families who made these tools supported themselves by hunting the large woodland species and gathering roots, nuts and berries. Their sites tend to cluster around substantial bodies of water, suggesting not only considerable exploitation of fish, but also major kills organized at watering holes. Evidence from modern hunter-gatherer bands suggests that game may have been a primary source of food in the colder periods, while during the warmer phases vegetable foods may have assumed a greater importance. We are still ignorant of the social patterns which such changes would involve, yet these patterns lie at the very roots of subsequent human development.

Upper Palaeolithic hunters

Little is known of human activity in Britain after this for a substantial period, but the picture fills out again during the last glaciation, which began around 70,000 bc and involved a sequence of colder stadials and warmer interstadials. Some heart-shaped hand axes and related, or slightly later, stone work belonging to the continental Mousterian

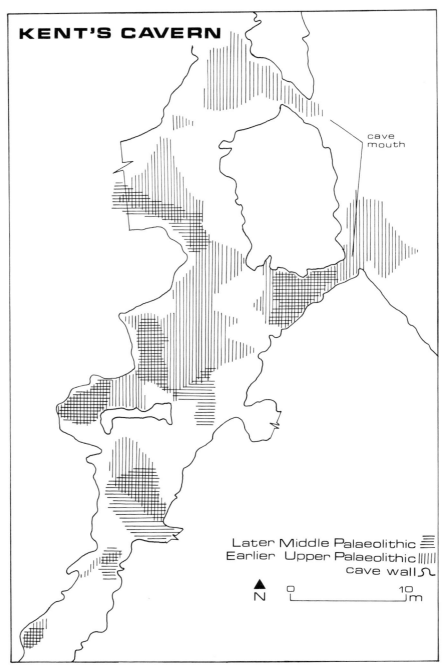

KENT'S CAVERN

cave mouth

Later Middle Palaeolithic
Earlier Upper Palaeolithic
cave wall

N

0   10
           m

tradition and dating to an early stage in the glaciation have been found at Kent's Cavern (*fig 1.4*), and Wookey Hole, Somerset.

Apart from these, it seems clear that there are two major phases of Upper (Later) Palaeolithic occupation in Britain, the earlier corresponding to the warm interstadial around 30,000 bc, and the later to the final late-glacial fluctuations which included warmer and very cold phases, all between about 12,000 and 8500 bc. The large, leaf-shaped and carefully flaked stone points, probably spearheads, distinctive of the earlier phase, have been found at Badger Hole in the Mendips, and Kent's Cavern (*fig 1·4*), where they were associated with scrapers, waste flakes, and a single but very interesting bone pin. Open sites are more elusive but one may possibly have been located at Bovey Lane, Beer.[3] All these must represent the activities of well-organized hunting groups.

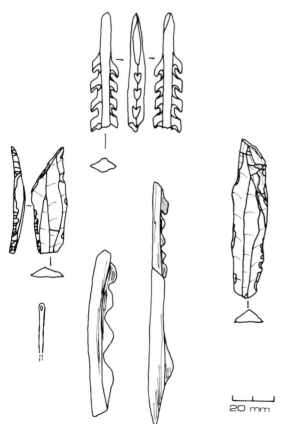

Fig 1·4 (*opposite*) Later Palaeolithic occupation in Kent's Cavern (*source: Campbell 1977*).

Fig 1·5 Later Upper Palaeolithic tool forms, including stone points, bone harpoons, and a bone needle, Kent's Cavern. (*source: Campbell 1977, fig 114, 115*).

20 mm

23

Although the stone industries of the later phase show a certain
continuation of earlier traditions, the tool kit also included curved and
straight-backed blades, large blunt-backed blades, and scrapers.
These have been found at a wide range of cave sites including Kent's
Cavern (*fig 1·5*), Brixham Cave, and Three Holes Cave, Torbryan (all
in south Devon), Gough's Cave, Aveline's Hole, and Soldier's Hole
(all in the Mendips), and open sites like those at Hengistbury Head in
Hampshire, Honiton in Devon,[4] and Gwithian in Cornwall.[5] With
these tools have been found bone harpoon heads at Aveline's Hole and
Kent's Cavern, perforated bone *batons* at Gough's Cave (*fig 1·6*), and a
sewing needle from Kent's Cavern, all of which suggest wide links
with continental groups who possessed similar equipment. The great
herds of horse, reindeer, and mammoth which roamed wild in the
area provided the hunters with meat, although they also ate smaller
animals, fish, and vegetable foods.

One of the many questions that we cannot yet answer is: to what

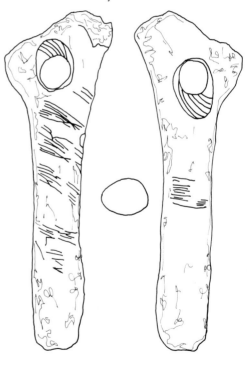

Fig. 1·6 Bone batons, Gough's
Cave (*source: Campbell
1977, fig 120*).

20 mm

use were the caves put, and what was their relationship with the open sites?[6] Do these together form a pattern of seasonal habitations, and did the hunters retreat to the cave shelters during the coldest part of the year? The excavation of more untouched sites may help to provide the answers.

The changing environment

At the end of the final glaciation a rapid and pronounced rise in temperature led to the growth of birch forest over north-western Europe, in the period 8500–7500 bc, followed by a growth in pine and, to a lesser extent, hazel (7500–7000 bc). With the forest came red deer, wild ox, and wild boar—a development of great importance to human hunters since the forest would support fewer herbivores than the open tundra plains.

The shift towards an early Mesolithic life style was a response to the changed environment. Hunting bands whose equipment had affinities with the Maglemosian groups of north-western Europe seem to have entered Britain by way of land bridges across what is now the North Sea. Their early Mesolithic tool kit was characterized by triangular blades known as 'microliths', which probably represent the points of wooden arrows, and by scrapers needed to work the hides of the large forest beasts.

Early Mesolithic sites are concentrated in south-eastern Britain, but are increasingly being recognized further west as at Shapwick and Middlezoy in Somerset, and Dozemary Pool in Cornwall.[7] Unlike the western sites, however, the eastern finds contain numbers of heavy flint axes: this has prompted suggestions that both sets of sites may have been occupied by the same families on a seasonal basis with varying tool requirements in response to the migrations of the red deer.[8] Worked bone and wooden objects recovered from eastern sites, especially that of Star Carr in Yorkshire, show the range of early Mesolithic technology.

Pollen studies show that throughout north-western Europe the steady climatic shift to warmer wetter weather resulted in the growth of oak-dominated deciduous forest, which was generally well-established by 6000 bc. The forest canopy probably inhibited the development of undergrowth species, producing a rather different type of woodland from that found in Britain today, and its growth both depended upon and helped to build up the fertile brown forest soils rich in humus. Nevertheless, there is still considerable room for argument about the density of the cover,[9] and the extent

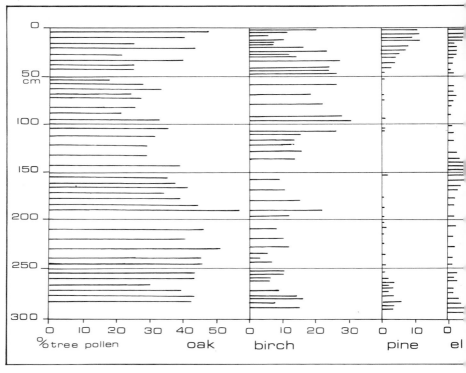

to which growth may have been delayed or inhibited in the upland zone.

Recent work on Bodmin Moor suggests that here the natural environment between 5000 and 3000 bc consisted of large open areas of grass and heath on the high ground, and oak and hazel scrub on exposed hill sides improving to oak forest on sheltered slopes, with birch and alder woods in valleys and peat bogs already developing in valley bottoms.[10] The surrounding lowland carried dense forest of elm, lime and oak. The same pattern seems to be broadly true of Dartmoor, where, however, the woodland areas may have been greater.[11] Pollen profiles from the Exmoor plateau of the Chains (fig 1·7) suggest a contemporary woodland cover dominated by elm and pine.[12]

The environmental history of the low-lying Somerset Levels between the Polden Hills and the Mendips shows a more complex sequence. A deposit of blue-grey marine clay reveals an early estuary-like environment with large expanses of bare mud. As the sea level fell, the drainage of the area remained poor, stimulating the develop-

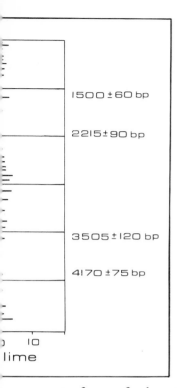

Fig 1·7 Diagram showing relative percentages of tree pollen, with radio carbon dates, from peat sample at The Chains, Exmoor (*source: Merryfield, Moore 1974, fig 1*).

1500 ± 60 bp

2215 ± 90 bp

3505 ± 120 bp

4170 ± 75 bp

10

lime

ment of open freshwater with reed swamp fringing the higher land. The gradual build up of organic debris, which was unable to break down into humic soil in the waterlogged conditions and which remains today as beds of peat, gradually shallowed the water level and allowed some growth of fen woodland dominated by birch and alder.

It is obvious that broad conclusions over-simplify what must have been a mosaic of complex localized environments. Nevertheless, the pollen studies seem to indicate a forest cover around 6000 bc broken by sea coasts and by areas of natural open upland, the original extents of which are uncertain. Evidence shows that as time passed the forest was vulnerable to a range of threats causing it to diminish and decline and the pollen samples also suggest some minor fluctuations in forest growth, followed by a consistent and major decline in tree pollen, especially that of elm, around 3000 bc or 3800 BC

Study of snail remains (*fig 1·8*) suggests a woodland cover on the Cornish coastal lands which diminished as the sand dunes advanced.[13] Study of upland soils has charted the steady progression to leached, acid and waterlogged soil types and the formation of deep peat beds on

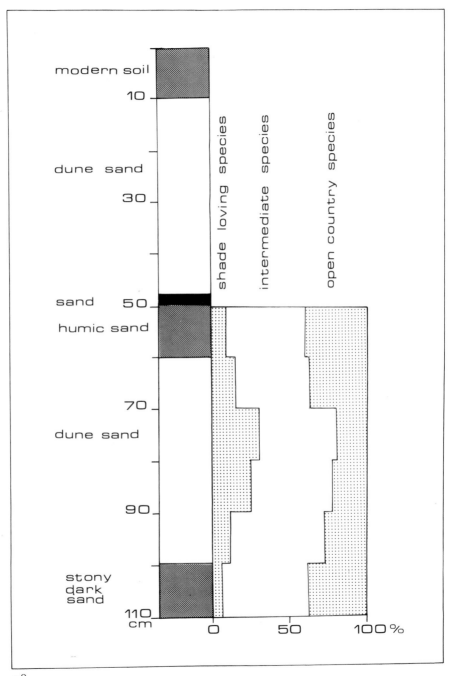

Dartmoor and elsewhere beginning soon after 6000 bc.[14] This created environments in which only typical moorland vegetation can survive. The most vexed question has been the relative roles played in this decline of the woodland by natural causes and human interference— interference that might be divided into an earlier phase pre-dating the major tree pollen decline and contemporary with later Mesolithic communities, and a later phase contemporary with the early Neolithic communities.

Later Mesolithic communities

The life style of the later Mesolithic communities around 5000 bc is typified by their production of a rich variety of tiny geometric micro-liths plainly intended to be mounted upon hafts to form a wide range of weapons and tools (*fig 1·9*). They also used triangular arrow heads, known as '*petit tranchet*' types, which were fitted into the shaft by the pointed end so that the impact was made by the square end, a curious arrangement perhaps intended to slice open the prey and cause the maximum blood-loss.

It has proved possible by study of the flints to suggest regional groupings across northern Europe characterized by small differences in the various assemblages. The finds from a large series of south-western sites along the north coast, as at Westward Ho! and Baggy Point, on Dartmoor, and on Bodmin Moor suggest that the south west represents a particular regional stylistic and therefore probably social grouping.[15]

The distribution of sites is distorted by coastal erosion and by the present upland peat cover so that over-precise definitions of Meso-lithic land use are not likely to be valid. However, it has been suggested that the bands moved in annual cycles. In late Summer, they hunted the red deer and the wild oxen then grazing on the upland; in Spring and early Summer, and perhaps in Autumn too, they lived off the sea food and the grey seals of the coasts and estuaries; while in Winter they inhabited bases from which they exploited the ground below 250 m. The successful exploitation of the large mammals was obviously crucial. The human bands must have had an intimate rela-

Fig 1·8 Histogram showing the distribution of snail species through a core sample 110 cm in depth, at Perranporth. The histogram shows how the relative percentages of shade, intermediate, and open country loving species differ in relationship to the soil types (*source: Spencer 1975, fig 2*).

tionship with the seasonal life of the herds, and manipulation of the herds of oxen, in effect a type of pastoralism, has been suggested by the quantities of ivy found at Westward Ho! which was perhaps fed to cows in milk.[16]

It has been shown that burning off patches of wood stimulates the growth of browse and consequently increases the carrying capacity of the area for ungulates, especially red deer.[17] Deliberate burning would thus bring a new dimension to the control of the animals, and also perhaps have a perceptible effect upon the forest cover. However, although charcoal and burnt peats were conspicuous in the pollen record at Dogway Pool, Bodmin Moor, and the evidence from Black-lane in Dartmoor was interpreted as representing clearance by fire, these occurrences may be rather later in date. It has not yet been

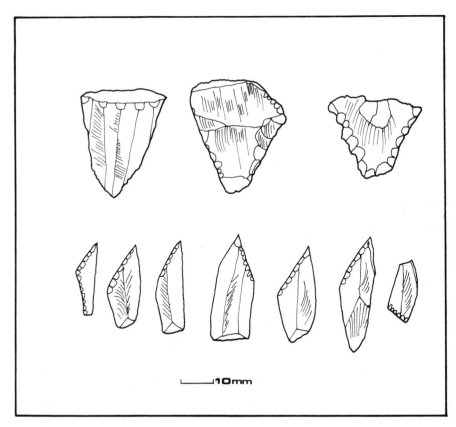

Fig 1·9 Later Mesolithic tool forms from East Week (*Exeter City Museum*).

proved that in the south west the woodland was affected by deliberate activities of Mesolithic men rather than by the natural effects of highland trends in climate and soil formation.

The social organization of the south-west Mesolithic community is, nevertheless, demonstrated in the trading or exchange networks for implements of Portland chert, south-western slate, and sandstone pebbles which have been charted across southern Britain. Comparisons with modern hunter-gatherers suggest that these may express gift-exchanging relationships with all the interchanges that this implies, and may relate both to the status of the south west (*fig 1·10*) as a distinctive culture province and to the suggested gathering sites within the annual cycle where the exchanges may have taken place. It would be unwise to underestimate the sophistication of the south-western Mesolithic bands' life style, even though they probably numbered in all only some hundreds of souls.

Plate 1 Baggy Point, north Devon. The present north Devon coastline took shape as the sea flooded the Bristol Channel in post-glacial times. Mesolithic communities lived near the present shore.

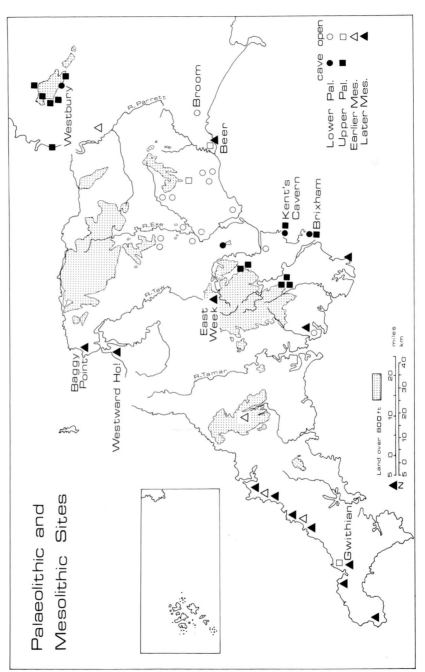

Fig 1·10 Palaeolithic and Mesolithic sites.

Neolithic pioneers

The culture of a hunting group may be very rich and satisfying to the individual member but its potential for development is restricted. The controlled harvesting of crops and the rearing of flocks and herds offer an alternative means of subsistence which permits infinitely more elaborate social organization (even though it may involve most members in harder work). Crop-growing gives a more intensive yield, making it possible for the community to grow and to be supported by a relatively small land area. The farming pattern may allow the accumulation of stored possessions and consequently the growth of new forms of authority and prestige. Pottery, although not an essential element, seems to have been possessed by all normal Neolithic peoples in northern Europe. Pots offer the best means of storing surplus food and liquids, including fermented liquids like beer and mead, and they are handsome objects in which to take a pride. Above all, the deliberate transference of wet clay by the use of fire into hard pottery marks an important stage on the long road which we call technology.

In the past, the acquisition of farming and other skills which are the hallmark of the Neolithic communities was regarded as a 'human revolution' which lay at the heart of all subsequent civilized development. 'Revolution' suggests too violent and sudden an image for what was a gradual, flexible, and infinitely varied process of change. Nevertheless, the new skills did unlock new resources and make new demands heavy with consequences for the future. Varieties of emphasis must have been dependent upon local circumstances and have differed from group to group.

The cereals which appear in the western European record as showing signs of human selection in their growth, like barley, emmer wheat and einkorn, all grow wild in a relatively restricted area including the coastal strip of the eastern Mediterranean and the upland beyond. In the same broad area flourished the ancestors of domestic sheep, goats, cattle and pigs. A range of peas or beans is also quite common on Neolithic sites, some species of which derive from the Middle East while others are indigenous to Europe. The inherent suggestion that all the plants and animals basic to western farming were first domesticated by human groups in the upland plains of the Middle East is confirmed from excavations at sites such as Jericho and Jarmo.

Through the joint processes of human colonization and diffusion the new techniques spread across central and western Europe. People subsisting by mixed farming, who are given the archaeological label of the linear pottery culture from the way they decorated their pots, appear to have been well established in north-western Europe by around 5000 BC. They seem to have lived in relatively stable settlements situated on fertile valley soils close to water where garden plots growing emmer, einkorn and peas could be cleared from the forest. Here they built substantial timber long houses and palisades. Their tool kit included arrowheads and stone axes with wide cutting edges, and they produced round-bottomed pots.[18]

By 4600 BC imperfectly understood pressures involving, perhaps, population growth, stimulated modifications in the settlement pattern. The landscape was more densely exploited within and beyond the old areas of settlement: the long house tradition apparently broke down, and various ditched enclosures, perhaps associated with cattle management, began to be constructed. It was at about this point, perhaps as early as 4500 BC, that the first bands of colonists from the Rhineland and from the area of what is now north France loaded their boats and crossed to settle in Britain. The immigration continued over a long period of perhaps several centuries. The immigrants represent one aspect of the expanding western Neolithic community: the society which they left seems to have been in a state of flux. They themselves had a range of mixed traditions, and it is likely that the upheaval of colonization disorientated old patterns and permitted new developments in the new country. So Neolithic culture in Britain is not exactly comparable to that of any specific area of north-west mainland Europe. Nevertheless, the generalized similarities between cultural development on the mainland and developments in Britain are clear enough.

Common sense suggests a period of several centuries between 4500 and 4200 BC when the pioneers explored the framework of rivers, hills, and natural resources, and organized their communications. The site at Ballynagilly near Cookstown in County Tyrone may show us a glimpse of this process. Here two pits and a hearth, which were associated with early Neolithic pottery, and which preceded the main Neolithic occupation, gave radio carbon dates of around 4500 BC.[19] In north-west Britain evidence has been found of some small-scale woodland clearance for crop-growing and pasture during this phase; it is possible, too, that the snail shell evidence from the north Cornish coast, as well as the pollen evidence from Exmoor and the granite areas, point to comparable early activity in the south west, although here the dating is very uncertain. It is during this period that the native Mesolithic communities are likely to have been absorbed.

The consolidation of settlement

In common with pollen profiles from north-western Europe generally, those from the Chains in Exmoor show a decline in tree pollen
around 3800 BC accompanied by an increase in herb pollens like plan-
tain, a development which also occurred in the Somerset Levels and
the granite uplands. At the same time, the formation was progressing
of sour, infertile peat and similar moorland soils. This decline in the
trees, especially on the upland forest margins, and the growth in
pollens from plants which may accompany or follow cultivation, have
been seen as evidence of steady Neolithic clearance in the interests of
agriculture and pasture. This would have directly eroded the woodland and stimulated the growth of peat.

No agreement has yet been reached on the methods by which the
Neolithic settlers cleared and cultivated the soil. Some groups may
have practised a 'slash and burn' technique, by which patches were
cleared in the forest through tree-felling, bark-cutting and controlled
fires. The ash-rich ground would have been cultivated by stone hoes
until the soil was exhausted, and then a fresh start would be made
elsewhere leaving the original patch to grow over. Evidence from
Wessex, however, suggests that primitive ploughs were in use at this
time; on the west coast of Ireland substantial field systems with arable
plots divided by stone walls built before 3000 BC have been revealed
beneath the peat. Early cultivation on this scale has not been recognized in the south west, but it is possible that some known field
systems are being dated too late.

Cultivation is likely to have begun on the lighter soils of the
hill-tops and upland fringes, and to have spread into the valleys. The
whole process, indeed, may have had a permanently degenerating
effect upon some areas of upland. At the same time, the natural trend
seems to have been towards the formation of peaty soils on the
upland, and drought and disease may have been hostile to the forest
trees. In all, the evidence suggests a complex situation, especially
along the woodland margins, within which clearance by the settlers
was one among several pressures upon the forest.

In the centuries after 4200 BC an impressive series of sites proves
the stability of the Neolithic communities and their ability to organize
complex social patterns. The classic occupation site is Hembury in
east Devon, excavated during the 1930s.[20] Hembury is on the tip of a
steep-sided spur of the Blackdown Hills, about 20 km from the coast.
The excavation located an arc of U-shaped ditch, interrupted by
shorter lengths of undug causeway, running around the plateau to cut

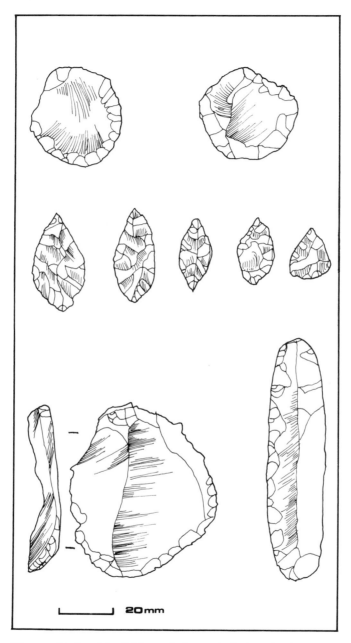

Fig 1·11 Earlier Neolithic tool forms including leaf-shaped arrowheads, scrapers and blades, Hembury (*Exeter City Museum*).

off the southern end of the spur tip. A further length of ditch to the north may signify a second outer arc. In at least three places there were dense clusters of pits, clay hearths, and stake holes, and much domestic rubbish. Immediately inside the western end of the inner ditch, stake holes showed the position of a sub-rectangular hut equipped with cooking holes and hearth.

The settlers had used thousands of flint blades for a wide range of domestic purposes, and they hunted with leaf-shaped arrowheads (*fig 1·11*). They had characteristic ground stone axes, and possessed beads of steatite and jet. Some carbonized remains survived of wheat, barley and perhaps spelt, and there was an assortment of saddle-shaped quern fragments and rubbing stones.

The shape of the pots showed that they functioned mainly as storage containers, sunk into the pits: large, round-bottomed jars and bowls of thin, well-fired, undecorated fabric, either smoothly curving to the rim or occasionally with a slight shoulder, and with pairs of simple lugs, sometimes perforated. A proportion of the pots, however, are a superior type characterized by elegant, long perforated lugs which have expanded ends, whence their usual description 'trumpet lugged'. Some of these have an internal and external black coating. From time to time rubbish seems to have been deliberately scraped into the ditches, burnt there, and then covered by earth pushed down from the bank. Neolithic Hembury was occupied around 4000 BC.

High Peak, on the cliff above Sidmouth, may well have been similar. Its settlers, in the centuries around 3500 BC, also dug cooking pits and used typical flints, stone axes and pots. A short length of ditch found on the cliff edge suggests that their settlement may have been enclosed.[21] Further north, on the edge of the Mendips overlooking the Somerset Levels, the earliest settlers on the hilltop at South Cadbury buried fragments of human skulls in some of their pits, while others contained the usual range of stonework and pots. Burnt hazel shell and antler gave dates around 3300 BC.[22] The hilltop at Norton Fitzwarren, with wide views south and east, has yielded similar tools and pots.[23]

The hilltop series continues west of the Exe. At Haldon, on the ridge overlooking the Exe Valley, the inhabitants built a substantial rectangular timber house, with a doorway in one wall and an inside hearth. At Hazard Hill above the River Harbourne excavation revealed a series of pits, cooking areas, and hearths, and some remains of indeterminate structures, together with finds like those at Hembury.

On the eastern summit of the triple-peaked granite hill of Carn Brea, important excavations have shown that the Neolithic settlers cleared the stones from a series of terraces around the summit, and

37

Plate 2 Carn Brea from the north. The central peak is marked by a monument erected in 1832 to a local mine owner. On the left the eastern peak, marked by castle ruins, was the site of Neolithic occupation. The eastern and central peaks were enclosed in the Iron Age. In the foreground is part of the fertile north Cornish plain.

there dug pits and built timber structures. One of these burnt down, and its charcoal gave a date around 3800 BC, a most important piece of information because, over its remains, the settlers had erected the most remarkable feature of the site—a massive dry stone wall which ran from outcrop to outcrop, and enclosed the summit top and most of the occupation (*fig 1·12*).

The Carn Brea people used characteristic pots, flints and axes. Few organic remains survived, but the stripping of a large area on the slope below the wall revealed an ancient land surface dotted with piles of stones dated by Neolithic artefacts, including a saddle quern. This looks like the original cleared land where the settlers grew their food.[24]

It is unlikely that this remarkable sequence of sites represents the true total of Neolithic-occupied hilltops. Further hill sites like Carn Brea probably exist west of the Tamar, and sites within this broad

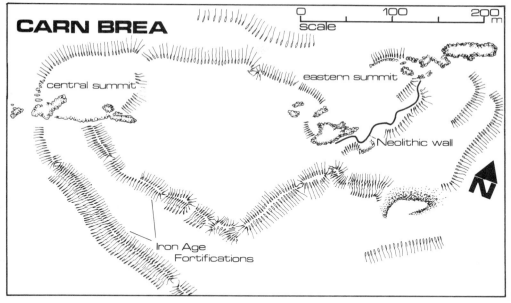

Fig 1·12 Plan of Neolithic occupation, Carn Brea (*source: Mercer 1974*).

group might be expected on the western and south-western flanks of Dartmoor. Similarly, more sites might be discovered around the rim of the Somerset Levels. Worlebury, which has produced Neolithic flint work, Glastonbury Tor, from which come flints and a stone axe, and Brent Knoll are three obvious candidates.

Hembury, and probably High Peak, fit into a series of sites known as 'interrupted ditch enclosures' or 'causewayed camps'. These have long been recognized on hilltops on the southern chalk downs at sites like Maiden Castle in Dorset and Windmill Hill in Wiltshire, and are now being discovered in river valleys near the Thames and in the east Midlands.[25] They can be broadly matched by contemporary enclosures in north-west Europe, and the whole series shows a wide range of plans, situations, and scope for possible functions, while each individual site may well have had a complex history of its own.

The sites in southern Britain are generally agreed to have been focuses of community activity. However, they have been variously interpreted as meeting places for ceremonial feastings, sacred enclosures connected with the cult of the dead,[26] and cattle pounds associated with seasonal grazing patterns across the whole landscape.[27] Recent work at Hambledon in Dorset, and Crickley Hill in Gloucester, suggests that substantial defences may have been erected at these sites some time after their use as causewayed camps. If early Neolithic communities really were fortifying hilltops here and at Carn Brea, this suggests a society already showing signs of strain.

In contrast to some of the sites further east, Hembury yielded sufficiently intensive occupation debris within the enclosed area to suggest that it was inhabited, although not necessarily permanently. Hembury, and perhaps High Peak, have enough in common with unenclosed sites like Haldon and Hazard Hill, and even with Carn Brea with its strong stone wall, even though they may differ in detail, to suggest that in the south west occupied hilltops as a group play a focal role. The cleared land at Carn Brea, the carbonized grain from Hembury, and the substantial house at Haldon suggest the existence of arable plots on the hill slopes.

In addition to the hilltops with their range of structures, there is a considerable number of occupation sites usually known as 'flint scatters', a term which precisely describes their appearance. Varying quantities of characteristic worked flint, often including a Mesolithic element perhaps reflecting long site use or a conservative approach to stone-working, are found strewn over an area of sometimes several hectares. Many of these sites, however, are only known through the activities of early collectors and few of them have been scientifically investigated. The flints are found chiefly in plough soil, and ploughing may have irretrievably destroyed evidence of pits and pottery.

The site at Churston Court Farm, in south Devon, which is in the process of being plotted, is typical of many.[28] About 2500 pieces of worked flint have been collected, including nearly forty arrowheads, mostly of the typically Neolithic leaf-shape, but some of Mesolithic and Early Bronze Age types. Twelve stone axes and axe fragments have been recovered, but no structural features or pottery have appeared in the small-scale excavations. The coastal site at Gwithian has produced a scatter of Neolithic flint material and sherds of early Neolithic character. The environmental evidence here suggests a local decline of woodland and subsequent development of open scrub, a process in which this occupation may have played a part.[29]

In Devon the known flint scatters are concentrated in the South Hams, in east Devon and the Exe Valley, on Dartmoor (except the highest north-west section), and in the valleys of the Taw and the Torridge; on Exmoor there is an important site at Milverton; and a number of sites are known from Penwith, Bodmin Moor, and along the north Cornish coast. The majority of these are on gentle hill slopes or in low-lying river valleys. The quantity of flint work recovered

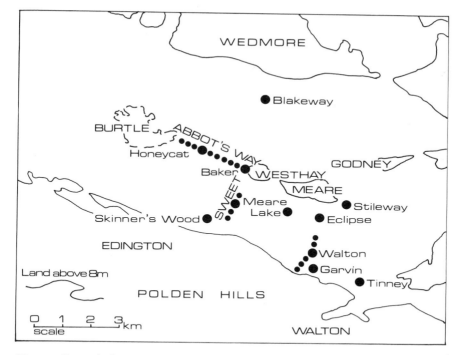

Fig 1·13 General plan, Somerset Levels (*source: Coles 1976, 1977*).

probably relates to the period of time during which the site was in use, and this means that the material discovered in the largest sites may represent the accumulation of more than two thousand years.

The Somerset Levels

The Somerset Levels, especially the area between the Polden Hills and the Wedmore Ridge, has proved to be most fruitful for the study of Neolithic communities. Settlement sites await discovery, probably on the areas of rock like Westhay, Meare and Godney, and on sand like Burtle, which stood out as islands among the surrounding fen woodland (*fig 1·13*). Linking these areas of higher ground have been found a series of trackways preserved in the peat which demonstrate a high level of community endeavour.

The Sweet Track, with its companion Post Track dismantled in antiquity, is the earliest so far discovered and has yielded a series of dates clustering around 4000 BC. The track ran south–north probably from the Poldens to Meare-Westhay, and crossed areas of wet fen woodland. Its construction (broadly like that of the slightly earlier Post Track) involved a rail laid on the contemporary peat surface which, with pegs and peat packing, supported a single plank (*fig 1·14*). The result would have been a narrow raised plank walkway across the marsh. The planks were chiefly of ash, and the builders used a variety of woods for the pegs and rails. In contrast to the other tracks, the Sweet Track yielded a range of exceptionally fine objects: pins of yew, and two axes, one of flint and the other of jadeite, both in mint condition and placed in a way which irresistibly suggests ceremonial observances. A range of at least seven pots was recovered, one of which had been full of hazel nuts. The pots were all of superior fabrication, and coloured inside and out with a black coating.

The Honeygore complex involves a series of tracks running east–west to connect Westhay, Honeygore Island, and Burtle, and has a date range suggesting that it was originally built around 3500 BC. The tracks were built on a brushwood base and had hurdles of slender birch and hazel stems laid longitudinally and pegged along the parallel sides. Further earlier Neolithic tracks continue to come to light as work proceeds.

The quantity of evidence which the Levels Project is producing is still being digested. Plainly, the tracks indicate a continuity of purpose among the inhabitants, suggesting established settlers who desired permanent communication, and access to the fishing, fowling, and vegetable resources of the wet fens at times when walking or boating was impracticable. Being fairly light, the tracks are unlikely to have been adequate for cattle-droving. It is likely, therefore, that the fens, and the islands and surrounding high ground, were exploited as parts of a coherent economic system in which stock-rearing on the hills was complemented by arable farming on the well-drained soils of the slopes, and by fishing and fowling in the fens.[30]

Study of the cut wood has shown that it was the product of sophisticated woodland management, probably on the fringing higher ground, by which the coppicing of hazel produced crops of hazel rods from the parent stumps or stools, and crops of leaves on the rods. Green foliage seems to have been a principle source of cattle fodder, and the managed woods may have assumed a much greater place in the Neolithic economy than the simple need for rods and workable timber. The surviving wood-work, both of the construction of the tracks themselves, and of incidental finds like yew bows and a ladle, shows the range of skills and objects which must surely have been available at all the main centres of Neolithic settlement.

Finally, the trackways underline the ability of the Neolithic groups

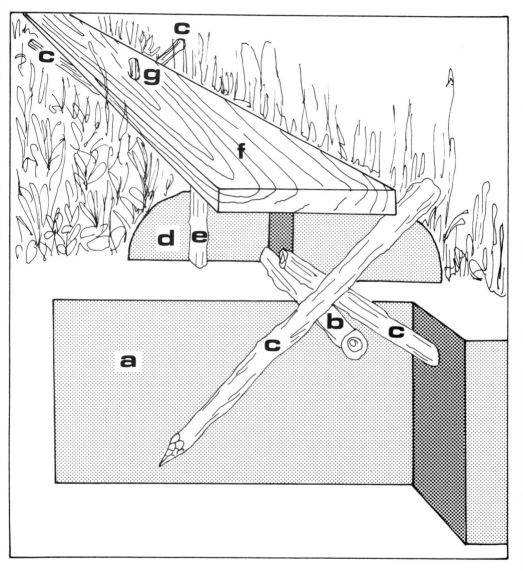

Fig 1·14 Schematic reconstruction of Sweet Track, to show major elements of construction: a: underlying peat; b: rail laid on contemporary peat surface; c: rail pegs driven into peat; d: peat-packing around and on top of rail; e: supporting plank peg; f: plank laid on peat packing (d), on plank peg (e) and on upper part of rail pegs (c); g: plank peg through hole or notch in plank. (*source: Coles Orme 1976, fig 20*).

43

to undertake substantial community projects, fulfilling a role in the yearly economy, which are an expression of successful settlement, and which, in the careful deposit of the Sweet axes and, perhaps, pots, suggest a recognition of the gods.

Exchange networks

Recent research has demonstrated that the Neolithic groups of the south west, like those in other regions, were knit together in a complex web through which goods were exchanged in organized transactions that took specialized products the length of the peninsula and beyond. Polished stone axes seem to have played an important role in this network. The superb jadeite axe from the Sweet Track can be paralleled by a jadeite axe from High Peak, and by several specimens known as 'stray finds' from the peninsula. The exact source or sources of the jadeite is not yet known but it is certainly continental, and serves as a reminder that the British Neolithic communities remained in touch with their continental cousins.

Work which is in progress on flint axes suggests other exchange lines running eastwards from the peninsula into the chalk downs. Flint workers were exploiting the bands of fine black flint which show up so clearly in the chalk cliffs of Beer Head. Flint-knapping floors are frequent on the Head, and Beer flint has been identified at Hembury, Haldon, Hazard, High Peak, and Carn Brea. Implements made from Portland chert have been found, among other places, at High Peak, and at the extensive flint scatter at East Week in Devon. Beer flint and Portland chert seem normally to have been used for small blades and implements.

Axes of igneous rock types broadly called 'greenstone' have been found on all the substantial south-western Neolithic occupation sites, and they occur frequently amongst flint scatter material or as casual finds (*fig 1·15*). Petrological analysis of the axes has broadly located the rock from which they are made, to a series of areas in Cornwall. About twelve Cornish groups have been identified and, of these, Groups II and XVII in Penwith, Group XVI near Carn Brea and Group IV on Balstone Down, seem to have been exploited during the early Neolithic.

Specialized axe manufacture was by no means confined to Cornwall; at Graig Lwyd in north Wales and Great Langdale in Cumberland the actual working sites have been discovered, marked by waste flakes and axe roughouts. No working sites have so far been found in Cornwall, and this is one of the reasons why some geologists have

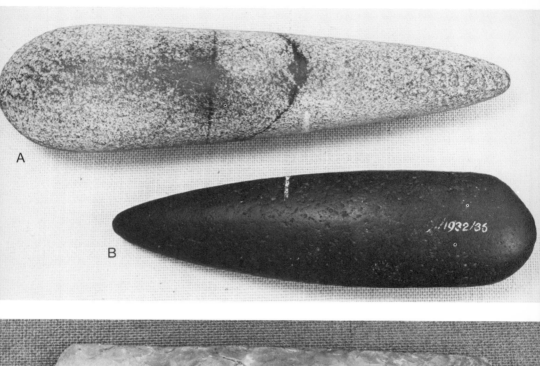

Plate 3 Neolithic axes. a: greenstone from Silverton, b: igneous rock from Seaton, c: flint from Hartland Point, all Devon. Lengths 275–217 mm. Exeter City Museum.

recently suggested that the axes were not made at 'axe factories' in Cornwall and distributed from there, but produced from boulders which may have been widely distributed in southern Britain as glacial erratics during the movement of the Pleistocene ice sheets. The published distribution map of the axes is cited in support of this view since it shows a concentration of finds in Wessex, and relatively few in the south west, nearer the supposed sources. However, material which

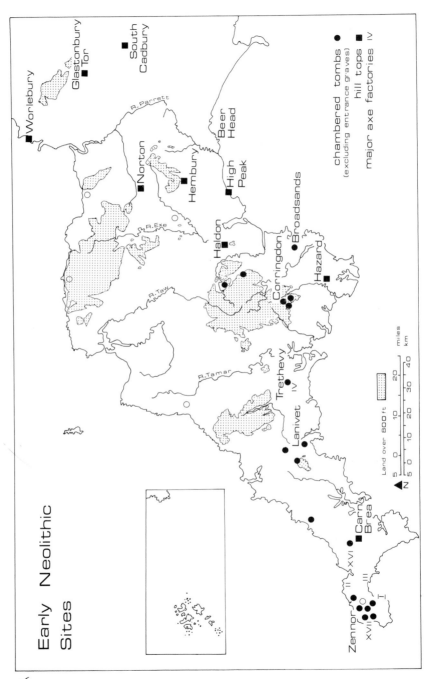

Early Neolithic
Sites

chambered tombs
(excluding entrance graves) ●
hill tops ■
major axe factories IV ■

Worlebury
Glastonbury
Tor
South
Cadbury
R.Parrett
Norton
Hembury
Beer
Head
High
Peak
R.Exe
Haldon
Broadsands
Corringdon
Hazard
R.Taw
R.Tamar
Trethevy
IV
Lanivet
Carn
Brea
Zennor
II XVI
III
I
XVII

Land over 800 ft
miles
km
20
10 20 30 40
5 0 10
5 0
N

Fig 1·15 Early Neolithic sites.

has been analysed more recently would help to fill in the blanks on the map, and the original view of the Cornish axe manufacture is surely supported by the known working sites elsewhere in the Highland Zone.

The accumulation of radio carbon dates has demonstrated that earlier Neolithic communities in southern Britain were using pots made in a variety of styles, and this has reversed the earlier view that the plain pots familiar from south-western sites were produced before the decorated types better known in eastern Britain. The ceramic style centred upon the south west is usefully called the Hembury style. It embraces plain round-bottomed pots of superior and coarse wares, occasionally shouldered, with lugs sometimes elaborated into the trumpet form.

It has been demonstrated that the clay from which the 'fine' or 'superior' Hembury vessels were made includes grit of such distinctive mineralogical character that it can be related only to the deposits of granite-derived gabbroic clays situated in the Lizard peninsula, since the shifting of this clay eastwards by glacial action seems unlikely. Pots of Lizard clay are found at Carn Brea, where they embrace both the shouldered and the trumpet lug forms; at Hazard, Haldon, Hembury, and High Peak, where the trumpet lug pots have been found; at Gwithian, and at the chalk down sites of Maiden Castle in Dorset, and Windmill Hill and Robin Hood's Ball in Wiltshire. The proportion of these pots to the known total from each site decreases progressively eastwards.[31] It seems, from the highly competent and similar appearance of the range of gabbroic pots, that the Lizard clay was being exploited by professional potters whose products were dispersed eastwards, although the working areas within the Lizard peninsula await discovery. In these superior gabbroic pots lies the origin of the Hembury regional style. The bulk of the Hembury coarse wares are local copies in local materials of the imported wares.

On the fringes of the south-western peninsula comparable contacts can be detected. Pottery from the Sweet Track and from Wiltshire was made from clay deriving from oolite limestone, perhaps from the Bath area. The facts that at Windmill Hill oolitic wares imitate Hembury gabbroic prototypes, and that the black coating appears at Hembury and at the Sweet Track, suggest competing influences, the intricacies of which have yet to be unravelled. The detailed design of Neolithic pottery, and its distribution, now seem to stem from fashion, professional expertise, and the practicability of cross-country movements, rather than from traditional patterns deeply embedded in the life style of a group.

The implications of this for prehistoric studies as a whole are profound, and they have stimulated recent research into the mechanics and the significance of what used to be called 'trade' but is now more frequently referred to as 'patterns of exchange'. Exchange of goods may represent much more than the simple transfer of commodities from one person to another. The giving of gifts may be an outward sign of superiority or dependence. Objects considered of value may be accumulated by a person or a group to be dispersed in a ceremonial way which brings prestige. Special pieces—and the jadeite and possibly some of the other axes come to mind here—may have been desired because special virtues attached to them.

One further point may be made. The finds from Hembury and elsewhere show that the exchange pattern covering the south-western peninsula and involving the Lizard pots, the greenstone axes, and the eastern flint and chert, had been initiated during the pioneer stage of Neolithic settlement and was to persist for at least two thousand years. Whatever its precise significance may have been, it was important and long-enduring.

The great tombs

Community effort is manifested equally strikingly in the erection of the great tombs. In the south west, as usually in the upland zone of Britain where building stone was freely available, the monuments consist of a chamber complex built of rough stone slabs, sometimes with lengths of dry stone walling. They are covered with a mound, often considerably more substantial than necessary, known as a barrow when it is of earth, and a cairn when it is of stone. The chambered tombs are sometimes known as 'cromlechs', or as 'megalithic' tombs from Greek words meaning 'large stones'. They appear to be the Highland equivalent of the Lowland earthern long barrows like that making up the first stage of the Wayland Smithy tomb on the Berkshire ridgeway, where a similar timber chamber or mortuary house was covered by a barrow. The north Cornish site of Woolley may be an outlying member of the long barrow group,[32] and it would not be surprising if further sites awaited discovery in east Devon: the long mound beside the River Lowman is a possibility.

Chambered tombs are relatively common in the peninsula, and the

Plate 4 Neolithic round-bottomed bowls from Hembury. That with trumpet lugs (*above*) is of gabbroic clay. Heights 148 mm, 125 mm. Exeter City Museum.

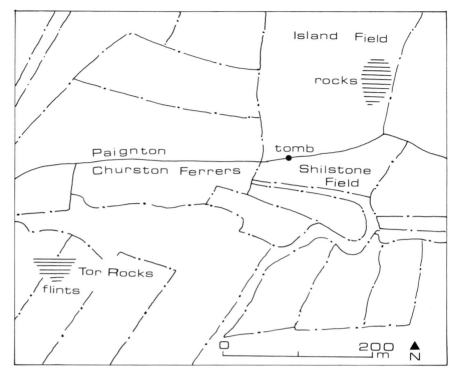

Fig 1·16 Area of tomb, Broadsands: the tomb is situated on the old parish boundary
(*source: Radford 1958; Ordnance Survey*).

known examples are only those that have chanced to survive. Unfortunately, many of the south-western tombs were ravaged in antiquity,
and most of them have been subsequently damaged so that frequently
they survive only as skeletons, denuded of all but their largest stones:
these are the monuments often in Cornwall given the name 'quoits'.
The placename *Shilstone* (*fig 1·16*) and similar forms recorded at least
eight times in Devon[33] derive from the Old English 'shelf stone' and
possibly refer to the existence of a chambered tomb, although in most
cases the tomb itself is now lost.

Within the tomb family a number of distinct designs is recogniz-
able, and in the past much effort was put into their classification.
Tombs with more or less elaborate chambers opening from a short
entrance under a long mound were grouped as gallery graves, while
those with a single chamber at the end of a long passage under a round
mound were called passage graves, and various sub-classes or hybrids
were given other distinguishing names. Modern approaches to the

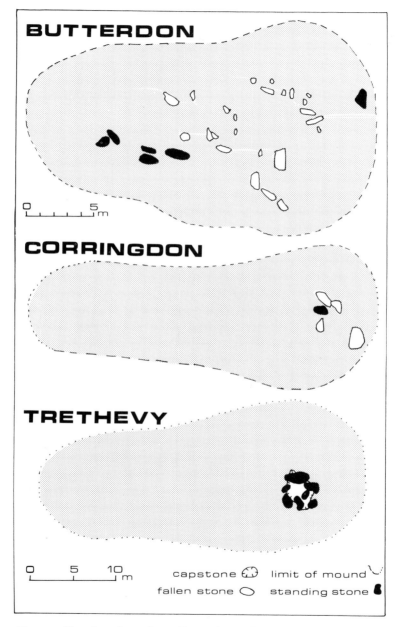

Fig 1·17 Chambered tombs at Butterdon Hill, Corringdon Ball, and
Trethevy (*sources: Butterdon, Fletcher, Grinsell, Quinnell 1974;
Corringdon, Fox 1973, fig 9; Trethevy, Hencken 1932, fig 16*).

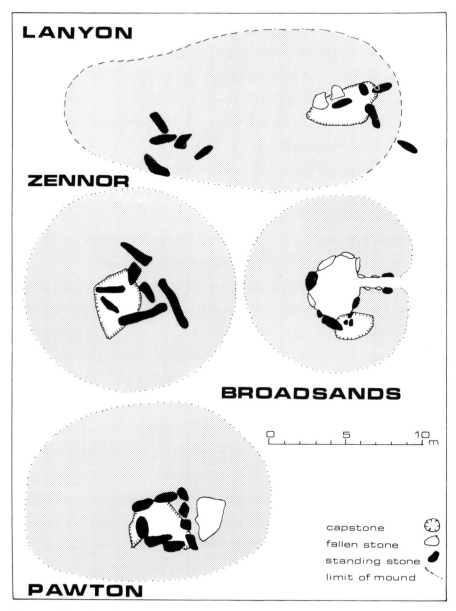

Fig 1·18 Chambered tombs at Lanyon, Pawton, Broadsands, and Zennor (*sources: Lanyon, Fox 1973, fig 9; Broadsands, Radford 1958; Zennor, Hencken 1932, fig 16*).

tombs, however, stress their social importance rather than their formal construction, and try to show how each group built its tomb as an integral part of its community life. The origin of barrow-building throughout north-western Europe seems to lie within the traditions of the expanding western European Neolithic communities, and perhaps the idea of barrows as houses for the dead reflects the early long house tradition.

Dating is difficult, since few tombs have been scientifically excavated and it is usually not clear whether datable finds belong to the early history of a site or to its later use. However, dates clustering around 4500 BC for some of the Breton graves, or a date of about 3500 BC from the old ground surface beneath the barrow at Ascott-under-Wychwood, Oxfordshire, show the broad time span. Finds from the tombs of Scilly and Penwith show that these were being used, and some of them probably built, well after 2500 BC. All in all, it is clear that many local variations were possible within the larger theme, and that the tradition was very long-lived in western Britain.

The Neolithic groups living around the flanks of Dartmoor built a number of tombs on the fringes of the high ground. The grave at Corringdon Ball is badly ruined, although its long, pear-shaped mound is reasonably preserved. This and the newly recognized long cairn on Butterdon Hill,[34] together with the possible site at Cuckoo Ball, form a tight group on the south-western slope of Dartmoor (*fig 1·17*). On the eastern side of the moor are the much denuded Spinsters Rock, the Meacombe burial chamber, and two simple tomb structures recently identified at Gidleigh.[35] South east of Dartmoor, at Broadsands, Paignton, there is a site with a round mound covering a passage running to a chamber. The earliest deposits in the chamber contained human bones and apparently shouldered black pottery of broad Hembury style.[36]

West of the Tamar, substantial remains may be seen at Trethevy, Zennor Quoit, and Pawton (*fig 1·18*). At Trethevy the chamber had flanking slabs placed at one end to give a portal effect, but access to the chamber was by a small gap at the bottom of the large granite closing slab. In the last century an oval mound enclosed the whole tomb. Similarly, at Zennor, which like Trethevy had a capstone tilted back from the portal, the chamber was entered by a narrow slit between two transverse slabs. Zennor's mound was round and about 37 m across.

Simpler box-like chambers survive at Chun Quoit and Mulfra Quoit, and many of the now ruined Penwith tombs may have been similar. The chambers were sealed by the erection of the mound

53

Plate 5 Trethevy Quoit, St Cleer, east Cornwall, from the south.

which must have been the last main act in the building sequence. Two stone slabs with round 'portholes' pecked out of them are known: the Men-an-Tol ('Stone with a Hole') at Madron, and the Tolvaen at Gweek. These may be closing stones from tombs, although no contexts for either have survived. Tombs at Carwynnen (Camborne), Lanyon, West Lanyon, and Lanivet are now very denuded, and the Exmoor site at Battle Gore (Williton) may be a ruined tomb.

A further group of tombs are those known as entrance graves because they consist of a short rectangular passage under a round mound. About ten of these have been identified in Penwith, of which that at Brane (or Chapel Euny) is sufficiently well preserved to be worth a visit. More than fifty are known on Scilly where they stand a better chance of survival. Work in progress suggests that the mainland entrance graves probably belong within the same broad period as the other great Neolithic tombs, although they were also in use in the Bronze Age. At the moment, however, it seems that Scilly may not have been colonized until around 2000 bc, and if this is so, then the Scilly entrance graves must be much later than those in Penwith. More radio carbon dates would clarify the picture.

Each tomb was an imposing monument while in use, and for each group the building represented both the expression of stable prosperity and the satisfaction of a spiritual need. The excavation of an unrifled tomb frequently shows it to have been a complex structure perhaps built in several stages before it achieved its final form, and this would help to explain how small groups could produce the necessary effort. Large quantities of human bones deposited with comparatively little in the way of grave goods are normal finds, and the fragmented nature of some individual skeletons has prompted suggestions that dead people were stored somewhere else until their flesh had rotted. At the right moment the accumulated bones would be gathered up and placed, with the correct ceremonies, inside the tomb.

With the potency of the dead was bound up the fertility of the living. Some ritual desposits suggest a desire to stimulate increase;[37] and the farmers seem to have sometimes placed the tombs deliberately on the edges of productive or abandoned corn patches, like that at South Street in Wiltshire.[38] Tombs may also have served as territorial markers on the edge of a community's land, and if so, the belief that a sacred grave protects a frontier had a long future. The ancestor worship which the tombs imply suggests that Neolithic society was organized in family groups or lineages in which descent from a common forefather gave individuals rights in the territory and the resources which each group controlled.

Neolithic lifestyles

Radio carbon has had the effect of extending the earlier Neolithic period in the south west, so that it spans a long time from roughly 4500 to 3000 BC. This perspective, together with recent work suggesting that woodland clearings and the growth of peat at the expense of the trees were natural features of the upland, implies a relatively thin scatter of Neolithic families, although their corporate undertakings show that they were mature, economically successful communities. The distribution of occupied hilltops, flint scatters and tombs shows that people were concentrated in the Somerset Levels, on southern Dartmoor, east Devon, the South Hams, and west Cornwall. They achieved some forest clearance in areas such as the coast lands, the Levels, and the South Hams,[39] but on the upland and in areas of present heathland like east Devon, the Hartland peninsula and much of Cornwall this activity may not have been extensive.

Neolithic life seems to have been organized around the exploitation of open clearings, either natural or artificial, and of the surrounding woodland. Families used the clearings as living and working areas which show up in the record as flint scatters, as corn-growing plots, and as centres for cattle-rearing and for the woodland management best demonstrated in the Levels. The tombs at Spinsters Rock and Meacombe are in an area where flint scatters are dense, as are those comprising the tight group of Corringdon Ball, Cuckoo Ball, and Butterdon Hill. Two flint scatters are known about 8 km from the Broadsands site. The area of landscape exploited by a single group may have been considerable and it is possible that its life style involved a pattern of cyclic movement in which cultivation, the exploitation of seasonal grazing, and ritual construction and observance all had their place.

All three of the Corringdon group of tombs are within 9 km north west of the hilltop settlement of Hazard Hill, while Broadsands is 18 km to the south east. Similarly, the potters, axe manufacturers, and tomb builders of Penwith and the Lizard were within easy reach of Carn Brea. Beer Head is relatively close to Hembury, and the hilltops of South Cadbury, Worlebury and Glastonbury Tor must surely relate to the groups who built the Levels trackways. These hilltops, varied though the picture they present may be, may play a vital part in the exchange network to which the dispersed pottery and stone bears witness. A cyclic life style would give scope for seasonal gatherings at focal points like the hills at which both ritual requirements and practical needs could be satisfied. Within the broad western Neolithic tradition, the communities of Britain developed a distinctive way of life. Within Britain a south-western province emerged, characterized by the series of occupied hilltops, and by the organized and influential exploitation of natural resources.

1. *Ashbee 1974*
2. *Stringer, Andrews, Currant 1979*
3. *Woods 1929*
4. *Field, Miles 1975*
5. *Thomas 1958*
6. *Campbell 1977*
7. *Wainwright 1960*
8. *Clark 1972*
9. *Barker, Webley 1978*
10. *Brown 1977*
11. *Simmons 1969*
12. *Merryfield, Moore 1974*
13. *Spencer 1975*
14. *Staines 1979*

15. *Jacobi 1979*
16. *Evans 1975*
17. *Mellars 1975*
18. *Whittle 1977*
19. *ApSimon 1969*
20. *Lidell 1930, 1931, 1932, 1935*
21. *Pollard 1965, 1967a*
22. *Alcock 1972*
23. *Langmaid 1971*
24. *Mercer 1974*
25. *Palmer 1976*
26. *Drewett 1977*
27. *Barker, Webley 1978*
28. *Pearson 1978*
29. *Megaw 1976*
30. *Coles 1978*
31. *Peacock 1969a*
32. *Higginbotham 1977*
33. *Gover, Mawer, Stenton 1931, 1932; Radford 1958*
34. *Fletcher, Grinsell, Quinell 1974*
35. *Turner 1978*
36. *Radford 1958*
37. *Ashbee 1976*
38. *Fowler, Evans 1967*
39. *Radford 1958*

CHAPTER TWO

The Monument Builders

Developments after 3000 BC

The archaeological record of events in Britain in the centuries following 3000 BC shows us an increasing complex society. People began to
make new kinds of artefacts, and to build ritual monuments of great
richness and variety. Foreign contacts come into play, and these are
bound up in the beginnings of metallurgy in southern Britain. New
land, especially the upland of the south west, was occupied for the first
time, and the settlers seem to have been anxious to exploit all possible
food resources. All these changes must have been the result of the
breakdown in later Neolithic society where the economic basis of the
old family groups seems to have become insecure. Perhaps soil exhaustion was becoming a serious problem in the ancient forest clearings of the southern Neolithic heartland, and perhaps the population
was increasing.

An important element in the social mix is represented by the
sudden appearance all over central and north-west Europe of handsome pottery vessels known as beakers. These are flat-bottomed,
frequently waisted jars, often more than 150 mm in height, and
characteristically decorated all over their outer surfaces with impressed patterns, often arranged in horizontal zones. They frequently
occur in graves together with small copper or bronze daggers, gold
ornaments, and archer's equipment, including barbed and tanged
arrowheads and stone wrist guards.

At present, it seems that pots with simple zonal patterns like that
from Langcombe in the Plym Valley should, on stylistic grounds, be
placed early in the sequence, while those with bold zones of chevron
or crosshatched decoration like the group of three from Wick on the
north Somerset coast should be later. Stylistically late beakers are
known from east Devon. That from Farway has a sagging profile and
is decorated with a series of horizontal lines with a little vertical

58

Plate 6 Beaker from Trevedra, St Just, found during ploughing in 1954, in a rectangular cist. Height 163 mm. Royal Institution of Cornwall.

Fig 2·1 Beakers from (left to right) Burnt Common, Try (Gulval, Tregiffian) (St
Buryan), and Farway (*sources: Burnt Common, Farway, Pollard 1967b, fig 4; Try,
Tregiffian, Patchett 1951, fig 1*).

ornament near the mouth. That from Burnt Common, Sidmouth, has
two cordons on a barrel-like body and poorly executed chevron
motifs. Even further out of step with the classic early forms is the
beaker from Try, Gulval, not dissimilar to that from Burnt Common
but with a strap handle set on one side (*fig 2·1*).

No radio carbon dates are available for south-western beakers.
Known dates suggest that beakers decorated in the 'all over corded'

style belong at least as far back as 2500 BC, but none of the south-western finds is likely to be quite as early as this. The upper fill of an early Neolithic enclosure ditch at Knap Hill in Wiltshire, yielded a date of about 2200 BC for beaker sherds, and material in the ditch of the henge at Durrington Walls also in Wiltshire, gave a date of about 2000 BC for beaker pot.

Controversy surrounds the significance of the beakers and their typical accompaniments. Some archaeologists argue that the beakers belong to immigrant groups who moved rapidly across Europe, and entered Britain in either one or a series of folk movements.[1] The beaker people, they say, were dominant archers and warriors with access to simple metal work, who were able to establish themselves as an aristocracy wherever they settled. An alternative view regards the superior beaker equipment as the prestigious possessions of local groups who emerged as dominant in the competition for land and resources in the late third millennium.[2] The beakers themselves were probably used as mead and barley-beer mugs in ceremonial and convivial drinking parties which were a social expression of an elite group. Whether they arrived from across the Channel or emerged locally—and of course both may have happened—the beaker people were among those who successfully established themselves on a broader economic basis in new environments, and were in a position to control many of the exchange networks.

Meanwhile, other new kinds of pots may represent similar new patterns which had been developing sporadically across the country. Recent research has focused upon a class of flat-bottomed Neolithic pottery involving low vessels decorated with narrow channels arranged in a variety of patterns from which it has been given the title 'grooved ware'. Grooved ware is best dated in Wessex, where a series of radio carbon dates suggests a range of use between 2700 BC and 1800 BC.

Some of the south-western material, although it belongs within the broad grooved ware tradition, is not quite like that from the classic sites further east. The best known is the bowl from Haldon which is flat-based and carries two bands of grooved decoration round its body. A similar vessel comes from South Cadbury (*fig 2·2*), and the sherd from Three Holes Cave in Torbryan was included in the original corpus of grooved ware.[3] One of the peculiarities of the ware is its wide distribution which falls (at present) most densely in Wessex and East Anglia, but extends northwards into southern Scotland and the Orkney Islands. Links with Ireland, where similar social upheavals were happening, are implied by the similarity of decorative motifs.

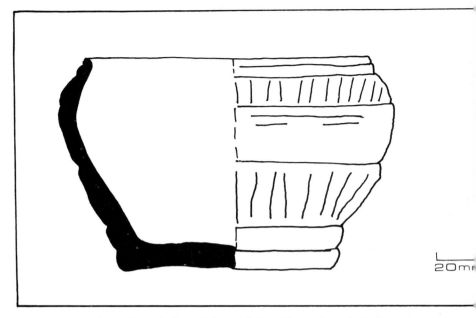

20mm

Fig 2·2 'Grooved Ware' bowls from (left to right) Haldon and South Cadbury (*sources: Willock 1937; Alcock 1972, fig 14*).

During the centuries after 1900 BC people began to require new pot types, which became known traditionally as 'cinerary urns' and 'food vessels', names which derive from what archaeologists thought were their functions and which have tended to obscure their considerable variations in form, background and context. The flat bottoms, zones of impressed decoration, and curved profiles of these pots suggest that the potters were drawing ideas from the beakers and the grooved ware. These potters may still have been professionals in the Lizard and elsewhere, supplying the market taste. Equally, the women in each group may have been the makers of some wares, and if social groups were exogamous, that is if women always moved to a new group when they married, this would help to explain how new ideas and customs could spread among neighbouring communities.

The evidence comes largely from burial sites. A food vessel with a flat base and wide flat collar shared the same flint cairn at Farway Down with the beaker already mentioned. A broadly similar pot came from Watch Hill, near St Austell, with a date around 1800 BC. A collared cinerary urn, of a type widespread through southern Britain, was one of four pots in a barrow at Upton Pyne in Devon, with a date

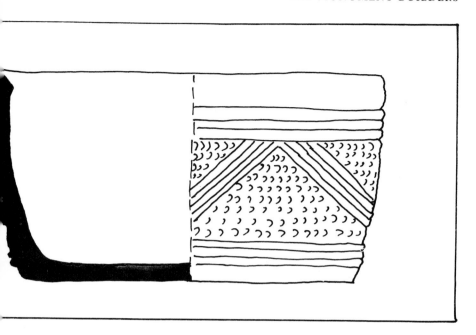

Plate 7 Urn from Crig-a-Mennis barrow, Liskey, Perranzabuloe. It is an elaborate 'Cornish' urn, and was found in a pit in the barrow floor. Height, 385 mm. Royal Institution of Cornwall.

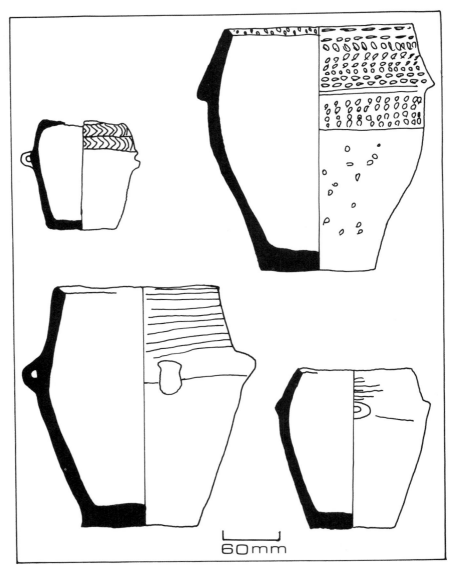

Fig 2·3 Pots from Upton Pyne barrow (*source: Pollard, Russell 1969, fig 6*).

around 1600 BC (*fig 2·3*). Conspicuous among the south-west pots are large, imposing vessels with narrow flat bottoms, lug handles, and broad zones of cord-impressed decorations set in zig-zag patterns below the rim. These are often known as Cornish Urns, and they

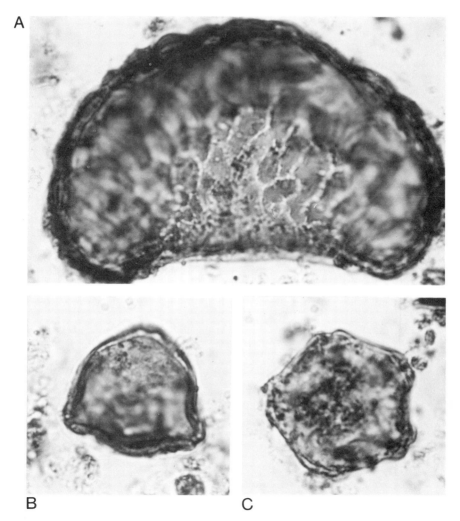

Plate 8 Fossil pollen grains from upper layers of soil buried beneath barrow at Colliford, Bodmin Moor, all at magnification × 1000. a: polypody fern, b: hazel, c: alder.

belong at the head of the Trevisker Ware series, named after the site where this ware has been most closely studied.[4] Good examples come from Tregaseal, from Crig-a-Mennis, Perranzabuloe,[5] and from Harlyn Bay, where the pot was accompanied by a bronze dagger and a small cup and dates around 1450 BC. The communities of Scilly pro-

E

duced their own styles, well preserved examples of which come from the Knackyboy chambered tomb on St Martin's, with their globular bodies, paired lugs, and rows of stab impression.

Pottery from settlements at Gwithian and Stannon Down, and from tombs such as Sperris Quoit in Penwith and Bant's Carn on Scilly, suggests that people were in contact across the Irish Sea. Behind all these local and regional pottery styles must stand economic and political arrangements at which we can only guess, but which may have involved hierarchical societies controlled by high status chiefs and priests.

Patterns of settlement

Soil pollen investigations at Innisidgen on Scilly revealed an old land surface under a fossil sand dune which yielded evidence of oak and hazel woodland subsequently replaced by open grass and heather heath with indications of corn-growing. This clearance may have been carried out deliberately by the local farmers.[6] The results of pollen analysis from old land surfaces buried under barrows on Hensbarrow Moor and the flanks of Bodmin Moor suggest that these ritual monuments were built in landscapes patched with light woodland and open heather, from which trees were being cleared. The evidence from Dartmoor may fit with this[7]—certainly cereal pollen was present in the area where the Cholwichtown stone row was built. Caution is needed in the interpretation of this evidence, however, and natural factors may have been at least as important as human activity.[8]

Some of the Cornish axe factories, like that producing Group IA implements in west Penwith, or that producing Group IIIA tools near Mounts Bay, seem to come into operation at about this time, perhaps in response to an increased need for edge tools. Similarly, the drilling of stone, perhaps by a bow drill, to produce the shaft hole implements with their 'hour glass' perforations, suggests the application of a different technique in the interests of more efficient production (fig 2·4). Nevertheless, as the barbed and tanged arrowheads witness, hunting remained an important food resource.

A series of recently investigated sites offers an insight into broadly contemporary settlement. At Topsham, on a sheltered estuary site just above the Exe flood plain, was found a scatter of sherds decorated in styles indicative of late Neolithic and grooved ware influence, but of a hard fabric which relates better to the solitary possible beaker sherd from the site. The mix of styles seems to be typical of ceramic assemblages from comparable south-western sites. The stone work

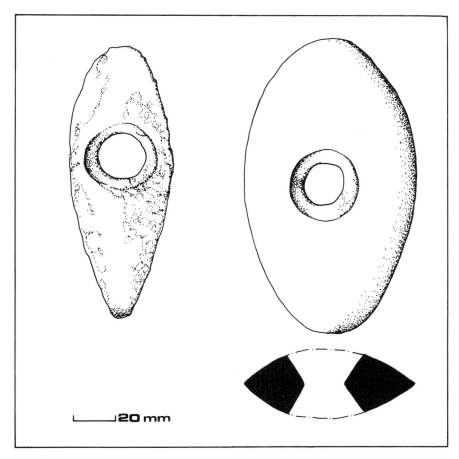

20 mm

Fig 2·4 Axe-head with shaft-hole perforation from a barrow at Woodbury Common,
found with a dagger and a cremation, and shaft-hole adze, with cross-section
showing typical 'hour-glass' perforation, found in the River Lew (*source:
Exeter City Museum*).

included a polished greenstone axe fragment and a broken perforated
sandstone pebble, and the range of worked flint included scrapers of
various types, flakes, knives, a single laurel leaf arrowhead and a
number of the mesolithic style '*petit tranchet*' arrowheads. All in all, it
was an assemblage typical of the late Neolithic/Early Bronze Age
communities (*fig 2·5*).

Associated with the pottery and the stone were clusters of pits and
undated ragged lines of stake holes, some of which may relate to
timber structures, although no plans could be recovered. The major-

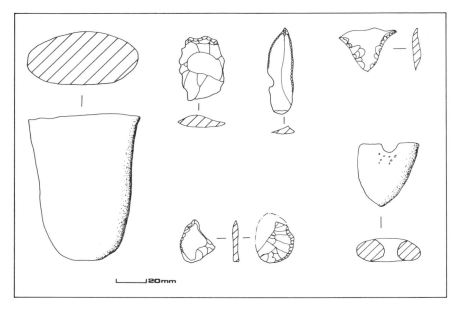

Fig 2·5 Greenstone axe fragment, perforated pebble, and flintwork from Topsham (*source: Jarvis, Maxfield 1975*).

ity of the pits are likely to have been used for storage, perhaps for grain. Unfortunately, no bone remains survived in the acid soil. The recovery of oak and hazel charcoal, and hazel nut shells, offers clues about the surrounding environment. So this site suggests a small group growing and storing grain, rearing cattle and preparing hides with scrapers, clearing woodland, knapping flint, and supplementing their diet with hunting and, no doubt, the seafood offered by the estuary. Their home or homes may not have been very substantial, and the polished Cornish axe head shows that they were in touch with other groups.[9] The beaker-type sherds and indistinct structural remains from the Honeyditches site near Seaton may suggest a second similar community in east Devon.

Further west is the important site at Gwithian near the sea where layers of occupation debris are divided by layers of sterile sands. Layer 8, the lowest level of occupation, yielded the scatter of beaker and locally developed pottery already mentioned, and similar ceramic forms persisted into Layer 7. In excavation Layer 8 showed a two-phase circular hut which initially had a diameter of about 0.5 m with one central and several radial posts, with an off-centre hearth, a free-standing entrance and various features represented by stakes. It was then rebuilt, larger, and with a double setting of stake holes but no central post, a central hearth, and a more elaborate entrance. Although the pottery was abraded, it seemed to be associated with the two-phase hut. Other finds included a Group IA greenstone axe, bones of sheep, pigs, and cattle, a saddle quern broken into fragments, a copper awl, and a pottery ring. The thinness of the occupation layer suggested a relatively brief occupation, and soil analysis indicated an environment of bracken and open scrub.[10]

At Stannon Down on the western edge of Bodmin Moor excavation has exposed a layer of organic cultivated soil which lay beneath the huts of the later village, and which, on the evidence of the pottery finds, seems contemporary with Gwithian Layers 8 and 7. A badly chipped greenstone axe at the base of the soil points to initial clearance, and a stone hoe found beneath one of the hut foundations suggests the cultivation methods employed. No settlement site was discovered which might tie in with this cultivation.[11] Less is known about likely similar sites on Dartmoor, but exploitation of the moor is amply demonstrated by the many flint scatters which contain barbed arrow-heads made by contemporary hunters.

The evidence for early settlement on Scilly comes from a series of somewhat confused sites, some of them damaged by sea erosion and by early excavating activities. Judging by the finds which have appeared so far of stone, bone, and antler equipment, and of pottery which belongs around 2300 BC, people first came to Scilly at this time. Original sites are difficult to detect because, apart perhaps from a certain increased sophistication of structural building, the way of life continued virtually unchanged until the latest prehistoric period. At least eighteen settlement sites are known which belong with this long period of continuity. A typical example is that on the cliff at Halangy Porth from which came a mass of charcoal and burnt material including limpet shells, pottery of general Knackyboy type, bones of seal and two varieties of deer, and saddle querns. Associated with this material were the remains of at least one sub-rectangular house, from the interior of which came two barbed and tanged arrow-heads. From a little distance away came flint flakes and tools, and a broken circular mace-head with an hour-glass perforation: this stonework may represent the earlier use of the site, and would fit happily into a late third millennium context.[12]

In the Somerset Levels the broad environmental change taking place around 2500 BC seems to have involved the gradual replacement of the fen woodland by bare, open raised bog similar to the huge bogs of central Ireland. Conditions on the ground differed according to the amount of rainfall: in wetter times, once the change was well under-way, there would have been deep pools separated by hummocks of dry land, and in drier times isolated pools separated by expanses of heather and ling. The phase of major clearance, represented by the decline of elm pollen, seems to have come to an end about 2800 BC. During the next two centuries or so the forest re-generated, and the record from sites at the Sweet Track, the Abbot's Way and Meare Heath shows that ash, elm and oak spread into abandoned clearings. Then, about 2500 BC, elm declined again, on a fairly minor scale this time, perhaps representing a composite picture of small local clearances.[13]

Radio carbon dates suggest that local groups were constructing trackways at a number of sites including Garvin's Tracks, the Baker Track, Walton Heath, and the Abbot's Way. Garvin's Tracks led straight out from the northern edge of the Polden Hills leaving dry land close to a spring which may have supported a Late Neolithic settlement. They were intended, as most of the contemporary tracks must have been, to give the settlers access to the rich marshland resources of wildfowl, fish and vegetables.

Garvin's Tracks were built of arm-loads of brushwood, laid longi-tudinally and with vertical pegs irregularly placed along the sides to prevent spread. They seem to belong to the earlier stages in the change to raised bog conditions. By contrast, the Abbot's Way, which runs from Westhay to Burtle, is a much more substantial construction involving transverse timbers, mostly of alder, laid flat. Pegs edging the roadway perhaps originally acted as survey lines. It is the heaviest track so far discovered in the Levels and could have supported traffic including cattle and vehicles like sledges. The Abbot's Way seems to have run through raised bog, and was in use around 2500 BC.

The evidence from sites scattered across the peninsula seem to tell a consistent story of occupation in the centuries after 2500 BC (fig 2·6). What proportion of the total may be represented by this handful of sites is difficult to estimate but probably many more await discovery, along the coast, in the river valleys, and on the higher ground inland. Clearance of wood and scrub created arable land cultivated by hoes, and cattle-rearing probably continued to be very important. Occupa-tion on the granite upland shown by Stannon Phase I and the Dart-moor flint scatters suggests that people were already exploiting high summer pasture, and it may yet prove that some of the known Dartmoor settlements were first occupied at this time. Nevertheless, occupation seems often to have been short-lived, like that at Gwithian 8, or lacking permanent home buildings, as at Topsham. As far as we

Plate 9 Abbot's Way, Somerset Levels, in course of excavation during 1974. Taken from the west and showing heavy timber construction.

know, no regular field systems were laid out in the south west at this time, and although this suggestion should not be pushed too far, it is possible that people were now finding their essentially Neolithic methods of food production inadequate, without yet having found any alternative.

Sacred circles and alignments

The social life of the late Neolithic people stimulated the erection of a complex range of ceremonial sites. The earliest of these, which seem to begin as a group before 3000 BC and to have continued for several centuries, are the eighty or so known henge monuments, so called because the earliest phase of Stonehenge is included in the group. The early, or Class I, henges are normally circular enclosures created by the excavation of a ditch and the heaping of the earth to form a bank. These henges usually have a single entrance, and many of them also

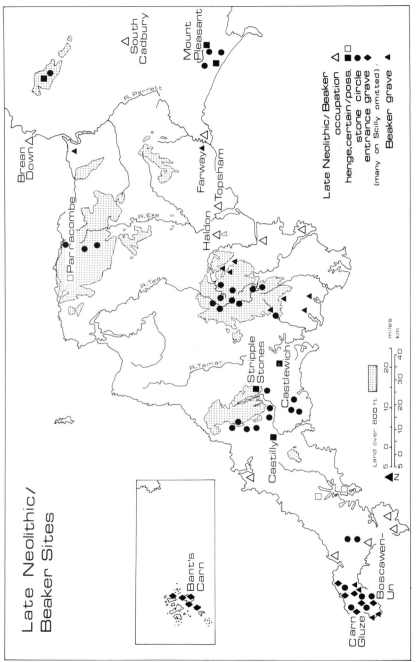

Fig 2·6 Later Neolithic and Beaker sites.

incorporated settings of stone or timber posts. A small number of much larger henges (Class II) with two or four entrances have been identified in central Britain, including one in Dorset at Mount Pleasant, three in Wiltshire at Avebury, Mardon, and Durrington Walls, and one beside the Icknield Way at Waulud's Bank in Bedfordshire. Finds of grooved ware have been a conspicuous feature of these super-henges, and the radio carbon dates suggest that they were constructed around 2500 BC.

The origin of the henges may owe something to the earlier Neolithic enclosures and round barrows, and they seem to have been peaceful gathering places where people might transact ceremonial and perhaps general business. Finds from some sites suggest that in their later phases, at least, rituals involved the burial of human remains. Perhaps the henges played a role in the exchange of stone tools and probably pottery. Equally, each henge may have been the ceremonial centre of a single group, and therefore their distribution may give us an insight into what almost amounts to the political geography of southern Britain around 2500 BC. This in turn leads to the suggestion that the building of the super-henges signals the emergence of larger power groupings at the time when pottery changes point to the rise of superior classes.

The known south-western sites fall into Class I, and unfortunately the finds from them are almost non-existent. West of the Tamar the sites at Castlewich, Castilly, the Stripple Stones and, less certainly, those at Cundodden in the Roseland peninsula and Halgarras near Truro have been recognized.[14] Castlewich lies on the south-west slope of Balstone Down looking over a small river valley and within easy reach of the River Tamar. The earthwork appears to be roughly circular with a simple entrance on the southern side although both bank and ditch have suffered serious plough damage (*fig 2·7*). No standing stones are now associated with the site, but any such may have long since disappeared into local buildings. Barely 500 m away is the outcrop of Balstone Down greenstone from which the Group IV implements were produced.[15]

Castilly lies on the weathered slate plateau of Innis Down in mid-Cornwall. The original earthwork seems to have been oval with an internal ditch and bank enclosing an area of 30 m by 49 m, and with an entrance on the northern side. Near the site are at least five burial mounds. The Stripple Stones site, on the western flank of Bodmin Moor near Hawk's Tor, reveals a low circular bank dug from a shallow external ditch with a single entrance at the south west enclosing a circle of originally twenty-eight standing stones with a single upright stone in the centre. The Stripple Stones suggest a local link between the embanked henges and the stone circles known through-out the south west which lack associated earthworks. No certain henges have been identified in Devon, but a site belonging to this group may be that on Parracombe Common in Exmoor, near the head of a tributary of the West Lyn, where a roughly circular earth-work has a bank outside the ditch.[16]

Stone circles and stone alignments are considerably more common than henges in the south west. The known examples are concentrated

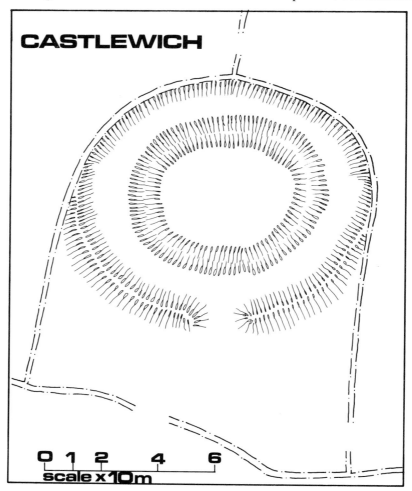

Fig. 2·7 Henge monument at Castlewich (*source: Fox 1952a*).

on the upland, but uneven chances of survival may come into the picture here, quite apart from the doubtful question of timber equivalents elsewhere. No radio carbon dates are available for the south-western sites. The rather sparse evidence suggests that stone cirles and alignments began to be built soon after 2500 BC, but there is no reason why their erection could not have continued for several centuries, or to doubt that people continued to pay observances at the sites. If we are right in regarding the henges as gathering places, the stone structures would fit as their equivalents, and perhaps successors. Their relationship to burial places, and the human bones found in some, give an idea of the rituals involved. Recently stone alignments have been seen as elaborate instruments aligned upon the movements of the heavenly bodies so that specialists might make astronomical and calendrical calculations requiring considerable mathematical knowledge and accumulated lore.[17] In its simpler forms, this theory probably has a good deal to recommend it, but it would be wrong to try to force one interpretation upon sites which may have had a wealth of meaning for their builders.

Several important monuments are concentrated in the Penwith peninsula and most of these are open to visitors. The Nine Maidens circle lies beside a ridgeway path and perhaps originally had twenty upright stones: a burial mound touches the circle. Boscawen-Un has nineteen stones and a central quartz pillar. Two circles used to exist at Tregeseal but only one partially survives. At the Merry Maidens, nineteen stones are still standing and a short distance to the east are two standing stones known as The Pipers. A number of standing stones are known in Penwith which are not attached to more elaborate alignments: some of these, as at Tregiffian, Trelaw, and Paul, were erected as grave markers. The excavation of the menhir at Try, Gulval, showed that a cairn had been erected beside it which covered a cist containing cremated remains and the handled beaker previously described.

Further east near St Columb Major is the only known stone row in Cornwall, also called the Nine Maidens because of its original nine uprights. On Bodmin Moor the Hurlers consisted of three large circles, the central one apparently paved with granite slabs. The Rillaton barrow is close by and further east on the Moor are the Trippet Stones, a well preserved circle of eight stones about 1.5 km west of the Stripple Stones.

The largest concentration of stone alignments is on Dartmoor, where about seventy have been recognized, some of them complicated sites covering considerable areas and incorporating a number of

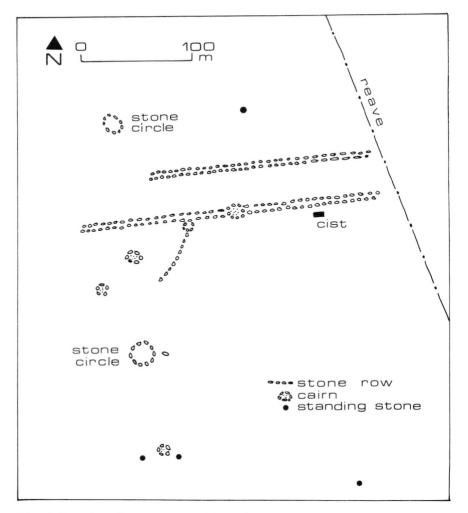

Fig 2·8 Complex of monuments at Merrivale (*source: Wood, Penny 1975*).

elements. Smaller stones are often covered by blanket peat, which suggests that the alignments were erected before the peat began to develop. The pollen evidence from the row at Cholwichtown suggests that the row was built in an abandoned clearing within woodland.[18] At Merrivale two fine double stone rows are side by side with a small third row set at an angle (*fig 2·8*). The southern row has the interesting feature of a cairn half way along it surrounded by a

Plate 10 Stalldon Row on Stalldon Moor, Cornwood, Dartmoor, looking south, in June 1903. This single row is one of the most impressive on the moor.

circular setting of kerb stones, and in the centre are the remains of a stone-lined pit or cist. Beside the row is a second large cist and further south are a number of cairns, one of them approached by a short stone alignment, a circle of eleven surviving stones, and a standing stone over 3 m high. Similar complexes are known at Drizzlecombe, Shovel Down, where the rows lie on the parish boundary between Gidleigh and Chagford, and Fernworthy, where one of the cairns yielded a beaker and a bronze dagger.

The characteristic association of stone settings and ritual mounds reappears at most of the simpler sites. At Watern Down near the Warren House Inn, for example, a double row of fifty pairs of stones

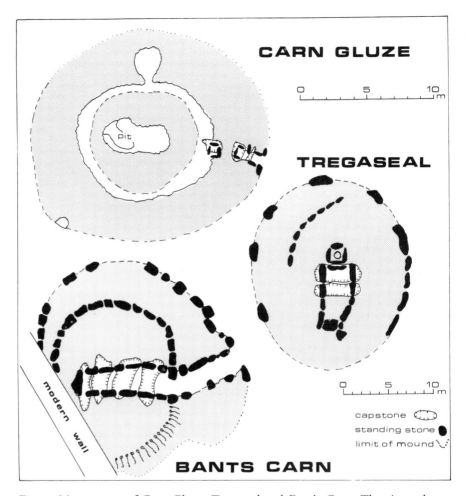

Fig 2·9 Monuments of Carn Gluze, Tregaseal and Bant's Carn. The cist and pot are shown behind the main chamber at Tregaseal (*sources: Carn Gluze, Tregaseal, Hencken 1932 13, 14; Bant's Carn, O'Neil 1961, fig 15*).

extends for 165 m to a cairn. Not every row is associated with a cairn: at Headland Warren, Challacombe, three rows converge on a standing stone. Several free-standing stone circles are known—at Grey Wethers, Langstone Moor, and at Scorhill near Gidleigh, a particularly fine example. There are various standing stones, of which that known as Beardown Man near Devil's Tor is the most impressive, standing over 3 m above the ground. A similar, although less rich, range of sites has been identified on Exmoor, including circles at

Porlock Common and Withypool, a row complex on Wilmersham Common, and several standing stones.

Chambered tombs

The great tombs built by the Neolithic settlers centuries before must still have been impressive monuments in the landscape. Pottery from Zennor Quoit,[19] and cremated bone from a pot set in a pit on the floor of the entrance grave at Tregiffian in Penwith (which gave a radio carbon date of about 1539 bc), show that the tombs were still being used. At Tregaseal near St Just, west Cornwall, a cist containing a Bronze Age pot was inserted into the mound behind the main chamber (*fig 2·9*) and the complicated site of Carn Gluze, or Ballowal barrow, near St Just, seems also to have been in use at this time. Here, the original builders dug a pit or shaft, perhaps representing entry to the underworld, which had four small cists around the top. Later, this was covered by a large, oval, double-walled cairn which still stands to a height of 4 m. Finally, the worshippers enclosed the cairn itself by a huge ring cairn, into the south-western side of which they built a chambered tomb that contained quantities of burnt human bones and broken pots. Traces of a variety of offerings and ritual acts were found at the site.

The entrance graves on Scilly mentioned in the previous chapter seem to have been built at this time. More than half the known tombs are concentrated into three linear cemeteries—on Gugh, and North Hill and South Hill, Samson—and they were probably erected over a considerable period. Architecturally, the most impressive tomb is that of Bant's Carn, Halangy Down at St Mary's.[20] The mound is more than 12 m in diameter and it possesses an inner and an outer retaining wall, hinting at two periods of construction. The entrance leads into a long, rectangular chamber built of large stone slabs with three rows of dry stone walling above, and roofed by four huge capstones. The tombs at Porth Hellick, Innisidgen and Lower Innisidgen, all on St Mary's, which may also be visited, are essentially of the same design, and generally most of the tombs represent simple variations of a similar plan. Excavations at Knackyboy Cairn, St Martin's, suggest that rites at the tombs involved the deposit of pots, burnt human bone, and charcoal.[21] Probably, the monuments were seen as the sacred places of the whole community, bound up in a concept of sacredness which embraced both the fertility of the living and the power of the dead.[22]

Barrows and cairns

The barrows and cairns which have been mentioned so far as elements in a variety of ritual complexes require fuller discussion. Throughout a long period beginning soon after 2500 BC and continuing after 1000 BC, the building of more or less complicated mounds was an important part of human religious activity. Solitary examples are known, but many of them probably formed groups, sometimes associated with other monuments, like the stone alignments. These barrows and cairns stud our present landscape, where they are often conspicuous features on crests and ridgeways.

Important concentrations were built on the heathland of Farway Common and its environs in east Devon where there are about a hundred; on west Exmoor where the group at North Molton is famous; and on Dartmoor where a particularly conspicuous line runs along Hameldown Ridge. A concentration of about thirty-five in the lower Exe Valley at Upton Pyne, however, shows that not all barrows were situated on high or marginal ground.

Further west, the group of some ten barrows at Pelynt in south Cornwall, or the row of at least seven on Taphouse Ridge, in southeast Cornwall, are all well known. Nevertheless, these are only the tip

Plate 11 Bant's Carn, St Mary's, Scilly, after replacement of fallen coverstone and jambstone in 1970.

of a potentially very large iceberg. Study of almost any area will reveal several possible new sites, suggesting the existence of many more examples. Barrows in general have suffered badly from the effects of early unscientific excavation and damage from ploughing. However, comprehensive lists compiled as a result of field survey and scrutiny of the relevant literature, together with important recent excavations, have helped to render much more intelligible the whole sacred mound tradition in the south west.

The classic form of beaker burial, demonstrated by discoveries made particularly on the chalklands of Wessex, involves a rectangular dug grave, sometimes slab-lined to form a cist, containing a single body buried while still complete, together with a beaker and other grave goods, all presumed to be the personal equipment of the dead. The grave might be covered by a mound. Some sites on Dartmoor, including that at Fernworthy with its beaker, bronze blade and characteristic V-perforated lignite button, or the archer's wrist guard from Archerton, or the equally characteristic barbed and tanged arrowheads from Langcombe and Lakehead, fall within this tradition, but generally in the south west traditions were different.

A range of important sites has been investigated on the heathland of east Devon. At Burnt Common beaker sherds, together with

Plate 12 Barrow cemetery known as Five Barrows, Western Common, North Molton, looking west.

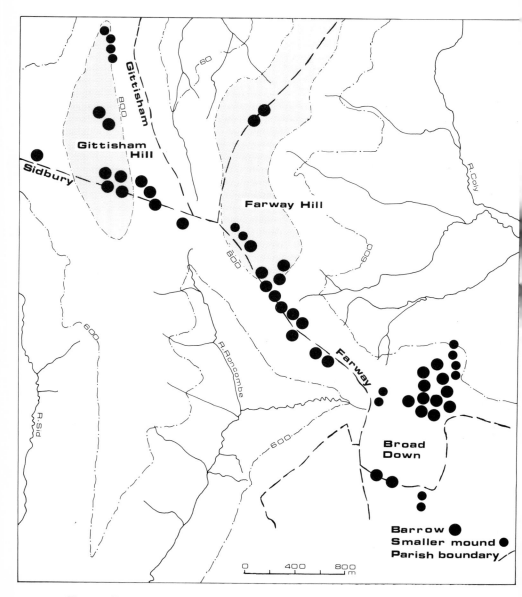

Fig 2·10 Barrow cemetery at Broad Down/Farway, east Devon (*source: Fox 1948, Ordnance Survey*).

quantities of oak charcoal, filled a sunken stone-lined pit, near which were two smaller charcoal filled pits and an area of burnt ground. After the burning a ring-shaped cairn of flint lamps, about 11 m in diameter, was built to enclose the pits, and this was left open and free-standing.[23] At White Cross Ring, south west along the ridge, a flint ring cairn surrounded a small cairn covering a pit containing six flint flakes and a fossil sea urchin: this seemed to have been preceded and accompanied by a series of small pits. On the opposite side of the River Sid two adjacent sites at Farway were essentially similar, one enclosing three probable cremations in pits.[24]

On the evidence of finds which seem to date around the fifteenth century BC, the Broad Down/Farway cemetery grew with the addition of a considerable number of cremations placed on pavements, or in cists, under cairns (*fig 2·10*). Some of these were covered with turf mounds sometimes ditched, or surrounded by a circle of standing stones. One cist held the cremated bones of an adult, and of a child with a segmented bone bead. Another of the group, at Roncombe Corner, was originally a cremation covered by a small earth mound, later enlarged by a deposit of burnt material within which was placed an incised cup containing a child's burnt bones. Finally, the whole was capped with chert boulders.[25] The local group seems to have added smaller mounds and pits throughout the life of the cemetery.

The Upton Pyne cemetery seems to have been much the same. A barrow excavated in 1869 produced burnt bone, a bronze dagger and pin, a necklace, and a small pot. A recently excavated barrow nearby had a range of pots and burnt material, including a child's bones, which the settlers had placed on the ground and subsequently covered with a mound of turf and clay. Oak charcoal, possibly from mature wood, gave a date representing about 1550 BC.[26]

The settlers built a number of barrows on the northern flank of Bodmin Moor. At Tregulland a central burial was enclosed by two stake circles 4 m and 7 m in diameter (*fig 2·11*). Outside the circles, the worshippers had dug a shallow pit in which they lit fires, and a pit containing cremated bone with two barbed arrowheads. Later, the stakes were removed and replaced by a ring of stones which included four slabs carrying cup-marks, small circular depressions signifying the magic of death and burial. A cremation in a pot was placed within the ring cairn, and then the whole thing was covered with a mound of soil dug from an encircling ditch.[27]

An important group of six mounds, which formed part of a considerable barrow cemetery on the Hensbarrow granite, has been excavated recently[28] and clearly shows what a wide range of ritual acts

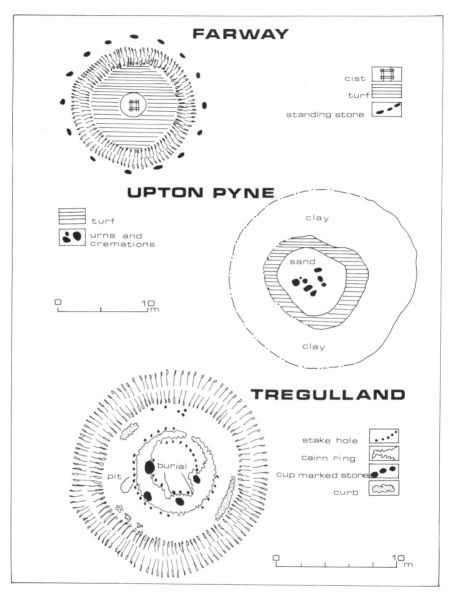

Fig 2·11 Plans of barrows at Farway, Upton Pyne, and Tregulland (*sources: Farway, Fox 1948; Upton Pyne, Pollard, Russell 1969; Tregulland, Ashbee 1958*).

such cemeteries represent. Cocksbarrow seemed to be the earliest site. Here the builders first dug pits, then erected a ring cairn with timber posts and an entrance on the south east. Some time later they dug a central slab-lined pit in which they put burnt human bone and a horn ladle, and then the whole was covered with a turf mound capped with eye-catching yellow clay, eventually masked with dark soil.

Nearby at Watch Hill, the original builders constructed a ditched ring cairn, with two rings of stones. The inner ring had a blocked entrance, and a scatter of sherds in the ditch, a feature noted at other south-western sites, may have been part of this ritual blocking. Radio carbon dates represent around 1800 BC or earlier for this primary phase. At a time when the ring cairn was partially ruined, two wooden coffins were placed one on top of the other in a central pit. The local group built a cairn of turves and granite lumps over this pit, and then constructed a turf stack which covered the whole ring cairn. Rather later they built the turf stack higher, capped it with yellow clay and filled in the ditch. Finally, the whole barrow was masked with dark soil.

Of three structures in line nearby at Caerloggas, one proved to be a simple mound, badly damaged, and another a similar mound constructed over a miniature standing stone. At the third site the builders had created a three-period ditched and banked enclosure circling a moorstone on the hill-top. Against the stone they had set a central pit, and inside the ring they deposited objects including flints, quartz pebbles, metal slag, parts of a bronze dagger which dates around 1450 BC, a fragment of amber, and a stone bead. The latest structure, on Trenance Downs, consisted of a cairn ring without a burial. Like Cocksbarrow and Watch Hill, the Caerloggas sites and Trenance were capped for a time with yellow clay.

On Dartmoor a combination of the very acid soil which destroys most artefacts except stonework, and the activities of generations of investigators, has left denuded monuments very difficult to interpret. Apart from numerous cairns and barrows, about a hundred cists—granite slabs forming a box-like structure—are known on the moor, chiefly concentrated in the valleys of the Dart, the Meavy and the Plym. These range in size from the large examples like that at Roundy Park, Postbridge, which was 2 m by 1 m, to the small ones like that on Langstone Moor which was only 0.5 m by 0.3 m. Some, although not all, of the cists were originally covered in mounds. Like other similar sites, they were sometimes built in groups, like the eleven in the valley of the Langcombe Brook, or as an element in standing stones complexes, like those at Merrivale. The earlier cists were erected by men with a beaker culture: the Archerton wrist guard, the Fernworthy finds and the Chagford beaker all came from cists. However, the likelihood is that cists continued to be built over a considerable period through the Bronze Age. Similar cists occur in Cornwall, on the granite moorlands and on the lower slate areas.

It has become clear that the older interpretation of barrow sites as the simple burial mounds of chiefs and heroes, derived essentially from written classical sources like the *Iliad*, is now inadequate. Bronze Age ritual needs further exploration to examine its religious and social implications. The building of a ritual site was plainly often a protracted business, involving fresh constructions perhaps over a considerable period, each accompanied by appropriate ceremonies which often seem to have included burnt human bones. The greater cemeteries were probably in use for some length of time, and perhaps each generation undertook the construction and maintainance of only a few barrows in each cemetery. Similarly, the great ritual complexes underline the fact that individual sites should not be considerered in isolation, even though we may not know what significance the juxtapositions had for their builders.

Although all these small monuments look like a break with the past when they are compared with the great tombs, and although the beaker ritual of individual burial in a well-furnished grave contrasts with Neolithic rites, nevertheless there is a clear element of continuity in the south-western monuments. People continued to place the remains of several human beings in the same mound, and to focus ritual effort upon the power of the dead. They continued to construct barrow ditches and post settings which recall the henges, and some of their ring cairns seem close in spirit to the stone circles. All these monuments are essentially sacred enclosures within which the worshippers carried out a wide range of ritual acts, and they embody a religious tradition which endured long in the peninsula.

Early Bronze Age society

Complex workings in European society during the third millennium BC, which are signified by the appearance of beakers and other new pots, in the ritual monuments, and in the settlement pattern, seem to have encouraged the emergence of new forms of social authority. The style in which these operated justifies the use of the term 'chief' with all its connotations of high barbarism, and the same men probably also acted as priests. Intimately connected with the rise of chieftains seem to be the means by which their status could be expressed, especially through the possession of highly personal, prestigious, and valuable objects, which could be re-distributed as gifts to symbolize dependence and superiority. A principal reason for the great development in metallurgical techniques—which we call the Early Bronze Age—may lie in the apparent *need* for such precious objects. In more precise archaeological detail, the process by which the working of gold, copper, and tin bronze was introduced into the south west (as elsewhere in Britain) is far from clear.

Two distinct strands seem to be involved. Beaker-using people often possessed small knife blades of copper or bronze, copper awls, pins, and occasional objects of sheet gold like earrings or the coverings of buttons. These are rare in the south west, but a knife was excavated from Fernworthy and an awl from Gwithian. It is generally agreed that the stimulus to the production of these pieces came from the continental mainland. However, at about the same time, heavy, roughly triangular axe blades made their appearance, like that from Drewsteignton in Devon. These were soon refined to thinner narrow-bladed pieces, a single valve stone mould for the manufacture of which was found at Altarnun in east Cornwall. Some were decorated in punched patterns which recall the design on beaker pots: an axe

Plate 13 Gold lunulae, Cornwall. The upper one was found at St Juliot, and the lower two together at Harlyn Bay, probably with a flat axe. Diameters 215–222 mm. Royal Institution of Cornwall.

with a 'raindrop pattern' came from Axmouth, while two with chevron patterns were found at Trenovissick in Cornwall.

Rather similar is the decoration found on the crescent-shaped collars or *lunulae* of thin sheet gold, which may well be chiefs' insignia. Most of the *lunulae* are found in Ireland, but four came from Cornwall—two from Harlyn Bay probably with a plain flat axe. The decoration on one of the Harlyn Bay *lunulae* matches exactly that found with unfinished pieces in a smith's box at Kerivoa in the Cotes du Nord in France, an eloquent witness to the mechanism of distribution. The axe blades also are extremely common throughout southern Ireland, and although knowledge of the technique may have come direct from the continent to the south west, it is possible that there were Irish intermediaries.

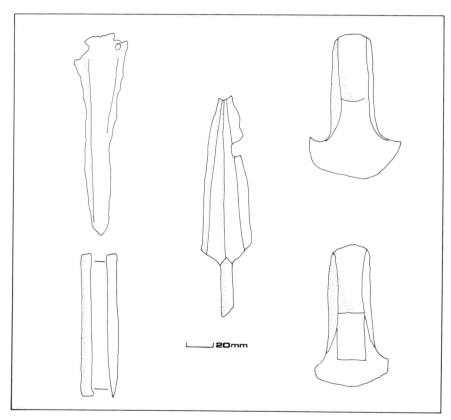

Fig 2·12 Dagger, punch, spearhead, and two flanged axes from Early Bronze Age metal hoard, Plymstock, Devon (*source: British Museum*).

People in the south west may have acquired a few of the early Armorico-British (AB) style daggers which developed from the knives, and certainly some of the improved axes with their edges hammered up to make flanges. However, it is not until the latest daggers, known as Camerton-Snowshill or Arreton types, together with cast flanged axes, appear around 1500 BC that metal workers seem to be active throughout the south west. An important discovery at Plymstock, near Plymouth, included sixteen flanged axes, three daggers, a tanged spear, and a punch, perhaps a metal worker's tool (*fig 2·12*). A similar dagger came from a barrow at Huntshaw, Torrington. The fragment from a comparable dagger with metal slag from the Caerloggas site is the first real intimation that smiths were exploiting the copper and tin ores of the south west. The axes and the daggers may have been used as tools, or as status symbols. Spears were new, and these daggers-on-sticks show us a society in which fighting and perhaps prestigious hunting, both typical aristocratic pursuits, have become important (*fig 2·13*).

This metalwork is broadly contemporary with those richly furnished barrows on the southern chalk downs which make up the often-discussed 'Wessex' culture.[29] These Wessex graves seem to build

Plate 14 Gold cup from Rillaton, Linkinhorne, Bodmin Moor, found in a cist within a barrow in 1818. Height, 83 mm. British Museum.

Plate 15 Shale cup from Farway, east Devon, found with cremated bone in a barrow. Height, 90 mm. Exeter City Museum.

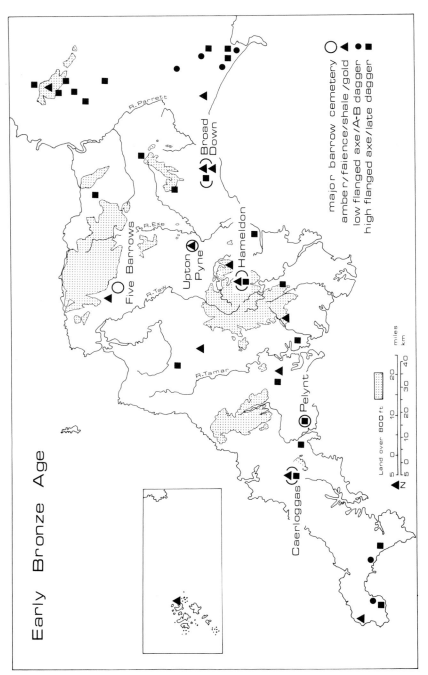

Fig 2·13 Early Bronze Age sites.

upon old beaker traditions: the glorification of the individual is expressed in a series of barrow burials in which the daggers, the goldwork, and the amber (probably from Jutland), demonstrate the farflung contacts of the chieftains. A few famous south-western barrow finds suggest similar aspirations: two fine shale cups, like that in amber from Hove, were deposited in two of the Farway barrows; one of the Hameldown group contained an amber dagger pommel decorated with inset gold pins; and from the Rillaton barrow in south Cornwall came a magnificent corrugated sheet gold cup.

Beads of the blue glassy paste known as faience sometimes appear in barrows. They formed part of a necklace in a grave at South Molton, and others came from Carn Creis in Penwith, and Knackyboy in Scilly. It is still not clear whether these were made in Britain, or manufactured in the eastern Mediterranean and imported together with the amber. A ritual site with beads on Shaugh Moor, Dartmoor, has given a radio carbon date of about 1480 bc.[30]

The indications that people were having difficulty finding enough food, and the appearance of chiefs as authorities replacing the old Neolithic family groups—chiefs who required expensive possessions to maintain their prestige—may point to a society under stress. These tensions may lie behind the outburst of religious ceremonies, which had the effect of reconciling groups with different interests, sanctifying economic arrangements, and offering a comforting link with the past.

1. Clarke 1970
2. Burgess, Shennan 1976
3. Wainwright, Longworth 1971
4. ApSimon, Greenfield 1972
5. Christie 1960
6. Ashbee 1976
7. Simmons 1969
8. Miles 1975a; Dimbleby 1963
9. Jarvis, Maxfield 1975
10. Megaw 1976
11. Mercer 1970
12. Ashbee 1974
13. Beckett, Hibbert 1978
14. Thomas 1964
15. Fox 1952a
16. Grinsell 1970, 25
17. Wood 1978; Burl 1979
18. Simmons 1969
19. Thomas, Wailes 1967
20. Ashbee 1976
21. O'Neill 1952
22. Ashbee 1976
23. Pollard 1967b
24. Pollard 1971
25. Fox 1948
26. Pollard, Russell 1969, 1976
27. Ashbee 1958
28. Miles 1975a
29. Piggott 1938
30. Wainwright et al 1979

CHAPTER THREE

The Farming Community of Later Prehistory

Later Bronze Age farmers

The long span of later prehistory, from about 1400 BC to the eve of the Roman Conquest, covers the conventional Middle and Late Bronze Ages and the pre-Roman Iron Age, so named from technological developments rather than substantial shifts in the patterns of farming life. Nevertheless, profound pressures for change were at work in late prehistoric society, for which these developments are important indications.

The chronological framework and the dating of individual sites during the earlier part of this time depends largely upon a few radio carbon dates, together with assessments based upon the pottery. A date from Trevisker in Cornwall of around 1250 BC seems to represent the end of the Bronze Age settlement. The Bronze Age farm at Gwithian in west Cornwall yielded a similar date. Both these sites produced a range of pottery types known as Trevisker style ware, which have cord-impressed decoration in the early phases and stamped decoration later.

Assemblages of broadly Trevisker ware make up the pottery normally found on Bronze Age sites throughout Devon and Cornwall (*fig 3·1*). Until a full-scale research programme has been undertaken it is impossible to estimate what proportion of these Bronze Age wares are of gabbroic clay (see p. 47), and were made in and distributed from the Lizard peninsula. Some pottery certainly came from this source, and further work will no doubt confirm other sources, including perhaps some on the flanks of Dartmoor, which may have a bearing on the history of the decorative fashions.

On Dartmoor considerable areas of ancient landscape still survive, now partially obscured by peat, which offer the fullest chance to appreciate the dynamics of Bronze Age society. By around 1300 BC the blanket bog was already well developed in areas above 440 m. Below this, open grass or heathland interspersed with patches of woodland extended down to about 160 m, and lower still, dense forest still flourished. A plot of the settlement pattern shows, as might be expected, that the farmers built most of their buildings in the open area. They built hundreds of round huts on the moor, each of which would have had a central post or ring of posts supporting a conical roof of wood or thatch, a doorway sometimes shielded from the elements by a curved porch, and if it was a living hut rather than a store or working area, a hearth. Huts with various internal fittings were excavated at Dean Moor.[1]

The huts sometimes stand alone, like tht at Rippon Tor, Ilsington, especially on the eastern slopes of the moor. Sometimes they are loosely grouped like the settlement on Horridge Common, where a bronze axe was found, or at Watern Oke where about ninety huts straggle over the hillside.

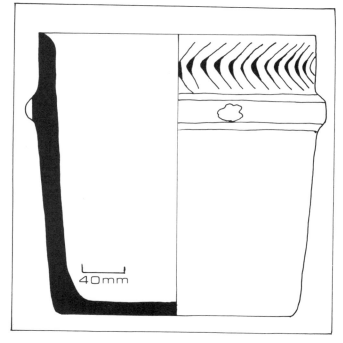

40mm

Fig 3·1 Pot with cordon and incised decoration, of broad Trevisker Style 4 type, from Raddick Hill, Dartmoor (*source: Radford 1952, fig 12*).

In contrast to the looser pattern are the hut clusters, frequently enclosed by substantial rough stone walls, locally known as pounds. Riders Rings (*fig 3·2*) in the Avon Valley has two distinct compounds with at least twelve hut circles distributed between them; Grimspound on the lower slope of Hameldown, and one of the easiest of the sites to visit, has about twenty-four huts and an enclosure which, although now renovated, must always have been impressive. The recently excavated pound on Shaugh Moor seems to have been occupied in the centuries either side of 1300 BC.[2] Pounds cluster thickly in the valleys of the Avon, the Erme, and the Plym, all on the southern part of the moor.

Aerial photographs show that many of the huts and hut groups are associated with field systems wherein the farmers grew the cereal crops witnessed by the saddle quern and corn rubbers of Dean Moor. The excavations at Gwithian showed remarkable details of Bronze Age fields: they were usually small and square, divided by banks or lynchets which developed as the stones cleared from the surface were dumped at the field's edge, and as, over the years, the turning of the ard or light wooden plough at each end threw up soil. Each field

Plate 16 Enclosure, or pound, with hut circles, Shaugh Moor, Dartmoor, in course of excavation in 1978.

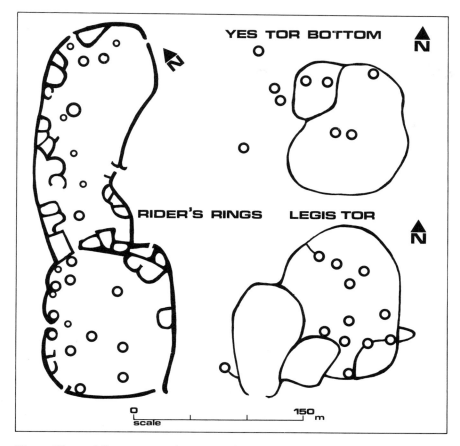

Fig 3·2 Plans of Dartmoor enclosures: Rider's Rings, Yes Tor Bottom, Legis Tor
   (*sources: Rider's Rings, Worth 1935; others, Worth 1943*).

probably had to be ploughed twice, once in each direction, in order to
disturb the earth sufficiently for crop growth, one reason why the
fields are square. The ard was drawn by cattle (*fig 3·3*), so that these
farmsteads must have included a range of byres, pens, fenced-off
fields, and the organization of a continuous supply of feed. Arrangements for the management of stock reared for meat, dairy produce,
and wool, must have been vital since the fields seem too small to
support the homesteads alone.

Recent field work has demonstrated that probably all the land on
Dartmoor below roughly the 400 m contour was part of a very large
allotment system, marked out by the linear stony banks known as

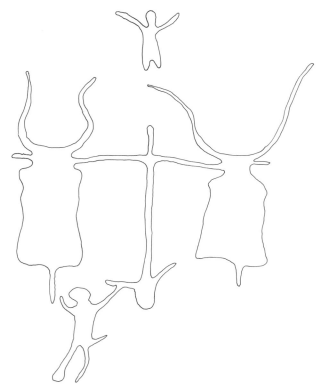

Fig 3·3 Bronze Age
plough-team
engraved on a
rock in the
Alpes
Maritimes
(*source: Clark
1952, fig 47*).

reaves. A typical landscape can be seen between White Ridge and Shapley Tor where a main reave runs along Hurston Ridge, and others across Shapley Tor and Birch Tor: these all have subsidiary reaves joining them at right angles, and some of the reaves have enclosures attached.[3]

A number of separate territories has been identified, each based on an upper river valley of the southern moor, like the Walkham, Meavy, and Plym (*fig 3·4*). Each territory is defined by main reaves and has three important characteristics. Each has access to an area of high moorland and this seems best interpreted as common grazing. Below is a zone thickly strewn with huts and enclosures. The Dean Moor excavation showed that the farmers pursued a range of activities which included spinning, perhaps potting, and possibly tin-working, to which should doubtless be added hide preparation, cheese-making, and wood-working. This zone may be subdivided by subsidiary or parallel reaves. The lowest zone is normally divided by a parallel reave system which seems to have included arable land, and in some areas,

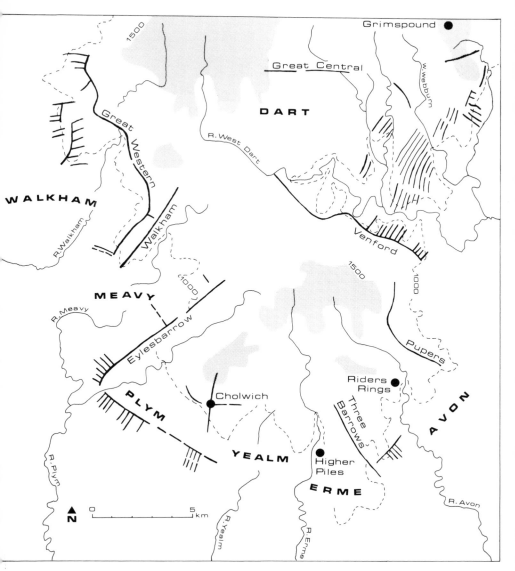

Fig 3·4 Diagrammatic plan of the reave systems on southern Dartmoor. Suggested prehistoric territories are marked in capitals. Major reaves are shown and named, and parallel reaves are shown. Major enclosures are marked (*source: Fleming 1978, fig 2*).

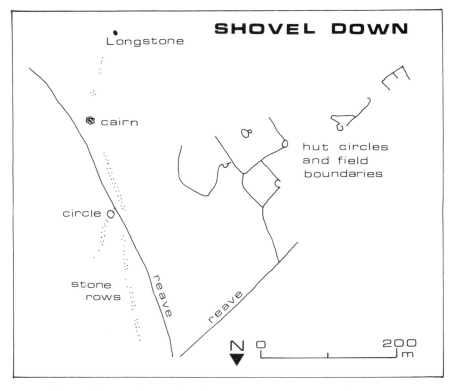

Fig 3·5 Plan of Shovel Down, Chagford, Dartmoor (*source: Ordnance Survey*).

like Shaugh Moor, the layout of the reaves may fossilize the boundaries of pre-existing fields.

The reaves bear a potentially interesting relationship to stone
rows. In some cases they ignore them altogether, but in others they
seem to have been deliberately laid out between them, as at Shovel
Down (*fig 3·5*), or at right angles to them, as at Merrivale, which may
suggest the perpetuation of earlier land allotments.

The territories seem designed to give each group a share in each
type of land, suggesting transhumance in which the cattle were taken
up to high summer pasture between sowing and harvest on the lower
land. The major pounds are conspicuous, and it is tempting to see
them as the centres of dominant families. The layout of fields and
settlements were changed as time passed. For example, the huts at
Shaugh Moor showed two periods of construction; at Legis Tor the
enclosed area was successively increased three times; and field systems

Plate 17 Section of Venford Reave, on Holne Moor, Dartmoor. The whole reave is over 7 km long. At this stage in the excavation original features are obscured by a mass of stones thrown over by Bronze Age farmers during field clearance.

Plate 18 The same excavation at a later stage. The original narrow main reave, with two carefully constructed faces, can now be seen. On the left, it is clear that a parallel reave joins the main one, and a circular hut was built in the junction of the two.

like that at Wotter show chronological depth. This underlines the complexity of the land management, and of the human society it reflects.

The settlement pattern on Bodmin Moor seems to have been broadly similar, involving hut groups and their fields in a landscape divided into complex allotments by boundary systems. Settlements are widely distributed over the western half of the moor. Excavations at Stannon Down (*fig 3·6*) showed that the inhabitants erected some eighteen huts, scattered among a strip system of cultivated fields, and three large enclosures, presumably for the cattle which calculations of cereal yield suggest would have been crucial. Climatic conditions probably matched those on Dartmoor, and excavation suggested that peat growth played a part in the abandonment of this particular settlement.[4]

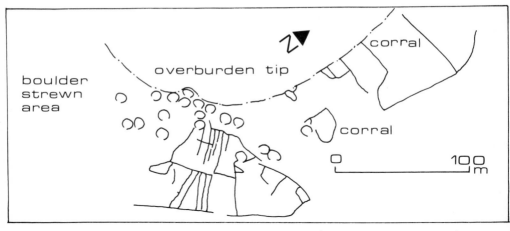

Fig 3·6 Plan of settlement at Stannon Down, Bodmin (*source: Mercer 1970, fig 6*).

Land management patterns as complex as those on Dartmoor and Bodmin Moor are in the process of analysis on Scilly.[5] On North Hill, Samson, a stone bank with pendant enclosures seems to run across country linking megalithic tombs, suggesting that settlers were utilizing the land for cattle-rearing. At Halangy Porth on St Mary's two megalithic tombs, a settlement and a field system are all elements in an integrated landscape.

This broad pattern of settlement, which accidents of survival have preserved so well in some areas, probably spread over much of the peninsula. In west Cornwall, the farmstead at Gwithian was just one of a range of similar sites. Trevisker, with its circular timber home and outbuildings, may have been one of a scatter of some forty farmsteads between the Valley of Lanhearne and Porthcothan.[6] Dainton Common in southern Devon has a characteristic field system, and here, around 900 BC, a smith cast an impressive set of bronze weapons and left behind fragments of his clay moulds.

Evidence of settlement on Exmoor continues to accumulate. In the Somerset Levels new tracks, like Viper's and Nidon's, were built, probably in response to renewed flooding of the raised bog. The pollen record at Abbot's Way suggests that local groups were clearing land, perhaps by grazing their beasts.

New developments

As for the earlier, so also for the later phase, pottery provides the best

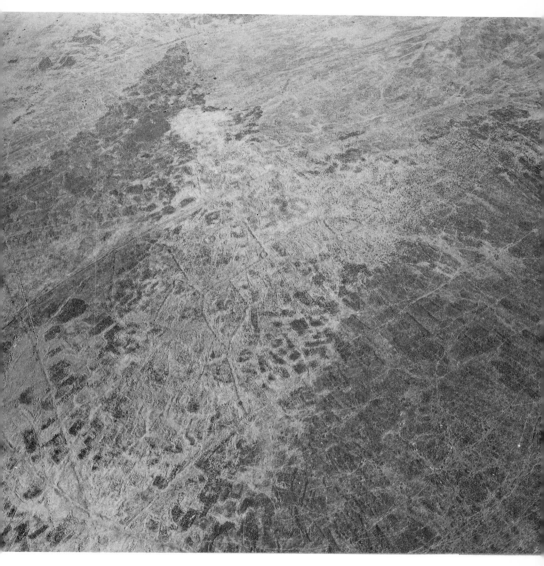

Plate 19 Shovel Down, Dartmoor looking south. In the centre are hut circles with enclosures or fields. On the left are a complex of stone rows, and the Longstone standing stone. Also on the left, a reave crosses the landscape between the rows, and another joins it in the foreground. Compare figure 3·5. Other features can also be spotted.

method of building up a chronological framework, assisted by the handful of available radio carbon dates. Throughout Cornwall and Devon, and into Somerset, pottery which can be described as 'latest Bronze Age' or 'earliest Iron Age' has proved hard to distinguish. The small amount of material available for study suggests that many communities were using pots which belong in the final phases of the broad Trevisker tradition, and some may have been virtually aceramic, using almost no pottery at all.

From around 400 BC vigorous novel pottery styles developed in southern Britain. These resulted in a number of broad regional groupings, including that of the decorated wares throughout the south west.[7] These south-western wares have normally been called 'Glastonbury wares' and as a blanket term, covering a range of dark, smoothly finished bowls and jars with boldly incised curvilinear patterns, the name still has validity (*fig 3·7*). However, it obscures the

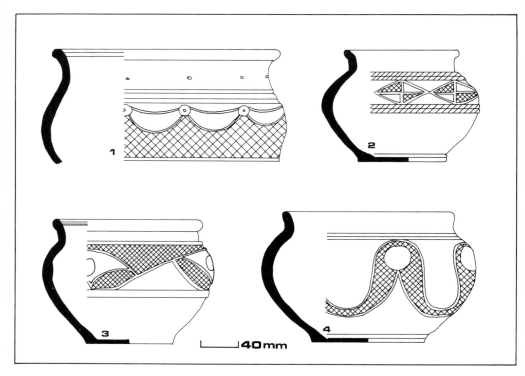

Fig 3·7 Glastonbury ware types, group 2, first century BC to first century AD: 1, 2, 3, Glastonbury: 4, Meare (*source: Cunliffe 1978, p. 375*).

fact proved by petrological study that the pots were made at and distributed from at least six centres, each based on a different clay type. One of these was sited on the gabbroic clay of the Lizard peninsula, and seems to have started in business around 280 BC. Its products have been identified at the Rumps, Caerloggas, and Castle Dor (Cornwall), further east at Meare and Glastonbury, and into Hampshire and Northamptonshire. Two centres were located in the South Hams, and their products have been found at Milber and Hembury. Three more, operating probably during the second and first centuries BC, were based on clays of the Mendip area, all with local distributions of their wares. It is from the appearance of these at the famous Glastonbury lake village that the decorated styles take their name.

In Cornwall a style of pottery known as 'cordoned ware' appeared around 70 BC and was superimposed on the earlier tradition. It consisted of wheel-turned jars and bowls, dark in colour and decorated with cordons or raised bands (*fig 3·8*). This was one element in a well-marked series of broadly contemporary ceramic innovations, which also included the Durotrigian wares of Dorset with their burnished bead-rim bowls and jars with counter-sunk handles, and the

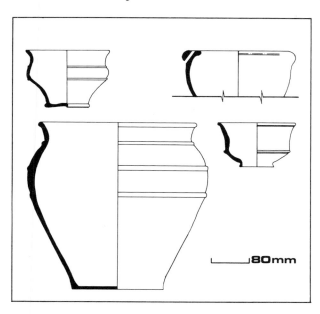

Fig 3·8 Cordoned ware types, about 50BC–43AD. All Caerloggas (*source: Threipland, 1956*).

Belgic wares in the south east with their pedestal urns, cordoned bowls and butt beakers. Like the Glastonbury pots, cordoned ware is likely to have been made at a number of centres, including the Lizard peninsula.

Armed with this broad pottery sequence, we can distinguish an increasing variety of settlement types in the centuries before AD 50, all of which are likely to be different responses to local conditions. In some—perhaps many—places, people continued to make their living from Bronze Age-style farms and fields, and a number of Iron Age sites have hints of late Bronze Age occupation in their near neighbourhoods. For example, at Bodrifty, near Penzance, from which came some Bronze Age sherds, the farmers built about twenty round huts, some of which they eventually enclosed in a pound wall. They grew corn, reared sheep, and finally acquired some Glastonbury-style pottery.[8]

Kestor, on north-west Dartmoor, appears to have been a broadly similar site. The one enclosed hut, known as the Round Pound, probably belonged to a blacksmith, judging by its iron slag and internal fittings. The plough soil overlay peat, suggesting that the settlers were already forced to contend with deteriorating conditions on the moor.[9]

Hill slope enclosures

Kestor seems to have been one of the last of the Dartmoor prehistoric settlements. A working hypothesis to account for this might be that the Dartmoor farmers and stockmen were forced to abandon the moor as a result of steadily worsening conditions, and that their new homes are to be found among the multiple enclosure forts or hill slope enclosures, which as a class of site seem to begin soon after 500 BC. This interpretation, of course, is not without difficulties, for environmental conditions and their causes on later prehistoric Dartmoor are not yet fully understood. Equally, few hill slope enclosures have produced datable finds, and research upon their origins and functions is still progressing.

Characteristically, the builders set these enclosures on the sides of hills, or on the spurs of ridges close to a water source, and not on hilltops, which suggests they were chosen for practical farming reasons rather than reasons of defence. Their typical form involves a central, roughly circular enclosure less than 2 hectares (5 acres) in extent and with an entrance, to which outer enclosures were sometimes later added (*fig 3·9*). Milber Down in south Devon[10] has two

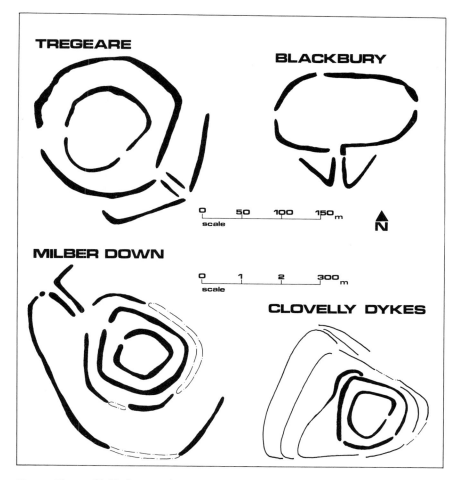

Fig 3·9 Plans of hill-slope enclosures (*source: Tregeare, Hogg 1975, fig 99; Blackbury, Young, Richardson 1955; Milber, Clovelly, Cunliffe 1978, fig 12·5*).

concentric enclosures surrounding the main enclosure, all with aligned entrances, beyond which is a fourth concentric enclosure set some little distance away. The finds from Milber included a range of Glastonbury ware. Clovelly Dykes near the north Devon coast is a similarly elaborate site where the plan provided for four separate enclosures apart from the central one.

Sometimes, as at Denbury in south Devon, or Castle Dor in south Cornwall, which produced Glastonbury ware and cordoned pots, the

Plate 20 The hill-slope enclosure at Milber Down, south Devon, looking
south east.

outer enclosure is pendant upon the inner, following its line for part of
the circuit and then belling out at the side where the two aligned
entrances are placed. Sometimes, as at Hall Rings, Pelynt, cross banks
were used to cut off substantial areas which often included a water
supply.

Hill slope enclosures appear in the South Hams, on Exmoor, and
on the fringes of the otherwise bare Culm measures which cover north
Devon. West of the Tamar they cluster especially thickly north and
south of Bodmin Moor. Their siting, their multiple enclosures, and
their relationship to water all imply that they were built by pastoralists
for the management of stock, although in the acid south-western soils
bone remains are sparse. This fits with the general absence of associated field systems, implying that beasts were the principal food
source. The central area is likely to have held the homestead of the
group, and although the record of material culture is generally poor,
the iron dagger handle from Milber or the glass, shale, and bronze
armlets and glass beads from Castle Dor hint at prosperity. The
construction work involved suggests a sizeable population acting

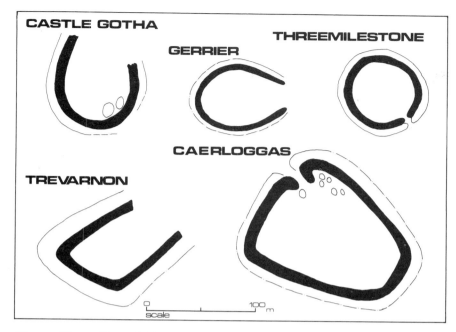

Fig 3·10 Plans of 'rounds' (*source: Thomas 1966*).

under authority, and the homesteads look like the settlements of socially superior elements in a community which, like many pastoralists, counted its wealth chiefly in flocks and herds.

Rounds

A similar type of site, and one with its roots clearly in Bronze Age society, is that known as a univallate enclosure, or more informally as a round. This is a simple banked and ditched enclosure, which may be of any shape, surrounding an area of usually no more than about 1 hectare (2 acres), normally sited on good arable land. Inside the enclosure, the settlers erected a number of huts and outbuildings. Many of these sites are still being located, and seem to be concentrated west of the Tamar and in north-west Devon, and it is likely that many more await discovery (*fig 3·10*).

Detailed survey in west Cornwall has shown that rounds were sometimes very densely distributed: in parts of west Cornwall they occur at the rate of one per 260 hectares (or 1 square mile).[11] However, it is plain from those few sites which have been excavated that rounds

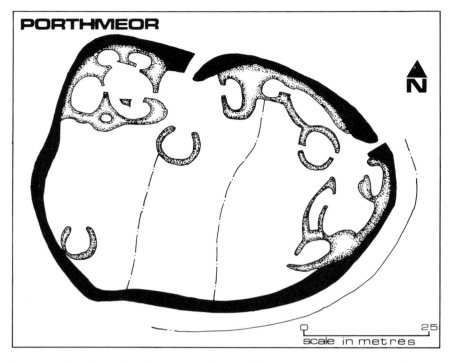

Fig 3·11 Plan of round and courtyard houses, Porthmeor (*source: Hirst 1936*).

were coming into and going out of use over a long period extending from about 500 BC to AD 400 or even later. Distribution maps, therefore, cannot give any real insight into the density of people at any given time, or the extent of the land which they were using.

Castle Gotha round yielded Glastonbury pottery, with hints of late Bronze Age activity on the site, and continued in use into the Roman period.[12] Caerloggas (St Mawgan-in-Pydar) is a large example of its kind set at the end of a low spur. Excavation[13] here showed that the first builders erected a number of huts from which came decorated Glastonbury style wares, and enclosed them by a single bank and ditch with a timbered entrance. Later inhabitants used much cordoned pottery of gabbroic ware in a variety of jar forms. One of their huts was equipped as a smith's workshop, with two stone-lined hearths and a furnace pit. Finds include tin ore, raw bronze, crucibles, and a decorated bronze shield mount.

At Trevisker the Bronze Age site was succeeded, after an apparently barren interval, by a new settlement first built around 200 BC,

Plate 21 Carn Euny settlement, west Cornwall, from the north, during excavation in 1972, showing courtyard houses.

and enlarged in the first century BC. The later settlers equipped their stone huts with slab-lined drains, suggesting that these may have accommodated cattle as well as men, and finds of spindle whorls imply that sheep were also kept. Rotary querns, a possible iron sickle blade, and clay ovens suggest cereal-producing fields. Iron slag showed that at least basic tools could be provided domestically, and stone, including the quartz porphyry milling-stones, came from nearby. The pottery included cordoned forms which closely paralleled those from Caerloggas.[14]

Courtyard houses

In Penwith and on Scilly, farmers built a related settlement type known as the courtyard house, which can be broadly paralleled at the same time elsewhere along the Atlantic seaboard. This was a roughly circular, earth and stone structure with a single entrance leading into a central courtyard, unroofed but frequently elaborately paved, off which opened a variety of roofed dwellings, byres and stores, built into the thickness of the bank. Courtyard houses occur singly as at Mulfra Vean, or in clusters as at Carn Euny. Scanty finds of querns and stone tools, and the apparently normal association of the houses with field systems, suggest agricultural communities.

The settlements with courtyard houses often seem to have had a complex history, like that at Porthmeor, where the houses were built into a round (*fig 3·11*). Again, like the rounds, some were in use over a considerable period (*fig 3·11*). That a Mulfra Vean produced cordoned pottery, suggesting that it was established some time in the first century BC. The excavations at Carn Euny, near Penzance, show that the history of this particular site covered a much longer period. The first main stage, dated around 150 BC, included circular timber buildings characterized by decorated Glastonbury type pottery, and a much coarser variant in the same tradition known as Carn Euny ware. Next, farmers who possessed cordoned ware erected four stone courtyard houses, all with labyrinthine interrelationships quite unlike the clear-cut structures known from most similar sites, although not so dissimi-

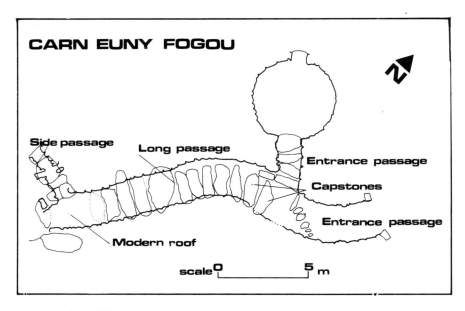

Fig 3·12 Plan of fogou at Carn Euny (*source: Christie 1978, fig 3*).

lar to the courtyard village on Halangy Down at St Mary's on Scilly. The settlers stayed until some time in the fourth century AD.[15]

Fogous

The curious structures known as fogous, from the Cornish word for cave, have been found in Penwith. They are normally attached to settlements, as at the courtyard villages of Carn Euny and Chysauster, or the round at Treveneague, St Hilary (*fig 3·12*) Like the settlements, they seem to originate in the late prehistoric period, but to continue in use into the Roman centuries. Fogous are galleries created by lining a trench with dry stone walling and roofing it with stone slabs, on to which the trench spoil is heaped back. The galleries are often curved, and usually open at each end. Sometimes the form is more elaborate: at Boleigh there there is a side chamber with a shaft hole, while at Halligey, Trelowarren, a second chamber joins the first at right angles.

Fogous seem to belong to a broad group of sites known as souterrains, which are widely scattered in time and space: in Brittany they tend to belong to the earlier Iron Age, predating the Cornish examples; in southern Scotland they seem to span the earlier centuries AD; and in Ireland they continue into the early medieval period. The function of these sites has been much debated. It has been suggested that they were refuges in time of attack, which seems unlikely since such structures would be death traps during a battle. Conceivably, they had a ritual function. However, a likely use was as well-ventilated barns for the storage of grain and other foods like preserved meat and fish, and milk products.

The Somerset Levels

The people of Penwith and Scilly seem to have built their courtyard houses as the best method of coping with the exposed and perhaps increasingly harsh conditions. At the other end of the peninsula, in the Somerset Levels, the pollen evidence similarly suggests wetter, colder weather in a landscape of raised peat bog dotted with pools of open water.[16]

This is the environment in which the famous 'lake villages' flourished, of which those at Glastonbury and Meare are the best known. At Glastonbury, on a shelf of peat near the original course of the River Brue, the Levels people founded a settlement which was complex, sizable, and successful. Eventually it included some ninety huts, not necessarily all in use at the same time, within a roughly triangular area enclosed by a palisade, built on an artificial platform of timber, brushwood, and clay at the edge of the Meare pool. A clay causeway with a landing stage ran out from the settlement into deeper water.

Waterlogged wooden objects, like tubs and buckets, preserved at the site give a rare insight into the details of the inhabitants' daily lives. Spindle whorls, loom weights, and weaving combs emphasize the importance of their flocks, although the wheeled vehicles and ploughs imply arable farming during at least the earlier stages of the settlement. The settlers used the decorated Glastonbury wares first defined at this site, and the bronze and enamel workshops demonstrate the high level of craftsmanship. The settlement was abandoned around AD 50, perhaps as a result of the rising water level.

Investigations at Westonzoyland, West Huntspill and Alstone have located further settlements on low sand islands in the Levels,[17] and more probably remain to be found. By the first century BC saltmaking had been established in the Levels, characteristic briquetage debris having been recognized at Quarrylands Lane, Badgworth. This industry, of great importance for the preservation of meat, was to continue through the Roman period.

Hillforts

Within the wide range of late prehistoric enclosures, the hillforts seem to constitute a separate group, even allowing for their diverse origins, changes of use, and overlap of functions with other kinds of enclosed sites. Hillforts, among the most impressive prehistoric monuments with their hilltop circuits of banks and ditches, may be defined as major fortified sites, defensible against human attack, and exploiting the natural terrain to this end.[18]

In the south west, the hillfort group is confined to a fairly small number of sites. These cluster most thickly around the rim of the Somerset lowlands, and in east Devon, where they form part of the band of classic sites which runs from the Devon/Dorset coast to the Mersey. Most hillforts were certainly constructed in several phases, but it is only when a site has been thoroughly excavated that any chronological precision can be achieved, and it would be rash to suppose that occupation was necessarily continuous. It is important to remember that a site is counted in the hillfort group chiefly on the strength of its late prehistoric plan.

Recent study has shown that the origins of some settlements

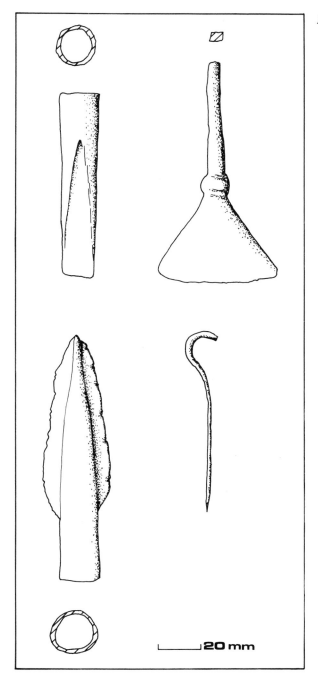

Fig 3·13 Late Bronze Age socketed gouge, tanged chisel, spearhead, and swans neck pin, from Ham Hill, Somerset (Somerset County Museum).

20 mm

H

which preceded hillforts must be pushed back to before 800 BC. A number of south-western hillfort sites have produced oddments of bronze metalwork dating around this time. At South Cadbury these came from unenclosed occupation. The material from Carn Brea in Cornwall, Ham Hill and Worlebury in Somerset and elsewhere points to a range of broadly similar hilltop settlements (fig 3·13).

Excavation and reinterpretation are giving us a clearer idea of the early defences which people built on some sites that later developed into full-scale hillforts, although, of course, not all sites so developed, and equally some forts may have been built on empty hilltops. At Hembury, in east Devon, a timber palisade preceded the dug defences.[19] At Woodbury Castle, not far away, the inhabitants built another palisaded enclosure, although it had a brief life. Akin to the palisades but involving the dumping of earth, and so the digging of a ditch, are the box-framed ramparts, where the space between timber walls was filled with rubble. At South Cadbury the settlers built one of these as their earliest defence, and they added an earthen rampart behind the inner timbers.

The palisades can be related to other sites in Britain, and as a group they seem to belong between 850 and 600 BC. The box-framed ramparts are broadly contemporary, but elaborate constructions like that at South Cadbury would belong late in the sequence, around 430 BC. It is difficult to show from the archaeological record how life in these enclosures differed from that in contemporary settlements on lower ground, but their history suggests that they must have been the centres of chiefs and nobles.

After about 350 BC social pressures stimulated the construction of more substantial and elaborately planned defences at many sites (fig 3·14). These involved the dumped earth ramparts and ditches, often multiple, which characterize the hillforts. The inhabitants modified their plans from time to time, until well into the first century AD. At South Cadbury the massive defences, still visible on the hilltop, were constructed gradually. Inside, the later inhabitants possessed a number of round huts, each with its own grain storage pit, and a range of characteristic bone-weaving combs, iron tools, and pots. A rectangular building on the summit seemed to be a shrine. South Cadbury was abandoned around 20 BC, but re-occupied from around AD 20.[20]

On the opposite side of the Levels, at Norton Fitzwarren, the principal defences seem to have been constructed around 200 BC. They stretch down on the south-eastern side to enclose a spring, which emphasizes the overlap between hillfort sites and hill-slope enclosures. The radio carbon date from Woodbury Castle suggests that the

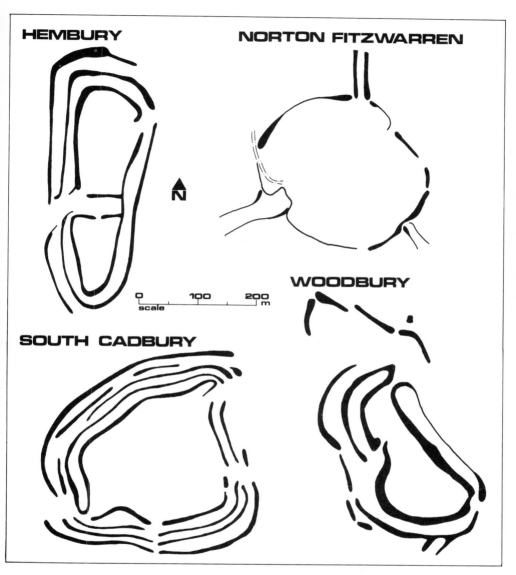

Fig 3·14 Plans of hillforts (*source: Hembury, Lidell 1930; Norton Fitzwarren, Langmaid 1971; South Cadbury, Alcock 1972; Woodbury, Miles 1975b*).

Plate 22 The hilltop of South Cadbury, Somerset, looking north east, showing some of the prehistoric defences and the village clustered beneath
the hill. The Somerset lowlands lie to the north west.

banks and ditches date before 300 BC. At Hembury a pear-shaped area
was enclosed with multiple defences.

West of the Exe, where the smaller enclosures abound, hillforts are
rather less common and generally simpler in form. At Carn Brea, the
central and eastern summits were enclosed by probably multi-period
fortifications. At Killibury, where the defences seem to begin around
250 BC, the settlers constructed two widely spread ramparts around
the hilltop.[21] Some sites have dry stone ramparts like Chun Castle,
near Penzance, with its massive inner wall and outer rampart.

The cliff castles, or promontory forts, which turn a coastal headland into an enclosed site by the construction of banks and ditches
across the neck, fit into this general picture. These sites appear all
around the coast from the Bristol Avon to the Dart (*fig 3·15*). They

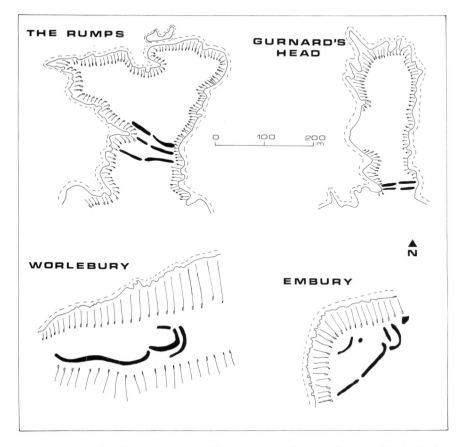

Fig 3·15 Plans of cliff castles (*source: The Rumps, Brooks 1974; Gurnards Head, Gordon 1941; Worlebury, Dymond 1902; Embury, Jefferies 1974*).

differ greatly in size and complexity, and so probably in function. The massive stone inner defences of the multi-ramparted fort on Gurnards' Head was provided with a fighting platform, and the site yielded Glastonbury style pottery. At The Rumps, St Minver, the three ramparts involved a number of structural phases and much cordoned pottery was found. The interior seemed to have been intensively occupied, at least at times. The finds of sheep bones and spindle whorls suggest the importance of flocks, while clay ovens and querns show that the settlers were eating grain.[22] On the other hand Embury Beacon, Hartland, a badly eroded site with two ramparts, seems to belong with the hill-slope enclosures: the interior yielded evidence of

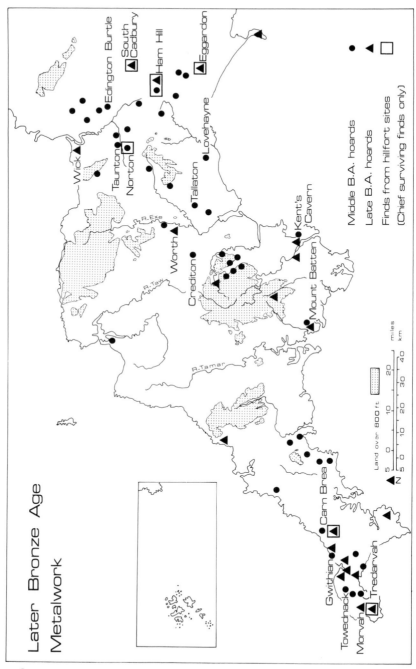

Later Bronze Age
Metalwork

Edington Burtle
South
Cadbury
Ham Hill
Eggardon
Wick
Lovehayne
Taunton
Norton
Tallaton
R.Exe
Worth
Kent's
Cavern
Crediton
R.Taw
Mount Batten
R.Tamar
Carn Brea
Gwithian
Towednack
Morvah
Tredarvah

● Middle B.A. hoards
▲ Late B.A. hoards
□ Finds from hillfort sites
(Chief surviving finds only)

Land over 800 ft
miles
km
N

Fig 3:16 Late Bronze Age metalwork.

various structures associated with Glastonbury style ware, and spindle whorls. [23]

The question as to what role hillforts played in late prehistoric society is proving extremely difficult to answer. Defended centres they certainly seem to be, and so the size of a hillfort might relate to the extent of the area under its protection or to the area over which a ruling chief exercised power. In this case, the small western forts and cliff castles (and some of the rounds and hill-slope enclosures too) would support the idea of fragmented political control here, which other evidence also suggests. The larger hillforts on the eastern fringe of the peninsula might fit, one way or another, with the bigger political units which were emerging at this time in southern Britain.

Within these regional variations, it is possible to explore ideas deriving from economic and distributional theory, and to see the forts as population centres, market places for distribution and exchange, locations for craft workers and, perhaps, religious focuses; as possessing, in fact, most of the elements which go to make a 'town'. However, distributional patterns in which forts are allotted territories may be treating evidence as contemporary when it is not and excavation in fort interiors has shown a variety of settlement characteristics. Investigations of the immediate surroundings of forts, linked with the finds from them, suggest that their inhabitants were farmers much like those at other sites. Nevertheless, the forts in the eastern part of the peninsula do seem to have fulfilled some of the roles suggested even if the range of sites in the western half suggests a less elaborate society.

Later prehistoric society

Through the creation of substantial, permanent farmsteads with well defined fields and grazing lands, the Bronze Age people first began to make a living from steady mixed farming, in a way which was to last comparatively unchanged for most people until recent centuries. Throughout southern Britain old and new land was transformed into productive arable. Although simple ard ploughs had been in use since the Neolithic, their increased use must be one factor behind the development of the new farms.

The appearance on Dartmoor, and elsewhere, of land divisions must reflect groups with sufficient stability to agree about rights, and to protect them afterwards by punishing transgressors. With the new solidarity and group confidence, people do not seem to have needed the support of ritual as they had done before. Many barrows were still being built, and some old monuments were still reverenced, but others were ignored by the new land arrangements.

The farming communities were prepared to spend part of their wealth on the acquisition of bronze ornaments, tools, and weapons (*fig 3·16*). From about 1400 BC south-western bronzesmiths began to turn out a range of the curiously clumsy axes known as palstaves, which seem to have been the normal all-purpose tools throughout southern Britain. A stone mould used for making palstaves was found at Bigbury near Plymouth. Also available were socketed spearheads, for fighting and hunting, and fine narrow-bladed rapiers, clearly intended for personal combat. All four of the known British stone rapier moulds come from the south west—from Holsworthy, Chudleigh (two), and Bodwen, and the rapiers themselves have been found at Tallaton, Devon, where there were six, Crediton, and North Crofty in Cornwall (*fig 3·17*). This suggests that the south-western smiths specialized in rapier production, and perhaps by now the social state had been reached in which every gentleman wore a blade.

Palstaves, spears and rapiers were the south-western smiths' bread and butter for a long time, until 1100 BC. However, their customers did demand some new designs, based on ideas produced by the innovating smiths of north-western Europe and south-eastern Britain, which were developed in response to local needs. Soon after 1300 BC the smiths marketed a new range of pins, elaborate neckrings and armrings, together with specialized tools such as sickles. All these were especially popular in the Vale of Taunton, where the famous Taunton Workhouse find included palstaves, tools, a spear, ornaments, and broken metal. Similar pieces came from Tredarvah, near Penzance.

Somehow, raw materials reached the smiths and finished products reached the customers, but how this was accomplished can at present only be guessed at. In most bronze alloys, tin comprises about ten per cent and the rest is of copper and other additions. Tin is a rare metal, and the most important north-western European source of its ore, cassiterite, is the granite of Dartmoor and Cornwall which also carries copper ore. As yet, surprisingly, no clear evidence has appeared to show that this ore was used to supply the southern British smiths during most of the Bronze Age, although it was probably used locally. Study of the contexts of bronze work, and of the multiple bronze finds known as 'hoards', suggest that the craft was organized on a 'village bronzesmith' basis. On the low hill at Norton Fitzwarren in the Vale of Taunton an enclosure was constructed at this time, from which came a hoard of armrings and axes dating around 1250 BC.

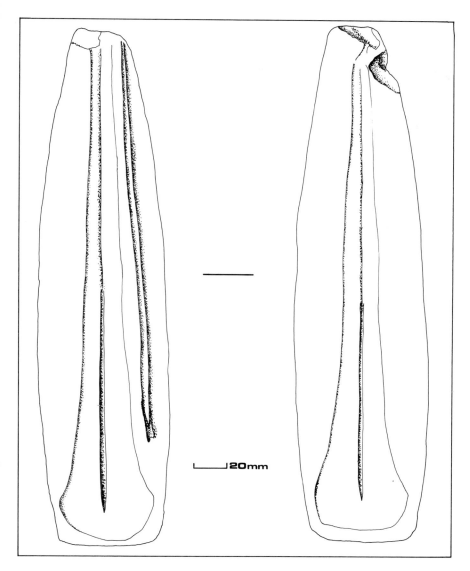

20mm

Fig 3·17 Stone bivalve rapier mould, Holsworthy, Devon. There is a matrix for a rapier blade on the face of each valve of the mould, and a second matrix for an ornamental strip on one face (*Holsworthy Museum*).

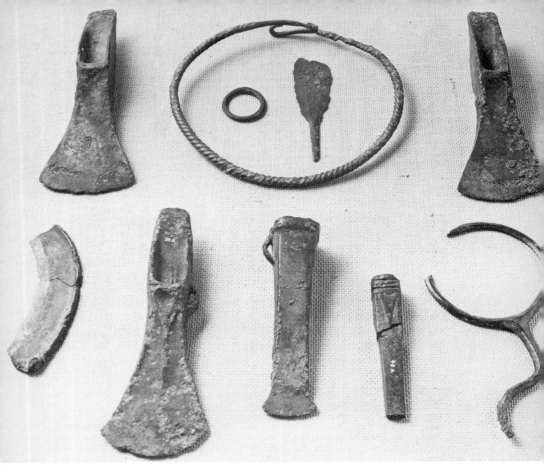

Plate 23 Objects from the Taunton Workhouse bronze hoard, including 3 palstaves, 2 early socketed tools, a sickle blade, a razor, a ring, a twisted neckring, and a 'quoit-headed' pin. Length of longest palstave, 160 mm. Somerset County Museum.

Bronze finds are especially dense in the area, and it is possible that the Norton enclosure acted as a centre where people gathered to make exchanges.[24] Further study of the metalwork is likely to suggest other possible centres throughout the peninsula, which must have an important bearing on the organization of Middle Bronze Age society.

Privileged people were able to acquire gold work, like the gold ornaments found in a field bank at Towednack, or the splendid neckring from Yeovil, most of which was likely to have been of Irish manufacture. From about 1100 BC weapons loomed much larger than before. New spearhead forms, with socket holes to take a peg and so

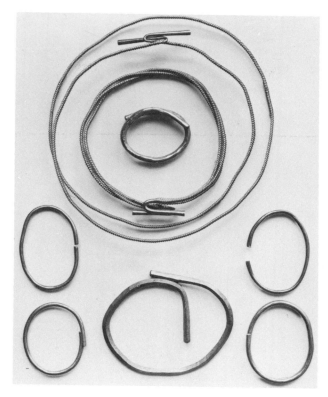

Plate 24 Eight of the nine gold pieces found in a field bank at Towednack, west Cornwall, including two twisted neckrings, four armrings, and two lengths of unfinished gold rod. Lengths 1160 mm–226 m. British Museum.

Plate 25 Elaborate gold twisted neckring, found doubled up at Yeovil, Somerset. Diameter 77 mm. Somerset County Museum.

123

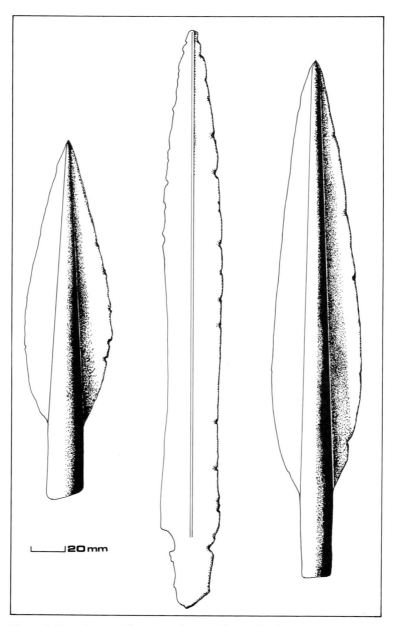

Fig 3·18 Hoard containing an early sword, two leaf-shaped spearheads and a flat bronze plate (plate not shown) from Worth, Washfield (*Exeter City Museum*).

fasten the shaft more securely, appear in the south west, and so do a few early swords with leaf-shaped blades. Two spearheads and a sword were found together at Worth, Tiverton (*fig 3·18*).

The south-western farmers participated in the great explosion of bronze-working around 750 BC, when market forces enabled the south-eastern smiths to turn out vast quantities of new designs, especially swords, tools, and the socketed axes which replaced palstaves. Much of this Late Bronze Age metalwork from the south west, especially from Cornwall, has been lost, but the group from Wick, Storgursey, in Somerset still survives. Knives and gouges become fairly common, especially from sites like Ham Hill and Mount Batten. Irish gold, best represented by the Morvah (west Cornwall) armrings, still arrived and eventually the metal merchants from Armorica began

Plate 26 Part of late Bronze Age hoard found at Wick, Stogursey, Somerset, showing a spearhead, the upper part of a sword, a palstave (*above*), a socketed axe and a socketed tool (*left*), a scabbard fitting or chape, and a broken socketed knife (*right*). Length of palstave 145 mm. Somerset County Museum.

to satisfy a metal hunger by selling the axe-shaped ingots which have been found along the south coast.

The territorial organization of the farming communities produced obvious sources of tension. Competition would have been almost inevitable, and in marginal areas like Dartmoor stress must have been heightened by probable climatic deterioration, stimulating the development of peat, and eroding available areas of arable and grazing. Both Kestor and Stannon Down seem to have been abandoned as conditions worsened. Equally, in some parts, over farming may have been causing soil exhaustion. The pattern of homesteads which developed as the centuries progressed shows the density of settlement, and their diversity suggests that farmers were exploiting as wide a range of land resources as possible.

People felt the need to assert or defend themselves, and perhaps were ready to sacrifice independence for security by joining larger units. Here must lie the origin of tribal consciousness embodied in the group name Dumnonii, which the people of the south west were using to describe themselves by the eve of the Roman Conquest. These troubles are the context of the development in bronze weaponry represented by the Worth sword and spears found in 'an ancient enclosure near the River Exe' (according to Exeter museum records) or the barbed spears, from Bloody Pool, South Brent, specially manufactured about 800 BC, which, like others of their kind, seem to have been offered in an effort to placate the water gods (*fig 3·19*). The first enclosures at Hembury and elsewhere were being constructed at this time or a little later, and their subsequent development suggests that the need for defended centres was becoming more urgent as society grew more complicated.

Among these pressures for change should possibly be included foreign bands, squeezed from their own homes by similar problems. The late bronze razors from South Cadbury and Ham Hill are certainly imported and might have been brought by incomers from north central Europe. At the same time iron working was spreading and new kinds of pots soon appeared. The old elaborate scheme of several 'Celtic invasions' has been largely abandoned by prehistorians, who now prefer to stress the significance of dynamic forces for change within British society itself. However, troubled times always offer scope to individual opportunists, both native and immigrant. In any case, the importation of Armorican metal around 600 BC represents co-operation between people on either side of the Channel, which may have continued in the following centuries with the famous tin trade between the south west and the Mediterranean via the Armor-

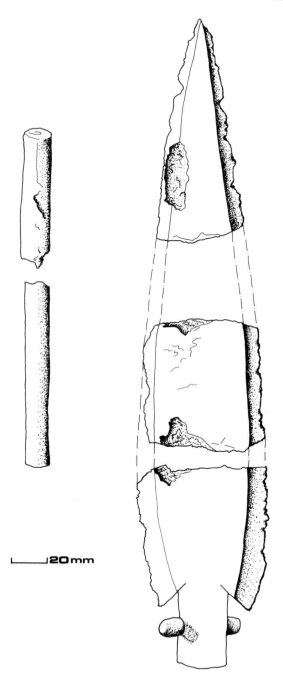

Fig 3·19 Barbed spearhead and ferrule for spear shaft butt, from the Bloody Pool hoard, South Brent (*Exeter City Museum*).

20mm

ican coast. Some historians have taken the extreme point of scepticism and doubt that the trade existed at all until the Roman period, while others accept that the H-shaped tin ingot dredged from Falmouth Harbour many years ago, which seems to match the shape of Mediterranean ingots, and the travellers' tales which the classical writers repeat, do give substance to the traditional interpretation of the trade, although its details remain obscure. Whether or not they accommodated tin merchants, a range of finds from around Mount's Bay in west Cornwall and Mount Batten in Plymouth Sound suggests that these coastal stations were important trading points throughout much of the period. They must play a role in the detailed similarities between Armorica and the south west which include prototypes for the early Glastonbury style wares before 200 BC, and, by around 70 BC, the technique of wheel turning and the appearance of the cordoned pottery.[25]

In the first century BC important bronze-smithing schools were established in the peninsula. This is proved by the finds of smelting gear from South Cadbury, Caerloggas, Castle Gotha, and Glastonbury, and their finished products are represented by objects like the Caerloggas shield mount, the animal figurines from Milber, and the bowls from Youlton and Rose Ash. The craftsmen's mastery of flowing forms created by engraving, hammering and a variety of inlays has attracted much admiration ever since.

The influence of the south-western smiths reached its peak in the conception of the 'mirror style' developed to decorate the backs of ladies' bronze mirrors, the manufacture of which continued until the Roman Conquest. Mirrors carrying characteristic motifs have been found in graves at St Keverne, Mount Batten, and, a particularly superb example, at Holcombe in east Devon, and further afield at Portsmouth and Nijmegen in Holland. These splendid objects were necessary to support the prestige of an aristocratic and war-like upper class.

The wooden fertility figurine from the River Teign, the place name element *nymet* from Old British *nemeton*, 'a sanctuary',[26] which appears in Devon names like George Nympton, and the Rose Ash and Youlton bowls, both of which came from bogs, all suggest that the Dumnonii, like most contemporaries, approached their gods by way of offerings made at sacred woods and waters. Much of the fine metalwork of the time probably has a religious significance (*fig 3·20*). The rite of burial in small cists was practised at a number of sites including the important cemetery at Harlyn Bay, where grave goods included fourth/third century ornaments. Nevertheless,

Plate 27 Bronze bowl, found at Higher Youlton Farm, Warbstow, Cornwall, while draining a bog. The escutcheon plate (inverted) may show a grotesque human head wearing a plumed helmet. Diameter 190 mm. Royal Institution of Cornwall.

these well furnished graves only account for a small percentage of the population, and the last rites for the others are a matter of speculation.

The evidence of coins and the record of Roman diplomacy show that between about 50 BC and AD 43 the tribes of south-eastern Britain were maturing into proto-states with kings, and urban centres like that at Colchester. Signs of self-conscious tribehood among the Dumnonii are limited to the use of their tribal name. Iron currency bars, like those from Holne Chase in south Devon, circulated during the second century BC, but the tribe never achieved a coinage of its own. A scatter of south-eastern first century BC gold coins has been found, chiefly at Carn Brea and Mount Batten.

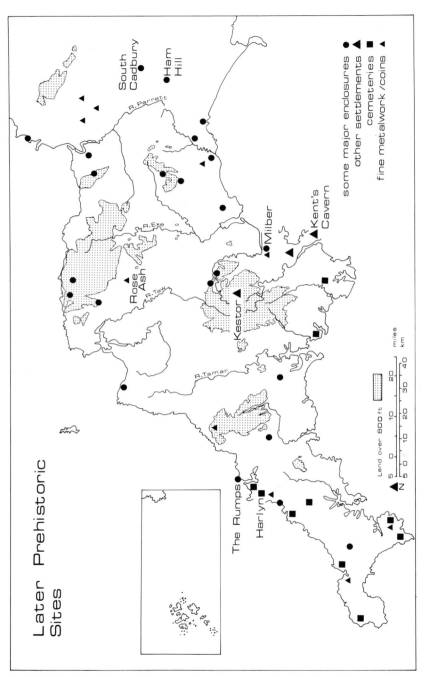

Fig 3·20 Later prehistoric sites.

From about 60 BC the peninsula (unsurprisingly) seems to have been part of the economic province dominated by the silver coinage of the Armorican tribes. Examples of these, and the comparable silver pieces of the Durotriges of Dorset, have been found at Mount Batten (both) and Cotleigh (Durotriges), while a block of argentiferous copper ore found at Hengistbury Head proved to be from the Callington district. The number and variety of enclosed sites suggest a conservative society on the eve of the Roman Conquest, supported by peasant farmers and herders, and dominated by local nobles, with whom lay the impetus behind the circulation of craft objects, and whose personal links with Armorica were strong.

1. *Fox 1957*
2. *Smith, Wainwright 1978*
3. *Fleming 1978*
4. *Mercer 1970*
5. *Thomas 1978*
6. *ApSimon, Greenfield 1972*
7. *Cunliffe 1978*
8. *Dudley 1957*
9. *Fox 1954*
10. *Fox, Radford, Rogers, Shorter 1950*
11. *Thomas 1966*
12. *Saunders 1963*
13. *Threipland 1956*
14. *ApSimon, Greenfield 1972*
15. *Christie 1978*
16. *Beckett, Hibbert 1978*
17. *Miles, Miles 1969*
18. *Avery 1976*
19. *Cunliffe 1978, 243–5*
20. *Alcock 1972, 1980*
21. *Miles 1977b*
22. *Brooks 1974*
23. *Jeffries 1974*
24. *Bradley 1978*
25. *Cunliffe 1978, 111–14*
26. *Gover, Mawer, Stenton 1932, 348*

CHAPTER FOUR

Roman Provincials

The military occupation

By AD 43, when the decision was taken by Emperor Claudius and his government to invade southern Britain, a quantity of information had been gathered about the island, its tribes, and its resources, especially the coveted metal wealth. Accordingly, once the Roman army had secured south-eastern Britain, a three-point offensive was mounted with three army divisions. Each division comprised a legion, together with auxiliary troops which included infantry and cavalry of lower status and different equipment. The Ninth Legion was eventually established at Lincoln, and the Fourteenth in the Midlands around Leicester. The Second Augustan Legion, under its legate Vespasian, the future Emperor (AD 69–79), marched west.

Suetonius, in his record of Vespasian's campaign, tells us that he defeated two powerful tribes, took over twenty hillforts, and conquered the Isle of Wight. His progress is probably recorded in the communications line which eventually became the west road out of London (as the major north and north-west roads mark those of the other two armies). This suggests that his route ran to Silchester, and thence perhaps to Old Sarum, Badbury Rings and Hod Hill, with thrusts north and south to Cirencester and Winchester: at all these sites early forts are known or suspected.

A fort was built at Waddon Hill in Dorset, and another may have been constructed in the Ham Hill area, possibly after the hillfort had been successfully assaulted.[1] Recent excavations at Ilchester revealed lengths of V-shaped ditch suggesting a fort on the site;[2] and Dorchester is still to be proved as a military point. Vespasian seems to have ended the initial westward thrust in the area of the River Axe. The Fosse Way, the military line of communication, ran from near the mouth of the Axe north east by way of Ilchester, Cirencester and Leicester, to Lincoln, and represented the frontier of the original south-eastern province, which had been achieved by AD 47.[3]

There is no reason to suppose that the Fosse Way was intended to be a permanent frontier. Apart from anything else, military intelligence must have known that the Welsh tribes were preparing for war. In AD 47 the Silures of south Wales, under the leadership of the refugee Caractacus, broke out into serious hostilities, which lasted with intermissions as late as AD 75. Similarly, unrest was mounting inside the province among the Iceni of East Anglia which came to a head in AD 60 with the revolt led by Boudicca.

There are hints from a number of south-western hillforts that occupation continued after AD 50. Norton Fitzwarren produced large quantities of early Romano-British pottery, but no coins or Samian wares imported from Gaul.[4] Hembury produced some scraps of early Samian,[5] and at South Cadbury, brooches and Samian sherds dating around AD 60–70 were incorporated into the final refurbishing of the hillfort defences.[6] The continued occupation after AD 47 of a strong hillfort like South Cadbury inside the Fosse Way, together with others in the area, needs explanation.

South Cadbury seems to have been within the territory either of the southern Dobunni, who occupied broadly what is now Gloucestershire, or of the northern Durotriges, who may already have been divided into the two groups whose later capitals were at Ilchester and Dorchester. It is possible that whichever tribe it was had come to an uneasy arrangement with the Roman authorities by which they continued to live as a client tribe, until political events, of which the most likely is the Boudiccan revolt, provoked a confrontation. Certainly, after a final but ineffectual strengthening of the defences, the fort was taken by Roman troops who massacred the inhabitants and left unburied bodies to decay in the south-west gateway, and who probably then occupied the site themselves for a short time.[7] The historical sources do not record the attitude of the Dumnonii, or details of any campaigns against them, but recent excavations have shown that the fortress at Exeter is likely to have been founded between about AD 55 and 60, and this must have been in response to the overall strategic situation.

The military presence at Exeter was first recognized in the excavation outside the later city south gate of a length of characteristic military ditch and the base of a timber-faced rampart, dated by an imported mid-first century wine jar.[8] Excavations during the 1970s have shown that this was part of a military installation contemporary with, and ancillary to, the main fortress which lay further to the north west. The fortress occupied a spur which overlooked the lowest fordable point on the River Exe (*fig 4·1*), ideally placed to control the

Longbrook Valley

Rougemont

via praetoria

High St.

via

via sagularis

Mount Dinham

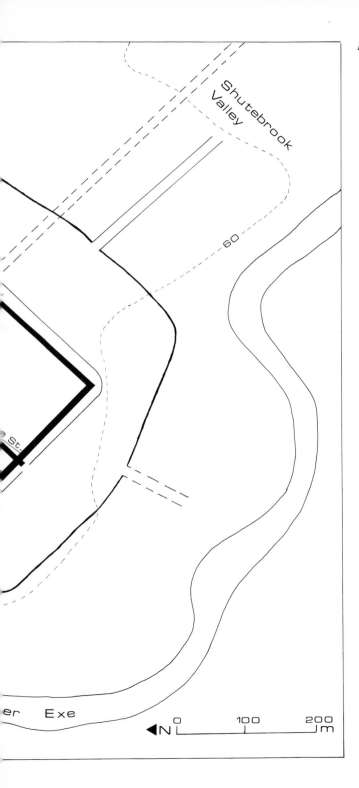

Fig 4·1 Plan of legionary fortress at Exeter. The outline of the later city wall, and the modern street plan and cathedral site are shown for comparison. Presumed approach roads are shown with broken lines (*source: Bidwell 1979, figs 1, 2*).

Shutebrook Valley

60

e St.

er Exe

0   100   200
◀N L_____I_____Jm

Exe Valley, which aerial photographs suggest was densely settled by native farmers.

The Fosse Way was continued to the fortress forming the main link with the east. The Exe was probably navigable as far as Exeter, so that the fortress could be supplied by water. At Topsham, further down the Exe estuary, recent excavation has revealed timber buildings dated AD 55–75,[9] but the direct evidence of a support base in the area is slender. On the high crest of Stoke Hill above the fortress, a fortlet or signal post seems to have been set up at this time which commanded wide views across the valleys of the Exe and the Creedy.[10] In spite of its excellent position, no archaeological evidence has been found which suggests that the site of Exeter was occupied when the military arrived.

Lengths of the fortress's defences found in excavation show that these consisted of a ditch and an earthen rampart. The evidence for the overall plan suggests that the fortress was about 430 m long, 350 m wide, and covered an area of about 15.4 hectares or 38 acres. It had typical rounded corners, and must have had four gates. The interior was divided by the normal military road system, and presumably held all the usual features, including a headquarters building, a commander's house, and various administrative buildings. Barrack-blocks were investigated in the northern corner of the fortress, some of which showed three building phases. These seem to form part of a series of pairs of barrack-blocks, each with centurions' quarters at the end, and accommodation for the men.

To the south of the barracks lay the *fabrica*—the work shop—the chief feature of which was an aisled hall 9 m wide with at least four bays. Its floor was covered in charcoal and slag, and equipped with a series of plank-lined troughs. Metal filings and off-cuts showed that part of it had been used for bronze-working. To the south east stood the granaries, supported on a grid of posts to help protect their vital contents from damp and vermin. Traces of various other buildings have been found from time to time, like the timber buildings, tile-roofed and equipped with verandahs, excavated in Fore Street in 1945–7, or the similar structures found in Bartholomew Street in 1959.[11] Further investigation would help to clarify their function. Finds of Samian pottery imported from central Gaul, glass cups from the Rhineland, and amphorae which contained oil and wine, suggest that senior soldiers, at least, were supplied with some home comforts.

A most important building, perhaps the only one built of stone, was the legionary bath-house, substantial remains of which were excavated in the Cathedral Close in 1971–7. (Unfortunately the site

Plate 28 First century AD ribbed cup of bluish-green glass imported from Gaul or the Rhineland, and found in the South Street excavations, Exeter. Height 115 mm. Exeter City Museum.

could not be displayed as a museum and was re-buried.) The baths were built on a vacant site in the centre of the fortress perhaps a decade after its establishment (*fig 4·2*). The whole complex occupied an area of about 0.4 hectares or one acre, and included on its south-western side a *palaestra*, or exercise yard, with a surface of rolled sand, equipped with what was probably a round cock-pit, a reminder of the Roman taste for blood sports. The bath building itself would have had a *frigidarium* or cold room, a *laconicum*, or dry heat room, a *tepidarium* or warm room, excavated in part, and a *caldarium* or hot baths room, the whole plan of which was recovered.

The *tepidarium* was a simple rectangular room, but the *caldarium* was elaborately equipped with two apses, each with hand basins, and two baths, one at each end, running the width of the room. The walls were decorated with painted plaster and veneers of Purbeck marble,

Plate 29 The caldarium of the legionary bath house, Exeter AD 60–65, looking south east, showing the tile stacks which supported the floor, the two apses and central recess at the south east, the white rectangular pier base, and the circular base of a wash basin. The wall of the basilica built about AD 80 runs SE/NW.

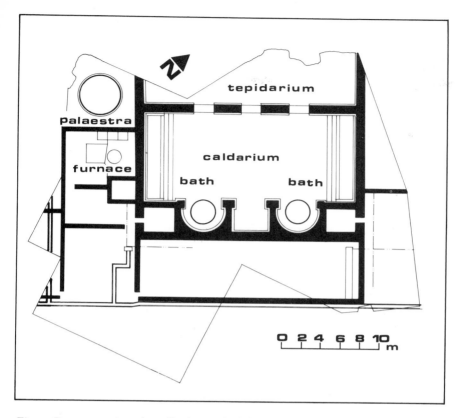

Fig 4·2 Reconstruction plan of legionary bath house, Exeter during period 1A (*source: Bidwell 1979, fig. 12*).

and the floors covered with white and grey tiles and at least one mosaic. The concrete barrel-vaulted roofs were painted internally, and externally protected by tiles supported on a timber framework. Tile antefixes, or plaques, decorated the eaves. Both rooms were heated by a hypocaust system in which the floors were supported on tile stacks allowing hot air from the furnaces (one of which on the south-west side was well preserved), to circulate beneath them. The hollow walls were connected with the system, making it yet more efficient. Altogether, the bath suite is likely to have been one of the most elaborate for its period north of the Alps, and provided splendidly for the off-duty relaxation of the troops.[12]

On the south east outside the fortress stood the ancillary installation: this might have been a store, or a works depot. The *canabae*, or civilian settlement, which served the needs of the military, seems to have occupied the level ground beyond the north-east gate of the fortress. Here have been found traces of timber buildings and early pottery. The find of two rich cremations dating about AD 65 suggests that a cemetery belonging to the fort lay on either side of the road leading to the south-east gate, and there may have been another to the north. Tile works and pottery kilns were set up outside the fortress.

Sadly, no inscriptions have so far appeared from the Exeter fort, but the Second Augustan Legion, together with auxiliaries, was still presumably controlling the south west when the fortress was built. Its identification as the Exeter garrison was confirmed by the discovery at Exeter of two antefixes made from the same mould as examples from Caerleon, to which the legion is known to have been transferred. The mould must have been part of the equipment of a legionary tiler who worked first at Exeter and then at Caerleon. The installations at Exeter seem to have been rather smaller than usual, meaning possibly that not all of the legion was intended to be housed within the fortress at the same time, although the size may simply have resulted from the choice of a hilltop site.

The legion's task seems to have been the annexation of the Dumnonian peninsula, made desirable by the unstable political situation and probably by the hope of exploiting the tin deposits. Recent work has given us a clearer understanding of how the troops went about their assignment. A small fort at Wiveliscombe seems to have been garrisoned through the 50s,[13] and a temporary camp recently identified near Tiverton hints at a military route running northwards up the Exe valley, conceivably striking eastwards to link with this fort. At Charterhouse-on-Mendip, the staff of the fort was responsible for the production of lead and silver: a lead pig stamped with the name of the Second Legion has been found near Boulogne in France.[14] The two successive fortlets on the north Devon coast must have formed part of the watch on the Silures. Excavations at Old Burrow showed that it was constructed about AD 50, and that it was replaced by the Martinhoe fortlet which was probably maintained until about AD 75. Martinhoe was equipped to house a century of eighty men trained in the use of signal fires.[15] The temporary camp site enclosing nearly 1.6 hectares (4 acres) detected by aeriel photography further west, between the estuaries of the Taw and the Torridge at Alverdiscott, may prove when examined to be a part of the same operations.[16]

Soon after about AD 55 a chain of forts seems to have been established down the spine of the peninsula, and, although direct evidence of roads within the peninsula is scanty, they were presumably linked

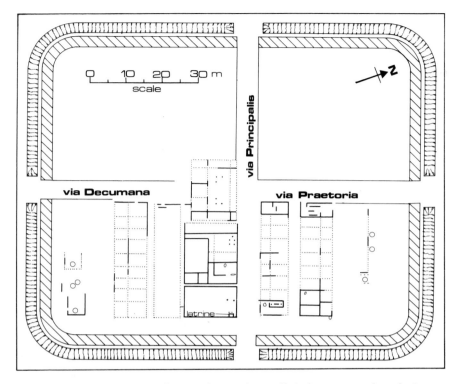

Fig 4·3 Plan of fort at Nanstallon, Bodmin. The small circles represent hearths (*source: Fox, Ravenhill 1972*).

by a military route. Best known of the series is the fort of 0.9 hectares (2 acres) excavated at Nanstallon on the River Camel (*fig 4·3*). Here, a fort housed a mixed auxiliary detachment of infantry and cavalry totalling five hundred men. The soldiers lived in wooden barracks, and the commander had a spacious house near the fort's east gate. Adjoining it, in the centre, was the headquarters building. The fort was defended by a turf rampart and ditch and four timber angle towers, and it had four double gates and was occupied until AD 75.[17] Traces of metalworking in one of the barracks may suggest attempts to exploit the Cornish ores.

Other forts in Cornwall doubtless remain to be found, and a military post must surely have controlled the Tamar crossing. In Devon in the North Tawton area[18] west of Exeter, aerial photography has recently revealed a large temporary camp, or marching camp, built as the brief stopping place of a Roman army on campaign.

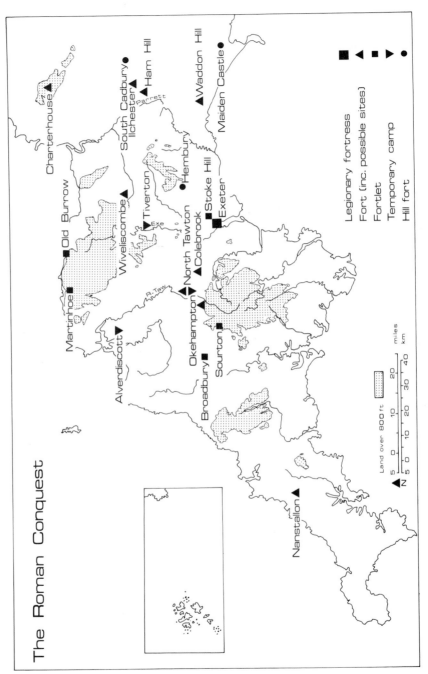

The Roman Conquest

Fig 4·4 The Roman Conquest.

Nearby, the possible fort site at North Tawton, which has an annexe, has produced first-century Roman pottery. On the eastern side of this site is a stretch of straight road, which may have linked with a possible fort at Colebrook.

The road continued west of North Tawton, to join the fort at Knowle, Okehampton, where trial excavation demonstrated a substantial clay rampart dated by early Roman pottery. It would then have crossed the Okement, or the East and West Okements if it ran just above their junction. A small earthwork south of Okehampton church might have been a signalling station.[19] The road may have continued to Sourton Down where a straight length of trackway and an adjacent earthwork have been interpreted as a possible fortlet and a stretch of military road.[20] It will then have turned slightly north west to the possible fortlet at Broadbury. Our knowledge of military activity in the south west is still fragmentary, and only more work will fill out the picture (*fig 4·4*).

Complicated inferences drawn from finds and structures at Exeter suggest that the legion pulled out about AD 75, and that until that date the garrison remained substantially at full strength. This clashes with the accepted view that the Second Augustan was responsible for the construction of the fortress at Gloucester about AD 66, but perhaps the truth will emerge when we know more of troop movements. Certainly, the legion was at Caerleon for the Welsh campaign of AD 74–8, and there it constructed the first phase of the fortress which was to be its home for the next three centuries. At Exeter, some of the timber buildings were dismantled, although the stone bath house was left. The signs all show that the garrisons along the Dumnonian peninsula were withdrawn at about the same time and, although the area may have remained under military goverment for a few years, the future was essentially with the civilian population.

Early Exeter and Ilchester

The policies inaugurated by the new governor, Agricola, during AD 80 were intended to encourage the growth of Roman-style city life in the emerging civilian settlements. It is reasonable to suggest that during the early eighties a pattern of local government was established in southern Britain: a series of broadly self-governing regions was created, each usually called a *civitas*, based on a pre-Roman tribal area, and centred on a principal city. The Dumnonii of the south-western peninsula formed an obvious unit with their capital at *Isca Dumnoniorum*, the original form from which the name of Exeter derives. In the south east, the territory of the Dumnonii probably extended as far as the Blackdown Hills; beyond lay the neighbouring tribe of the Durotriges with their initial tribal capital at *Durnovaria* (Dorchester). The north-eastern boundary line is less certain, but it may have run along either the River Parrett or the River Axe in Somerset.

At Exeter the ruling Council (*ordo*) of the Dumnonii would have met, composed of magistrates drawn from the local important families and charged with the administration of the city and its dependent population. This included the raising of taxes, both to make up the tribe's imperial quota to be forwarded to London, and to be spent on local projects. Very little detailed information is left to us of this process, but two third- or fourth-century inscriptions from Hadrian's Wall at Carvoran and Thirlwall show the corporate act of the *civitas Dumnoniorum* as it supplied resources to aid the northern defences.

Agricola's encouragement stimulated a considerable programme of civic public building at Exeter which was completed by the end of the century (*fig 4·5*). The main building of the old legionary bath house, which had been turned over to civilian use for the past decade or so, was gutted. Within its shell the builders created a large hall or *basilica*, comprising a nave with a row of rooms behind it and a large room interpreted as the *curia*, or council chamber, the whole suite to be used for the transaction of public business. The west wall was rebuilt, and pierced with a series of arches which led, by way of short flights of steps, to the old *palaestra* area, now reconstructed as a *forum* or market place—an open space covered with a thick layer of mortar surrounded on three sides by rows of shops and offices behind a colonnade. A passage with a dignified entranceway connected the complex with the road on the south-east side. The forum-basilica buildings seem to have occupied an area about 67 m wide and more than 106 m long.[21]

An additional open area seems to have been provided south west of the central block, which may have been a cattle market. To the north and south were two pairs of *insulae* (building plots) each about 70 m square. Three of these apparently passed into private ownership, but the south-western plot, where the Deanery now stands, became the site of the public baths. Temple sites remain elusive, although the city must surely have possessed some. The River Exe was probably crossed by a series of wooden bridges extending from island to island; a stone-based structure may have been necessary over the main stream, but so far no traces of this have been discovered. Shops and private houses seem to have been mostly still half-timbered buildings with stone foundations and concrete floors. The quantities of Gaulish

Samian pottery show that the citizens were benefitting from the flow of imperial trade. Coin finds are as common as in most Romano-British towns, and altogether Exeter seems to have been as prosperous and sophisticated as most *civitas* capitals.

In accordance with imperial decree, the city was defended by the erection of a rampart at the end of the second century (but see Bidwell, 1980). This took the form of a massive bank, originally about 4.5 m high and 8 m broad, consisting of clay and gravel dug from an external ditch. Its course was later followed by a stone wall, and it was pierced by four stone gates. At the South Gate, excavation showed the bottom courses of the 5 m square western gate tower; and possibly the round arch shown on nineteenth-century prints of the inside of the medieval South Gate was a Roman survival.[22]

At Ilchester, excavation within the central area and within the southern suburbs has added considerably to knowledge of the town's development.[23] Its civic growth plainly resulted from its position at the junction of the Fosse Way and the link road to Dorchester. Finds of pottery suggest that the fort lasted until towards the end of the first century, when the palisade was dismantled and the ditches filled.

Plate 30 Small head of Italian marble, 1st century AD, found in the Pancras Lane excavations, Exeter, in 1971. It may come from a family shrine. Height 70 mm. Exeter City Museum.

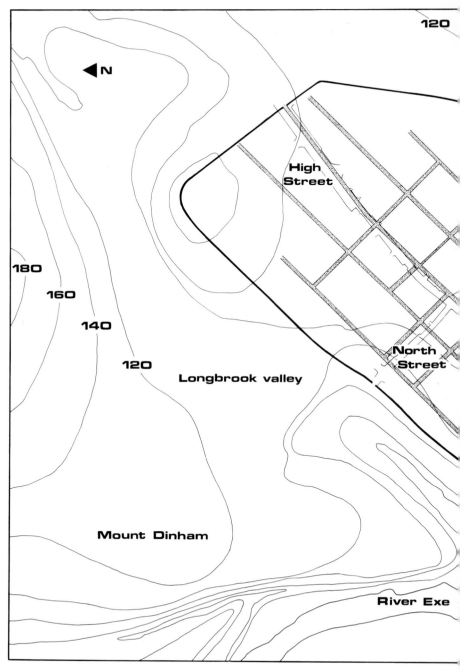

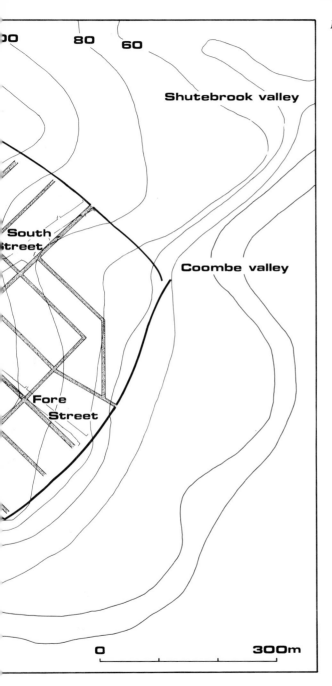

Fig 4·5 The Roman city
of Exeter
showing Roman
streets and
modern street
plan for
comparison
(*source: Exeter
Archaeological
Field Unit*).

00   80   60

Shutebrook valley

South
Street

Coombe valley

Fore
Street

0   300m

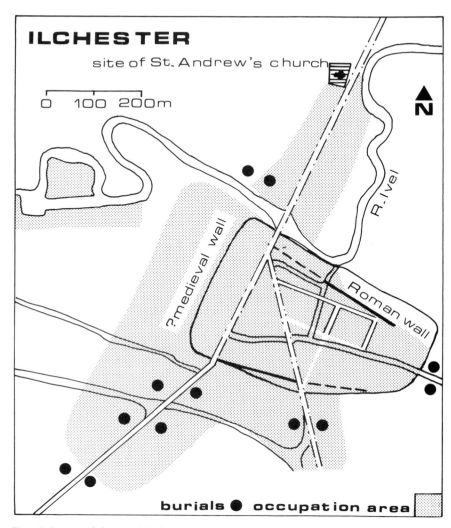

ILCHESTER

site of St. Andrew's church

0   100   200m

N

R. Ivel

?.medieval wall

Roman wall

burials ● occupation area

Fig 4·6 Roman Ilchester. The known and probable courses of Roman roads and streets are shown, and the modern street plan is shown for comparison (*source: Aston, Leech 1977, maps, 27, 28*).

During the same years timber buildings, perhaps already related to plot boundary ditches, were being built along the sides of the two roads south of the junction (*fig 4·6*).

From the early second century, activity in the settlement area becomes clearer. Fronting the northern side of the south-western

Fosse Way were two lines of ditches linked by cross ditches, clearly defining two zones of rectangular enclosures, and a similar pattern probably existed on the opposite side of the road. The road frontage was occupied by sophisticated stone and half-timbered buildings, and the rear zone by workshops, barns and outbuildings. This general pattern endured until the late fourth century.

Meanwhile, about the middle of the second century, the citizens erected a massive turf and clay rampart to define the perimeter of their town. A section of this was excavated and its line can be picked up in the town as a break in the slope, lying substantially inside the previously projected Roman wall line. The building of the rampart may have stimulated urban development, which can be seen in the erection of intramural stone buildings with plastered walls, stone floors, and stone roofing slabs, put to a variety of private and commercial uses and implying a stable street pattern.

Roads, towns and industry to AD 200

Exeter and Ilchester apart, the indications from both archaeology and the surviving Roman road-books, which list the main roads and the towns along them, suggest that urban settlement in the region was very limited indeed, in contrast to, say, the valley of the Somerset Avon where a string of small towns has been identified. One problem, which applies especially to central Somerset, is the difficulty in deciding whether a substantial group of structures constitutes a small town or a large agricultural unit. Combwich has been classed as a 'town',[24] while the settlements around Ilchester may be better regarded as agricultural[25] (see below).

Both the third-century *Antonine Itinerary* and the *Ravenna Cosmography*, compiled in the seventh century from older material, mention *Moridunum*, a still unidentified site somewhere in east Devon. The *Cosmography* also lists *Nemetostatio*, probably to be linked with the surviving central Devon names containing the element *Nymet* and so conceivably representing the North Tawton fort, *Deventiasteno*, possibly somewhere in the Mount Batten area which has produced a scatter of Roman material and fourth-century coins,[26] and *Tamaris* which looks like the place where the road line crossed the Tamar. The possible suffix *statio* in the first two of these may suggest that they were tax-collecting stations. The remaining ten or so place names preserved in the *Cosmography*, or by the geographer Ptolemy, are unidentified. They may refer to rivers, and native settlements like Carvossa, Probus, which seems to have served as a local centre.

This bare picture fits with the slight indications so far revealed of the road network within the peninsula, since flourishing market towns and good communications would have gone hand in hand. A number of routes eastward out of Exeter have been suggested, like the final section of the Fosse Way between Exeter and Ilchester, or a road connecting Exeter and Dorchester, perhaps branching from the Fosse near Honiton, or Axminster. However, although a stretch of the Exeter–Honiton road has been recognized at Rockbeare,[27] no typical carriage-way, side ditches, or metalling appeared when the M5 road-works cut the road's supposed line at Sowton. During the same operations, no sign was observed of the proposed roads running from Exeter towards the south coast, or from Exeter to Topsham.[28]

West of Exeter, the old military works imply a road of some kind running around the northern rim of Dartmoor towards the Tamar and beyond, and a length of road has been claimed in the area of Stratton in north-east Cornwall.[29] A similar route may have run around the southern flank of the moor, although excavation on Haldon Hill produced no evidence for the Roman road previously claimed on the basis of superficial indications.[30] Altogether, the number of roads in the peninsula may have been overestimated, and those that did exist were perhaps largely left as unmetalled tracks for most of the period.

Only on the eastern rim of the region, at Charterhouse-on-Mendip, was there a substantial industrial complex, comprising the small town with its amphitheatre, and the installations connected with lead-working and silver extraction, all on a branch road linking with the Fosse Way. Production was leased to civilian operators from about AD 60. The finds of lead pigs or ingots make it plain that the metal was exported to the continent via the port of *Clausentum* at Bitterne outside modern Southampton.[31] No signs have been traced which suggest exploitation of the Cornish or Dartmoor tin (or any other metals) during the late first and second centuries on a scale beyond that needed for local consumption, in spite of the early hopes of mineral wealth.

Commercial or surplus production does not seem to have been part of the Dumnonians' way of life, although salt-working sites like that at Trebarveth in the Lizard may be exceptions. Here the remains of two superimposed stone rectangular ovens were found, together with a large quantity of coarse briquetage vessels used in evaporating sea water.[32] The site was probably working during the second century. Its operators had inherited a long local tradition of refining raw materials for the market, and the clay desposits nearby continued also to be utilized on a small scale, since some pottery from the Lizard reached Exeter in the first century.

The countryside

Everything that we know about patterns of settlement in the south
west from the later first to the later fourth centuries AD suggests that
most people were living in a style which had its roots deep in prehistoric society, and was to endure into the post–Roman period. With the
exception of eastern Somerset, this life style centred upon a homestead with its outbuildings, all enclosed within a single bank and ditch
intended primarily not for defence but for domestic convenience.
These sites relate to the broad group of similar raths or cashels in
Ireland, raths in Pembrokeshire, and enclosed hut groups in North
Wales, which together represent the settlement pattern around the
shores of the Irish Sea during the Roman period and beyond.

Over recent years many of these small univallate enclosures, or
rounds, have come to be recognized through cumulative programmes
of field work and the study of aerial photographs, and their potential
range and variety, as well as their considerable numbers, are now
better realized. The conservative nature of these sites brings its own
problems: without vast programmes of excavation we cannot know
how many of them were in use in the period after the Roman Conquest. The relationship of the structures to the landscape is still difficult to ascertain, and only more detailed field work, of the kind being
undertaken in the Gwithian area, will provide facts about important
matters like the extent of the related arable and how it was cultivated,
and the proportional importance of pasture and woodland. Still less is
known about the patterns of economic dependence and land right. The
later Welsh Laws and relevant Roman legal fragments hint at family
land-sharing systems, and settlement units with land held in common, which depended upon a landlord and ultimately upon the ruler.

At Caerloggas in the parish of St Mawgan-in-Pydar, the inhabitants re-modelled their gateway and built new huts about the middle
of the first century and acquired some Roman pottery, but their
settlement continued essentially unchanged until around AD 150. At
Castle Gotha, St Austell, the round began before 100 BC and occupation continued well into the second century AD. Timber huts were
built in the shelter of the bank, and the group included craftsmen who
could work tin and bronze.[33] The story seems much the same at Three
Milestone Round near Truro, and at Crane Godrevy, Gwithian,
where the round fits into a complex pattern of local settlement.

In contrast, the round at Trethurgy, St Austell, started in the third
century AD, when the rampart and ditch were completed. The central
area was roughly cobbled and kept as a yard. Five oval huts, rebuilt

many times, were in use during the later fourth century, together with various farming buildings, all set close against the inside of the bank. Finds included local pottery, scraps of early Samian pots, and fourth-century Romano-British black burnished ware.[34]

Similar problems of dating apply to the courtyard houses. Nearly forty sites of this kind are known. At Chysauster, Gulval, (*fig 4·7*) eight houses arranged in pairs to create a village have survived and can be visited. A field system is attached to the settlement, and the finds show an occupation during the first and second centuries AD coming to a peaceful end in the third. At Carn Euny and Mulfra Vean, people stayed at old sites well into Roman times, while at Goldherring, Sancreed, and Porthmeor, Zennor, they built new courtyard houses around AD 250. At both Porthmeor and Goldherring part of the field systems attached to the settlements can be traced.

Various rectangular enclosures seem to belong within the 'round' tradition, their shape possibly influenced by that of Roman forts. Two have been excavated west of the Tamar, at Trevennick, St Kew,[35] and at Grambla, Wendron, where the enclosure surrounded two boat-shaped houses, and finds suggested an occupation from the second century into the post-Roman period.[36]

Fig 4·7 Plan of courtyard house settlement, Chysauster, west Cornwall (*source: Hencken 1933*).

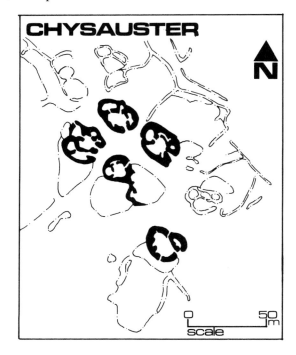

A few sites are known in the South Hams, like that at Stoke Gabriel. In the Exe Valley the broadly comparable site at Pond Farm, Exminster, belongs in the second century,[37] and aerial photographs have revealed further similar sites in the same area.

In the eastern part of the region the settlements appear by contrast to be unenclosed. In the low-lying land around the lower Parrett and the Brue, a scatter of small farms and settlements is known, if not well recorded. The extent to which this land suffered flooding from the sea in the later Roman period is still uncertain,[38] but the area of marsh may have increased and drainage been impeded.

Around Ilchester and south to the River Yeo an important group of large agricultural settlements has been discovered, including Catsgore, Charlton Mackerell in Somerset, Pinford Lane, Castleton in Dorset, and a dozen or so more.[39] Catsgore, the most thoroughly examined of the series (*fig 4·8*), proved to have been established about AD 80, possibly deliberately to absorb people dispersed from hillforts. About AD 150 the settlement was extended. In the north, three separate properties were laid out, and to the south other buildings included dwellings, stores and a byre all well built in rectangular style. If Catsgore is typical, then perhaps all these settlements came into being early in the Roman period and continued into the third and fourth centuries, when they must have related to the *villa*-type establishments created in the area about that time.

Plate 31 Cropmark north east of Exminster near Exeter, showing a double rectangular enclosure, possibly of a Romano-British farmstead. Other cropmarks may also be seen.

153

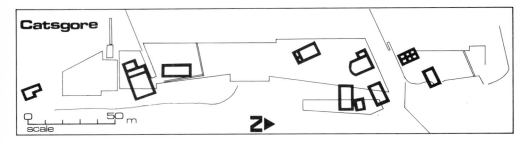

Fig 4·8 Plan of settlement at Catsgore, Somerset, about AD300–370 (*source: Leech 1976, fig 33*).

Generally, as far as is known, the group of *villas* in the Ilchester area did not develop from pre-300 origins, with the possible exception of Littleton, but the two excavated examples of the few sites in Devon which make up the south-western fringe of the group certainly began earlier. At Honeyditches, Seaton, the first-century occupation was that of a normal native farmstead, succeeded possibly as early as the second century by a group of Roman-style buildings including one with a hypercaust.[40] At Holcombe, Uplyme, the inhabitants continued to live until about 200 in rectangular timber-framed buildings erected within a rectangular enclosure. Extra stone-built rooms and a verandah together with a timber barn were added during the second/third centuries, and the prosperity of the farm must have made possible its future growth as a villa. The remote villa at Magor near Camborne was erected in the mid-second century and included rooms along both sides of a corridor.[41]

Inevitably, it is the larger or more easily recognized sites which have always attracted attention. Humbler sites, which only occasionally appear within the archaeological record, such as the hut at Gulval occupied during the second/third centuries, or the enclosed single hut at Porth Godrevy,[42] presumably the smallest kind of enclosed site and interestingly close to the Magor villa, may have been much more common than we sometimes imagine. Caves, too, like those on Mendip, or the south Devon coastal fringe, were put to a variety of uses, as burial grounds or perhaps as living sites. The real density of settlement, and so of people, still eludes us.

Third/Fourth-century towns and industry

In probably the third century, the administration of the Durotriges, like that of some other British tribes, was re-organized and Ilchester seems to have been raised to the status of the *civitas* capital with responsibility for a northern group of the Durotriges whose territory must have covered the low-lying area of central Somerset.[43] By about 312 Britain itself had been re-divided into four provinces each with its own administrative staff. The whole south west was probably a part of *Britannia Prima* with its capital almost certainly at Cirencester. In marked contrast to the military installations established during the later third/fourth centuries around the coast of south-eastern Britain, and to a lesser degree that of Wales, no late military activity has been recognized in the south-western peninsula, although the intriguing site at Oldaport in south Devon, with its curious defences, should not be forgotten.[44] A probable fleet patrolling the Bristol Channel must have given protection to the northern shore.

During the third century, and probably by AD 235, a massive wall was erected around Exeter, set in the front of the existing earth rampart. It was about 3 m thick, and faced on its outer side with square-cut blocks of trap quarried on Rougemont within the city, set as a chamfered plinth at ground level. The core was of rubble, left rough where it backed against the rampart. Above the rampart, the wall was narrowed and faced inside with small trap blocks up to the level of the wall-walk about 6 m above the plinth. Little Roman masonry now survives, but the entire 2.3 km course of the wall can still easily be traced on foot, and this is the best way to appreciate the effort and skill of the construction.

Within the city, more rooms were added to the basilica complex around 200 by converting adjacent areas of the forum and the open space to the south. These look as though they were intended for administrative use at a time when bureaucratic work was steadily increasing and public office becoming a greater burden. Around 350 this civic block was modified again, in markedly inferior workmanship, in part to create a tribunal or magistrates' rostrum.

The timber buildings were gradually replaced by structures of stone with mortared walls and cement floors. Mosaics and under-floor heating arrangements are relatively rare, but the new buildings are substantial courtyard-type houses, which seem to represent consolidation of land holding, and presumably therefore the gradual emergence of a small class of wealthy citizens. By the fourth century one of these houses, excavated in old Trickhay Street, showed rural-type barn and byre buildings suggesting the growth of self-sufficient villa-like households within the city, such as have been found at Cirencester, for example. The coin supply at Exeter and elsewhere seems to have dried up very abruptly about 370, reflecting perhaps

Plate 32 Bowl with lid, found at Treloy, St Colomb Minor, Cornwall, about 1830. Believed to be nearly pure tin, probably 3rd or 4th century AD. Diameter 352 mm. On loan to Royal Institution of Cornwall.

deep-rooted problems within the Western Empire rather than local poverty or crisis. Surprisingly, no civic cemeteries have yet come to light, although the area outside the North Gate may be a likely site.

At Ilchester a wall was constructed during the late third/fourth centuries, which cut into the outer face of the earthen rampart. Possibly later bastions were butted onto this wall. As at Exeter, stone courtyard houses were built within the defences. Land use along the road ways south of the city changed dramatically during the fourth century with the establishment of substantial inhumation cemeteries. The one found along the south-western Fosse Way revealed that the dead had been buried in wooden coffins accompanied by hobnail boots (usually worn), coins placed on the mouth, food offerings, and small possessions, features which are all paralleled at other fourth-century cemeteries.[45]

The extinction of the Spanish tin supplies in the mid third century, coupled with the greatly increased production of debased silver coins (*antoniniani*) at the Gallic mints which required quantities of tin, quickened official interest in the Cornish supplies. Five mile-stones of the third/fourth centuries, and the fourth-century stamped tin ingot from Carnanton, St Mawgan-in-Pydar, show that the metal was smelted and transported under imperial control. A fine tin bowl with moulded handles and a close-fitting lid was found at Treloy, St Colomb Minor, closely resembling granite bowls made at Trethurgy. Lead production on Mendip continued, and the manufacture of pewter, an alloy of tin and lead, within the peninsula, is demonstrated by the finds of pewter moulds at St Just-in-Penwith, and at Camerton to the east of Mendip. Vessels of pewter or tin have been found at St Stephen-in-Brannel and Carnon (Devoran), and flagons come from Carhayes (where the piece was filled with 2500 *antoniniani*), and from the shore at Goodrington, Torbay.

The economic effects of the massive manufacture of black burnished pottery around the Poole (Dorset) area may have had some spin-offs among the eastern Dumnonii, and these wares are found at virtually all fourth-century sites. In the Lizard peninsula, the South Hams in Devon and the Somerset Levels, potters continued to produce wares for local consumption. South Hams pottery has been found in quantity in Exeter, and some reached Taunton and east Devon. Pots from the Levels also reached Exeter. In the Levels several scattered industrial areas were producing iron and, as at Chilton Polden, salt.

Villas

Nothing suggests major changes in the overall pattern of rural settlement during the last two centuries of Roman rule, but in the eastern part of the region a further element was added to the countryside which must have had far-reaching implications: the increased development of villa estates. In archaeological terms, villas are differentiated from other homesteads by the more or less elaborate Roman-style buildings which they possess, involving hypocaust heating systems, bath houses, mosaic floors, and suites of rooms often arranged along a corridor, to which similar suites were sometimes added at right angles creating a courtyard plan. Economically, villas seem to have been regarded both as gentlemen's residences and as investments producing a marketable surplus (*fig 4·9*).

Villas tended to occupy low-lying positions in easy reach of rivers. Their economic and social functions show clearly in the way in which they cluster along the main roads and around some of the southern cities. More than twenty villas have been recognized within a 16 km radius of Ilchester, and although the Ilchester pattern is especially well marked, similar obvious constellations surround Bath, Cirencester

157

and Dorchester. The lack of similar sites around Exeter is a long-standing puzzle. The only villas in Devon are a few in the eastern strip of the county, chiefly at Holcombe and Seaton. One reason why the suitable country of the Exe Valley was not exploited may have been because some of the best land belonged to the *territorium* of Exeter, land attached to the city itself.

Full examination of a villa site is rare, although several important excavations are proceeding or have recently been completed. Rather unusually, most of the Ilchester group appear to have been newly established in the late third century, prompting the suggestion that some of them may represent an extraordinary influx of Gaulish capital and settlers.[46] At the villa in Lufton near Yeovil, for example, the twelve rooms along a corridor with a bathroom extension at the north-west end were all built during the fourth century.[47]

Holcombe followed the more normal pattern where in the fourth century new rooms, one with an elaborate geometrical mosaic floor, and an octagonal bath house, were added to the existing third-century corridor house, itself a building of some pretensions incorporating

Plate 33 Roman villa, Lufton, Somerset, from the west, during excavation in 1946, showing in the foreground Room I with fine mosaic pavement, and beyond the plunge bath and *frigidarium*.

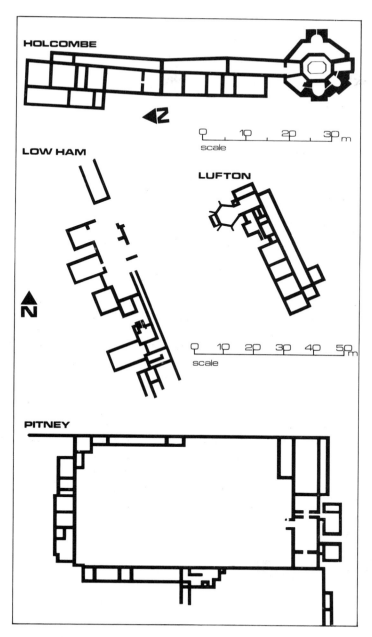

Fig 4·9 Plans of villas (*source: Holcombe, Pollard 1974, fig 3; Low
Ham, Lufton, Pitney, Leech 1976, fig 39*).

rooms built about 200.[48] At Seaton, the bath house was demolished in the late third or fourth century.[49] Especially fine mosaics were installed at Pitney, showing the 'Gods and Seasons'; at Low Ham, with scenes from the story of Dido and Aeneas; and at Frampton where Latin couplets were included. The small bronze figure group featuring the young Achilles and his tutor Cheiron found on Sidmouth beach was designed as a tripod mount and may derive from a local establishment.

Farmyard and outbuilding arrangements are less well understood than house plans, although the reconstruction of the Pitney courtyard complex suggests barns, granaries, and byres opposite the residential wing. Structural remains at Pitney, Lufton, Halstock, and Low Ham suggest that wheat production may have exceeded what was needed for home consumption, possibly aided by improved ploughs, but generally the impression is of mixed farming with pigs, cattle (per-haps pastured on open moor or hillside during the summer), and garden vegetables and fruit.

Villa estates must have been sizeable households of family, slaves, and labourers, producing food for sale and offering a stimulat-ing market for pewterers, masons, and other craftsmen. Each estate must have been a legally defined unit, but the tenurial relationships between the owner and his workers remain unclear. What we do know is that the marked trend of fourth-century imperial legislation was to increase the authority of the landlord. Intriguing hints are sometimes offered by the juxtaposition of sites: at Catsgore the villa was a short distance from the agricultural settlement, while at Magor the villa was in the near vicinity of a round.

Branigan[50] has made a case for supposing that a number of the Somerset villas were badly damaged in the great barbarian raid of 367. Most villas continued to function after about 370, but occupation gradually sank to the lower social level suggested by the hearths built in corridors at Lufton, or the iron-working furnaces erected among building debris at Holcombe. Nevertheless, unambitious occupation may have continued for a number of decades, and the survival of some estates as recognized units is a distinct possibility.

Religion

The pagan sacred places of the south west show up in the archaeolo-gical record most clearly in the third/fourth centuries, which seem to have witnessed a revival of interest in this direction, possibly reflect-ing increased prosperity. The sites themselves may have been holy for a long time, as the gods worshipped are plainly local native fertility

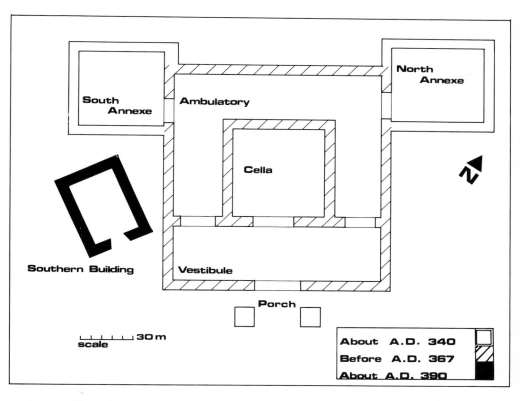

Fig 4·10 Plan of temple on Brean Down. The original temple was augmented by lateral annexes and a porch, probably before AD 368. It was abandoned and finally demolished about AD 390, when the southern building was erected. This was used for domestic occupation, and it too was demolished sometime in the fifth century AD (*source: ApSimon 1965, fig 50*).

and underworld powers, sometimes civilized by identification with a member of the Roman pantheon.

On the eastern fringes of the region, the worshippers built a temple at Brean Down (*fig 4·10*), which was in ruins by the late fourth century, and another at Henley Wood close to the Congresbury hillfort, which was still in use around 400. A temple has been excavated at Lamyatt Beacon near Bruton, and another possible site may have existed at South Cadbury.[51]

Further west, temple buildings are rare, but two shrines are known, both with shafts into which offerings were dropped. Inside the enclosure at Cadbury near Tiverton was a shaft over 15 m deep wherein had accumulated a quantity of bracelets, beads, and other votive objects of later Roman date, all normal offerings.[52] At Bosence, St Erth, a similar shaft in the corner of a hilltop enclosure yielded a pewter jug, and a pewter dish with an inscription showing that it was dedicated to Mars, a god often identified with Celtic deities. An undiscovered site may exist in the area of *Nemetostatio* since the first part of the name means 'sanctuary'.

The important site at Nor'nour on Scilly, which revealed two substantially built rooms and a number of other structures, and which yielded a quantity of coins ranging from 69–371, numerous pipe clay figurines featuring goddess types, and a large collection of personal ornaments, has been interpreted as a cult centre, possibly with a workshop attached.[53] A significant number of the sacred sites occupy prominent hilltops, frequently, as at Henley Wood, South Cadbury, and Cadbury near Tiverton, in or near the sites of pre-Roman hill-forts. This arrangement appears again to the east at Lydney, Maiden Castle, and elsewhere, and it sheds an interesting light on what late Romano-Britons regarded as fitting (*fig 4·11*).

By 315 the Christian Church, with its catholic scope and its far-reaching demands upon the individual, was on its way to becoming the official religion of the Empire. Cirencester, the provincial capital, possibly became the seat of a metropolitan (senior provincial) bishop. The important and largely Christian cemetery at Poundbury, just outside Dorchester, together with the Christian mosaic from the villa at Hinton St Mary, show that Dorchester probably also possessed a Christian bishop and his flock. The existence of either still cannot be proved at Exeter or Ilchester, the other obvious centres for a city-based church. The excavated cemeteries at Ilchester have a pagan appearance, although poorly recorded, but clearly impressive burials outside the city at Northover near the site of the later (perhaps much later) church could be significant. Exeter has produced only an odd-ment of pottery scratched with a chi-rho monogram, formed by the superimposition of the first two letters of the Greek spelling of *Christ*. Outside the cities and villas, the country people, as far as we can see, were wholly pagan.

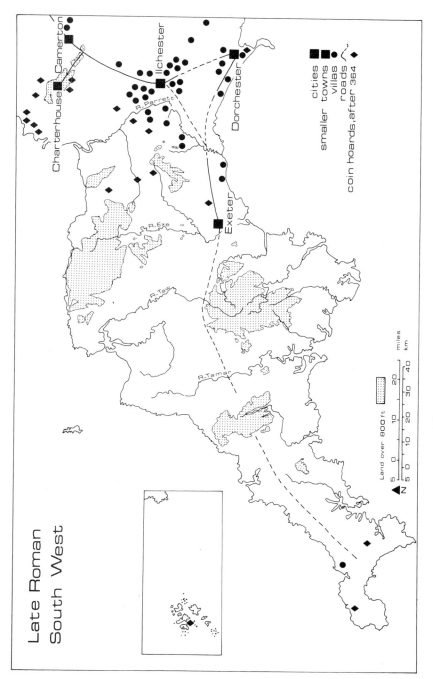

Fig 4·11 Late Roman south west.

1. *Manning 1976*
2. *Leach 1975*
3. *Bidwell 1979*
4. *Langmaid 1971*
5. *Lidell 1935, 164*
6. *Alcock 1972*
7. *Campbell, Baxter, Alcock 1979*
8. *Fox 1968*
9. *Jarvis, Maxfield 1975*
10. *Fox, Ravenhill 1959*
11. *Fox 1973*
12. *Bidwell 1979*
13. *Webster 1959*
14. *Elkington 1976*
15. *Fox, Ravenhill 1966*
16. *St Joseph 1977, 126*
17. *Fox, Ravenhill 1972*
18. *St Joseph 1977, 125–6*
19. *Balkwill 1976*
20. *Balkwill, Silvester 1976*
21. *Bidwell 1979*
22. *Fox 1968*
23. *Leach 1975*
24. *Rahtz, Fowler 1972*
25. *Leech 1976*
26. *Clarke 1971, 154–5*
27. *Fox 1973, 169*
28. *Jarvis 1976, 54*
29. *Jermy 1969*
30. *Miles 1977*
31. *Elkington 1976*
32. *Peacock 1969c*
33. *Saunders 1963*
34. *Miles, Miles 1973*
35. *Fox, Ravenhill 1969*
36. *Saunders 1972*
37. *Jarvis 1976*
38. *Hawkins 1973*
39. *Leech 1976*
40. *Miles 1977a*
41. *O'Neill 1934*
42. *Fowler 1962*
43. *Wacher 1975*
44. *Farley, Little 1968*
45. *Leach 1975*
46. *Branigan 1976*

47. *Hayward 1972*
48. *Pollard 1974*
49. *Miles 1977a*
50. *Branigan 1976*
51. *Alcock 1972*
52. *Fox 1952b*
53. *Ashbee 1974*

CHAPTER FIVE

Continuity and Change
400–900

Pottery and chronology

The most important finds which enable archaeologists to distinguish fifth century and later sites are, as usual, pots; but during the post-Roman period special problems arise. The period is marked by a low level of material prosperity, and the household tools of bone and iron are difficult to date with any certainty. Surviving fourth-century goods, including pots and dishes, were still being used, and the extent to which it was possible to replace them as they broke is still unclear.

This means that sites are very difficult to date. The archaeologist may be faced with scraps of fourth-century wares, pieces which look like late Roman vessels but could in fact have been manufactured later, and pieces of very coarse pottery, not fashioned in any datable style. Stoke Gabriel near Totnes in Devon can be shown from the coin evidence to have been occupied into the later fourth century. The finds included a range of rough cooking pots and storage jars in the usual late Roman forms, wheel-made, but apparently manufactured locally. Porth Godrevy, Gwithian, produced a similar range. Sites like these are conventionally regarded as 'fourth-century' but they could have continued in occupation beyond the Roman period.

Pottery in the Roman tradition certainly continued to be made in Cornwall through the fifth century and beyond, both on a strictly local scale and perhaps on a slightly larger scale at a centre in the Lizard peninsula. The earliest post-Roman levels at Gwithian revealed stone huts associated with locally made fine pottery in the Roman style, accompanied by examples of imported pottery. Trethurgy, near St Austell, has yielded sherds which included copies of late Roman forms and large storage jars. These seem to have been made in the area during the fourth century but their currency and perhaps their manufacture may have continued into the fifth and sixth.[1] Little as yet is known of any similar fifth/sixth-century wares from Devon, or from Somerset west of the Mendip edge.

It is easier to define the foreign imported wares, and this pottery found in western Britain forms one of the main struts in the chronology of the period from about 450 to 700.[2] The wares imported from the Mediterranean basin fall into two main groups: the fine wares and the coarse wares. The fine wares, known as 'A wares', consist of a series of bowls and dishes, often of reddish fabric, and occasionally stamped on the base with a symbol, usually a Christian one. They belong within the large and very varied groups known as 'Late Roman C ware', which was manufactured in the Aegean/Dardanelles area, and 'North African Red Slip ware', made along the eastern North African coast.[3] The British vessels seem to lie within the 460/70 to 600 phase of the Mediterranean industries. Finds of A ware are fairly rare, but some pieces have been discovered at South Cadbury, Gwithian, Tintagel, and Porthmeor.

The coarse wares, known as 'B wares', include a range of handled amphorae intended for the bulk transport of dry goods and liquids, especially oil and wine. They seem to derive from the Black Sea area, where similar types were made from about 400 to 700. B wares have been found on a considerable number of south-western sites, including all those named above and others like Bantham and Mothercombe in south Devon. Amphorae and their contents were also coming in from North Africa, since fragments of North African wares have been found at Cheddar, and Gloucester (*fig 5·1*). Other classes of pots imported into south-west Britain will undoubtedly be recognized as work progresses. A limited range of other goods, like oddments of glass, accompanied the pottery.

Nothing suggests a very frequent, regular, or indeed necessarily direct contact with the Mediterranean. The trade involved luxury goods rather than subsistence material, although the oil and wine was needed by the Church, and its social importance was greater than its economic.

Hilltops

The dramatic excavations at South Cadbury in Somerset focused attention on a wide range of potentially exciting hilltop sites, many of which had been enclosed in the prehistoric period. At South Cadbury around AD 500 a new stone and timber rampart was built on the inner ring of the prehistoric defences and at least one substantial timber

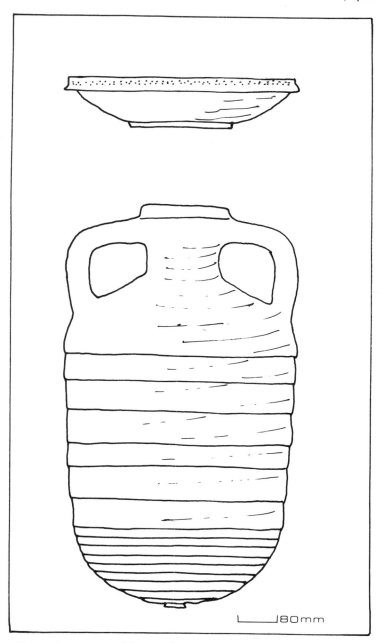

Fig 5·1 Reconstructed forms of a coarse-ware amphora and an A ware bowl (*source: Alcock 1971, fig 14; Radford, Swanton 1975, fig 1*).

167

building was put up inside the fort. The hillfort at Cadbury Congresbury in north Somerset seems to have been similarly refortified and occupied. These two must surely have been the fortified centres of men of importance in the military and political affairs of the fifth and early sixth centuries.

Elsewhere, however, the picture is less clear. A range of sites, including Berry Head or Membury in Devon, and Cadbury Tickenham in Somerset, have produced scatters of late Roman pottery and coins. These may provide a link with the hilltop temples already mentioned, and religious activity represented by fourth-century finds may, for all we know, have continued well beyond 450.

People were making use of sites like High Peak (Sidmouth), Chun Castle in Penwith, Glastonbury Tor, and Killibury in north Cornwall, since all these have produced oddments of imported pottery; but nothing proves contemporary occupation on any large scale. Nevertheless, there are hints, like the number of parishes which take their name from a hillfort, which suggest that these ancient sites may sometimes have been embedded in the structure of post-Roman landholding arrangements.

Inscribed stones

In the post-Roman period, for the first time, we have inscriptions which give us the names of some of the inhabitants. About forty-five inscribed stones are known from the south west, although they continue to come to light. These form an important group within the wider series distributed chiefly in south Wales, north Wales, and southern Scotland.

The inscriptions are normally in Latin and cut upon substantial pillars of roughly trimmed local stone. Their general purpose was commemorative, although they do not seem to have been set necessarily over an actual grave. As a class they owe something to the elaborate funerary monuments erected by wealthy western late Romans, Christian or otherwise, in the cemeteries which lined the roads leading to the gates of their cities. Equally, the erection of simple inscribed pillar stones had become an Irish custom, possibly also as a result of Gaulish inspiration, so that complex influences can be detected in the development of the British custom.

None of the south-western stones can be directly dated, as can a few from Wales, so their dating is dependent upon comparison with the Welsh stones, and upon the character of the inscriptions and the form of their letters. We know that the earlier are those whose letters take the form of good Roman capitals, set, sometimes roughly, in horizontal lines. Inscriptions like these can be ambitious, although they are relatively rare. Four only are known from the south west, the most elaborate being that from Carnsew near Hayle which probably reads something like 'Here lately went to rest Cunaide. Here he (or she) lies in the tomb. He (or she) lived 33 years.' As a class these early monuments belong to the decades either side of AD 500. Phrases like HIC IN TUMULO (Here in the tomb lies . . .) are known to be specifically Christian, having been customarily used during the late fourth/fifth centuries in the great cemeteries of North Africa and Gaul.

As the sixth century progressed the inscriptions became much simpler. The forms of the letters show the influence of contemporary handwriting styles. They are often poorly cut and the words run vertically down the stone. These inscriptions begin after AD 530, but

Fig 5·2 Stones with vertical inscriptions. CARAACI NEPUS (probably 'grandson of Caratacus'), Winsford Hill, Exmoor. CUMREGNI FILI MAUCI (The stone of Cumregnus son of Maucus), South Hill, Cornwall. RIALOBRANI CUNOVA-LI FILI (The stone of Rialobranus son of Cunovalus), Men Scryfa Down, Penwith (*source: Macalister 1945, nos 499, 486, 468*).

they may have gone on being produced into the early eighth century (*fig 5·2*). Sometimes they employ the Christian formula HIC IACET (Here lies) which was as stereotyped as the modern R.I.P. Sometimes the pagan-looking X FILIUS Y (X Son of Y) was used, the phrase implying a pride of ancestry at variance with Christian piety. A typical example is the stone from Parracombe near Lynton, which reads CAVUDI FILIUS CIVILI (The memorial of Cavudus son of Civilis).

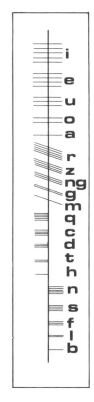

Fig 5·3
Ogam
script.

Plate 34 (*Opposite*) Inscribed memorial stone in churchyard, St Clement, Cornwall. The main inscription on the shaft reads VITALI FILI TORRICI (The stone of Vitalus the son of Torricus), and dates about 550. Above it, a later inscription reads IGNIOC, a personal name.

Plate 35 Inscribed memorial stone from Buckland Monachorum (now at Tavistock), dating about 550. It carries a version of the Irish personal name Maccudecceti, meaning 'devotee of the god Deiche'.

171

The stone from Sourton near Okehampton has three vertical lines of fairly good Roman capitals, but the inscription is difficult to read, except for one word, PRINCIPI meaning 'prince' or 'chief', an interesting assumption of Roman-style authority on the part of the local ruler about AD 550.

The stones are found in two quite distinct locations. Some were deliberately set beside tracks, in the Roman tradition. The memorial in honour of Caratacus, as his name seems to have been, still stands beside the ancient path over Winsford Hill in Exmoor. The Penwith stone inscribed RIALOBRANI CUNOVALI FILI (The memorial of Rialobran son of Cunoval) stands on Men Scryfa Moor to which it has given a name, 'Men Scryfa', meaning 'written stone'. Nearly half the stones, however, seem to have been set in graveyards, irrespective of whether they bear specifically Christian formulae or not, and their presence, as will be seen, is most significant.

Irish settlers

The inscriptions in Ireland already mentioned are cut not in Latin but in an Irish script known as ogam, where letters are represented by groups of strokes cut against one of the long edges of the stone (fig 5·3). The Irish inscriptions cluster most thickly in southern Ireland, and generally belong in the late fifth and sixth centuries.

About sixty of the British stones are bilingual, carrying more or less identical inscriptions in both Latin and ogam. The bulk of these are in south-western Wales, but a significant group of seven has survived from the south west, from Ivybridge and Buckland Monachorum in Devon, and from Lewannick, where there are two, St Endellion, St Kew, and Worthyvale in Cornwall. With these belong a small number of stones, including that from Bleu Bridge in Penwith and another from Buckland Monachorum, which carry single Latin inscriptions where, however, the personal names involved are linguistically Irish.

The south British ogam stones fit into a considerable body of documentary evidence which makes it plain that, during the sixth century, southern Irishmen from Munster were settling in south-western Wales, just as Ulstermen were settling in what is now western Scotland. The whole tone of the inscriptions implies that the Munstermen were concerned to integrate themselves into British society, and the Irishmen commemorated on the south-western stones may have come by way of south Wales (fig 5·4).

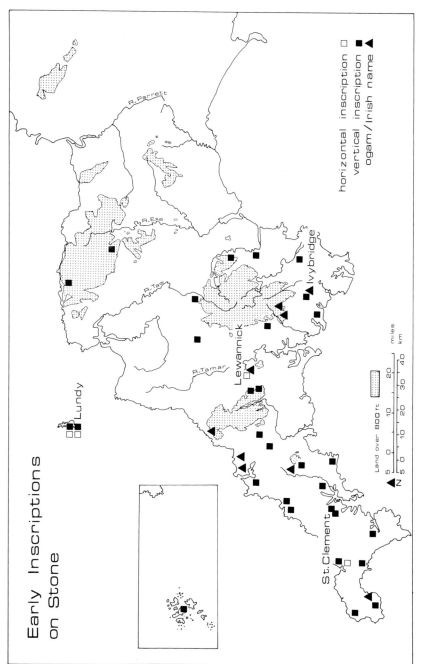

Fig 5·4 Early inscriptions on stone.

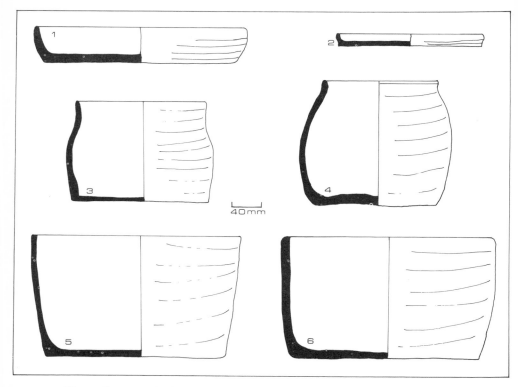

Fig 5·5 Grass-marked pottery. 3: Chun Castle; others: Gwithian (*source: Thomas 1972, fig 4*).

Much more difficult to assess is the significance of the grassmarked pottery, so called because the vessels bear on their bases the impressions of the chopped grass on which they were rested before firing (*fig 5·5*). Early examples of this ware, dated to the sixth century, have been found in the far west of Cornwall at Gwithian,[4] and at Tean on Scilly, and it has appeared also at the Cannington cemetery in Somerset. Similar pottery had a long currency in Ulster, where it is known as souterrain ware, and may have begun as early as the sixth century. However, it now seems unlikely that the pottery represents incomers into the south west from Ulster.

Nothing, then, suggests that the Irish immigration into the south west was considerable or had far-reaching consequences. The importance given by tradition to 'Irish' saints in the early south-western church is largely the result of conscious effort on the part of writers from about 800 onwards who wished their saintly heroes to share in the glamour of the Irish 'Age of Saints'.[5] No individual place names deriving from Irish speakers have been convincingly identified as yet in the south west as they have in Wales, although Thomas has made the interesting suggestion that the fresh terminology required to describe new farming arrangements may owe something to Irish influence.[6]

The Kingdom of Dumnonia

What is now Cornwall and Devon, possibly together with part of west Somerset, formed the Kingdom of Dumnonia, one of many similar kingdoms in post-Roman Britain. Pitifully little is known of its history. About 550 the monk Gildas was able to list a Constantine of Dumnonia as one of five contemporary kings. There survives among the traditions of south Wales what seems to be a genealogy of Dumnonian rulers, together with a body of poetry and story which grew up around their names. The interpretation of this material is not easy but, considered together with the inscribed stones, it suggests a society where the aristocratic ties of blood and honour were very important. It is reasonable to suggest that the Constantine of tradition, the man who called himself 'prince' on his memorial, or the Rialobran whose name, recorded on the Penwith stone, probably means 'Royal Raven', were the men who controlled local strong points, drank the wine which found its way along the trade routes, and generally filled the positions of authority vacated by the imperial officials. These men, too, must have provided the economic and political support behind the monastic foundations.

In later medieval tradition Arthur was made a member of the Dumnonian royal house. Story-tellers linked his history with a number of west country sites, especially Tintagel, where he was said to have been born, and Glastonbury, where he was believed to have been buried and where his supposed last resting-place can be seen to this day. Similarly, the tragic love story of Tristan and Isolt was set at Tintagel, and in the area around Fowey. These tales all belong in the world of medieval romance, and their relevance to genuine sixth-century occupation at Tintagel and Glastonbury is highly debatable.

If Arthur did really exist, he probably lived around 500. He may have operated as a war leader in the south west; but a good case can be made for locating him in northern Britain. Equally, he may have been a mythical hero, stories about whom came to be attached to prominent places throughout Britain, like South Cadbury where 'King

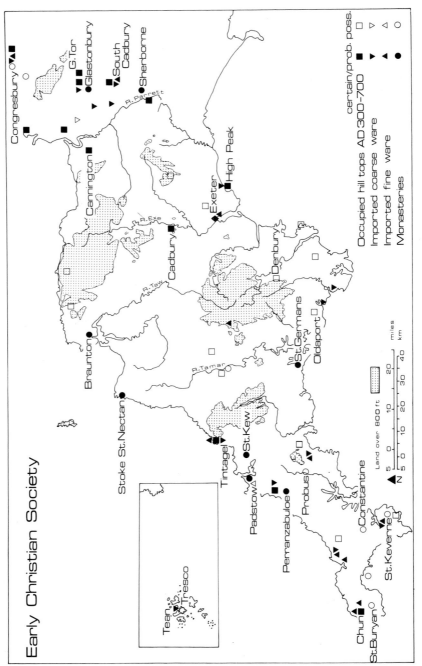

Fig 5·6 Early Christian Society.

Arthur lies asleep'. From around 950, Welsh story-tellers spoke of Arthur as if he had lived in the south west, perhaps because at this time the real Dumnonian kingdom was coming to an end (*fig 5·6*).

The West Saxons

By 400 groups of Germanic settlers—Saxons, Angles, Frisians and the rest—had begun to infiltrate Britain, settling in a piecemeal fashion into varying relationships with the British, and only gradually merging into kingdoms like Wessex which show up in the historical record. Early Germanic material, suggesting a range of possible contacts from settlement to casual trade, has appeared in Somerset in graves from the later stages at Camerton cemetery, and from Queens Camel, and in a scatter of chance finds including three brooches from Ilchester. The burial in a prehistoric barrow near Charmouth in Dorset of German jewellery and weapons represents the most westerly of the splendid warrior graves.

These finds fit the record in the *Anglo-Saxon Chronicle* of West Saxon victories over the British in 577 at Dyrham near Bath and in 614 at *Beandune* (perhaps Bindon in east Devon).[7] About 700, Ine of Wessex seems to have been fighting Gereint of Dumnonia along the south Tamar line, implying that by then the whole of Devon was included within Wessex. Germanic rather than Irish antagonism in south-western Britain during the late fifth and sixth centuries may have been the cause of the considerable British emigration to Brittany, and the lesser one to Galicia in north-west Spain. Linguistic and documentary evidence show that the bulk of the settlers came from Dumnonia, although so far the complementary archaeological evidence cannot confirm this.

Fighting continued intermittently between Wessex and Dumnonia. The south west suffered during the ninth-century Scandinavian raids, but the lack of Scandinavian place names in the peninsula shows that the Norsemen did not come to settle. These troubles preoccupied the West Saxon kings and delayed the final conquest of Cornwall. A cross fragment preserved at St Cleer carries an inscription referring to *Doniert*, possibly the Dumgarth king of Cornwall, who is recorded in the *Welsh Annals* as having been drowned about 871. The inscription on a cross now standing in Penlee Gardens, Penzance, may refer to a King Riocatus (or a similar name). After Athelstan's reign (924–39) we hear no more of Cornish kings, and his statesman-like arrangements settled the political affairs of the peninsula for a long time to come.

The evolution of the rural landscape

Meanwhile, what was happening to the food producers upon whom the higher levels of society depended? The landscape now around us displays an infinite variety of fields, boundaries, lanes, woodlands, and unenclosed grazing, within which are set farmsteads, hamlets, villages, and towns. The broad lines of much of this rural pattern had been achieved by about 1100, but exactly how and when are still open to question. How dense was British settlement around, say, AD 500? Did people live in villages or scattered farms, or both, and how were these organized into estates productive enough to support a land-holding class? Were the Anglo-Saxons able to take over going concerns, or did they found new settlements of their own? In any case, how many Anglo-Saxons were there? The answers will undoubtedly differ from area to area along the length of the peninsula. The best approach is by way of place name studies, and documents like the royal Anglo-Saxon land-granting charters, *Domesday Book*, and later estate records, together with archaeological and topographical information.

We now know that, even though place names east of the Tamar are overwhelmingly English, and must represent substantial numbers of English-speaking settlers, and those west of the Tamar are mostly British or Cornish, it would be an over-simplification to regard the English names as indicating new settlements created by Englishmen after about AD 500.[8] A charter of King Centwine of Wessex, dated about 682, refers to Creechbarrow in Somerset as 'in the British language Cructan, among us Crybeorh' suggesting that many places had two names for a while, until the British version (usually) was lost, and that many English-looking settlements may have been originally British.

A framework for dating elements in the settlement pattern between, say, 500 and 1100 is still elusive. Pottery and other datable small finds are rare, and accumulating evidence suggests that settlers quite frequently rebuilt their homes, either on the original site or elsewhere within their settlement territory, leaving a misleading impression.[9] Place names in themselves certainly do not offer a straightforward chronological sequence for the early period. Similarly, a late name, like that of Goodcott in Ashreigney parish in Devon, which takes its name from a woman called Godgiefu, recorded in *Domesday Book* as in possession of the estate in 1066, may represent a new settlement, but it may just as well represent the re-naming of a much older one.

The early documents do not facilitate the dating problems. Charters and *Domesday Book* may be referring to a large estate by the name of just one central settlement, when in fact the property included a number of settlements, so giving an erroneous impression of the density of settlement at that time. Obviously, also, the date of a surviving record is not necessarily the foundation date of the settlement, which may have been much earlier.

Detailed local studies, which can take into account all the evidence together with environmental factors like good and poor soil, offer the best chance of creating an understanding of settlement chronology and character, but few of these studies have yet been undertaken. It may emerge that the Anglo-Saxon settlers made their way into a landscape quite densely populated, with a range of settlement types, within which people gradually cleared more woodland and established new homes.

The landscape of Cornwall and parts of Devon seems to have formed a pattern of dispersed farms and small hamlets, joined by a network of lanes, with only a few large or nucleated villages. Certainly, in the later medieval record individual farms and hamlets predominate throughout Cornwall and much of Devon, in contrast to the villages of Somerset and east Devon, but the history of settlement in the South Hams and parts of north Devon poses unanswered questions. The origins of the villages remains one of the most vexed problems of settlement history. Some, in south or east Somerset, may have their roots in the Roman period, while others may be much later.

Little is known about the early history, or original layout, of west country villages, because what we now see may well be the result of post-1066 reorganizations. The position of a church can provide significant clues towards the location of the Anglo-Saxon or early medieval focus of settlement.[10] An isolated church may suggest a shift in the village settlement pattern. At Curry Mallet and Seavington St Mary, both in Somerset, isolated churches are surrounded by village earthworks, while others, like Beercrocombe and Knowle St Giles, are not. A churchyard within its own special enclosure may mean an early foundation, whereas a churchyard which occupies one plot within a regularly laid out village, as at Long Load, may not occupy the original site.

In Cornwall and parts of Devon a crucial but gradual change seems to have taken place in the organization of the isolated farms. During the post-Roman centuries, settlers gradually deserted the old enclosed homesteads or 'rounds' and began to establish open farms. At Goldherring, Sancreed, occupation of the courtyard house continued into the fifth century; at Halangy Down on St Mary's, Scilly, pottery showed that occupation had continued into the sixth century at least. Trethurgy round yielded about fifty sherds of A and B wares, and the story was the same at Grambla, where the sub-rectangular enclosure had imported wares associated with what seems to be the latest use of the site.

The open settlements seem to have been larger and sometimes occupied newly cleared land. The excavation at Gwithian revealed such a site on the coast. The inhabitants built round huts with turf walls on a stone foundation, and their settlement continued until the eleventh century. They worked iron and, during the first phases, they possessed some imported vessels. Later they produced grass-marked ware, and by about the early ninth century a new improved feature known as the 'bar lug' was added to the cooking pots: high 'ears' were built up over the bridges intended to take suspension strings, so that the strings might be better protected from the fire. The idea seems to have come from the Low Countries, and it was generally adopted in southern Britain.

Some of the hamlet and farmstead settlements on the modern map

Plate 36 Bar lug pot from medieval settlement, Gwithian, Cornwall. Width 270 mm. Royal Institution of Cornwall.

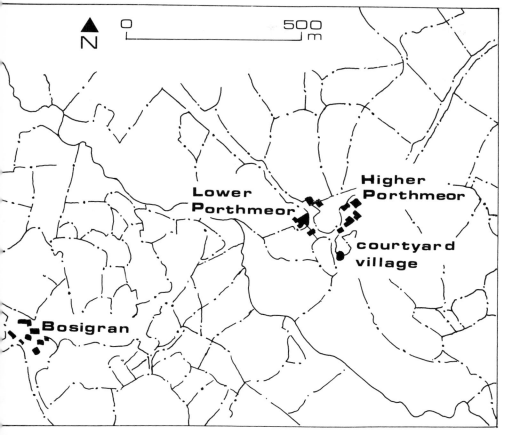

Fig 5·7 Fields and settlements at Porthmeor, Zennor (*source: Ordnance Survey*).

are still surrounded by what seem to be prehistoric fields, eloquent witness to the potential antiquity of the settlement pattern. At Sherril, on Dartmoor, the reave pattern seems to underlie fields in much later use, while at Horridge, on the eastern edge of the moor, the small square fields of the prehistoric settlement on the higher ground merge into, and seem to underlie, the pattern of lower fields still in use.

In contrast to these small square fields are larger, rectangular fields which seem to have come into being during the later Iron Age and Roman period, and which could be—although further evidence is required—related to the acquisition of improved iron tools. At Porthmeor in the parish of Zennor the small rectangular fields with their massive boundary banks of granite rubble probably represent the surviving fields originally attached to the adjacent courtyard house, which the finds of imported Mediterranean pottery show was occupied into the sixth century. Rather later, possibly as part of the change from enclosed to unenclosed settlements, the two farmsteads now known as Higher and Lower Porthmeor were created, as well as the hamlet of Bosigran; but the ancient fields remained (fig 5·7).

The excavations at Gwithian have shown important details of the cultivation of two rectangular fields belonging to the homestead, the first used from the late sixth to the ninth century, and the second from the ninth to the eleventh. These suggest that the development of such field systems is intimately connected with the availability, probably increasing throughout the early medieval period, of the improved plough equipped with a mould-board to turn a furrow slice. The second field showed narrow parallel rigs or 'ridge and furrow', the alternate peaks and dips which develop lengthwise down a field as a result of earth movement over the years of ploughing.[11]

These farmers seem to have managed their fields in the system known as 'infield and outfield', which is typical generally of the British Highland zone. The infield, comprising the fields nearest the settlement, was normally permanently under cultivation. A rotation of crops probably helped to preserve fertility, as would the grazing of beasts in the stubble during the winter. Beyond lay the outfield, patches of which would be broken up and cultivated for a few years and then allowed to revert to rough grazing. Beyond again was the waste, offering wood for all purposes, food for sheep and pigs, and opportunities for further intake of arable.

The use of the improved plough may have been one factor in the development of strip cultivation within large subdivided fields of the kind that are often called 'open', although in fact most of them may have been hedged. This system is, of course, the classic pattern of medieval English agriculture, in which each settlement had two or three large fields divided into strips, each theoretically of roughly an acre, separated by unploughed areas or balks, and grouped together in batches. Each occupier's holding, including that of the lord, comprised a number of scattered strips allocated so that each man had a share in every kind of available land. Dating is difficult, but shareholding field systems like this seem to have been in existence at least as early as the eighth century.[12]

Areas of relict strip cultivation appear in field plans from many parts of the south west around villages and hamlets, although maps used without assistance from documents may be misleading and there is a need for detailed study on a regional basis. It has been argued that

Plate 37 Part of Braunton Great Field, looking north. The strips, arranged in bundles, can be seen plainly. Compare figure 5·8

in Devon subdivided fields were the normal early medieval agrarian pattern east of the Exe, south of Dartmoor, and along areas of the north coast.[13] In Cornwall the distribution seems to have been general, with a certain increase of density in the east of the county, in and near the Roseland peninsula, and in Penwith.[14]

The Great Field at Braunton in north Devon, to the south west of the village, is a rare example of a surviving subdivided field, where the pattern of strips divided by balks still remains (*fig 5·8*). Further west, on the north Cornish coast at Forrabury near Boscastle, a broadly similar survival has been studied.[15] The fifty acres of arable, landwards of the rough grazing offered by Willipark headland, is divided into cultivation strips, or 'stitches', as they are called locally. The original allocations seem to have been based upon acre strips but subsequent

Fig 5·8 Plan of Braunton Great Field (*source: Slee 1952, Pl 5A*).

amalgamations are clear in the plan. The strips were grouped in seven bundles defined by trackways, and originally each strip seems to have shown a slight twist in its plan, known as the reversed S, which made it easier to turn the mould-board plough at the end of the furrow.

Field systems like Forrabury may have been worked according to the method typical of much of the English midlands, whereby part of the arable was left fallow each year while the rest was cultivated, or else linked with infield–outfield exploitation. In the subdivided field, each man probably worked his own strips, intermixed as they were, but in winter there would have been common grazing rights on the stubble.

184

Subsequent enclosure and alteration have obscured the early medieval picture so much that it is difficult to estimate the extents of the different types of land use or to make confident assertions about the types of settlement to which the various fields may have been attached. Nevertheless, the landscape of the south west around 900 would certainly have involved areas of enclosed squarish fields, some already very ancient, and rectangular fields, attached to hamlets and farmsteads, together with areas of strip cultivation around some of the hamlets and many of the larger villages.

These settlements and their appurtenances were part of an intricate network of legal and administrative arrangements which have themselves often left their mark on the landscape. Recent studies suggest that a basic unit may have been the multiple estate, which included a number of scattered farms and hamlets, each with its own organization appropriate to the terrain it occupied, together with a centre which might be a socially superior farmstead or a sizable village, from which the whole took its name.[16] The charters show that even as early as the seventh century many estates were large and well-developed, with all their various resources thoroughly exploited. This suggests that they were then already organized units which must have originated in the pre-English period. Many of the smaller manors which gradually appeared, like Goodcott already mentioned, would then have been fragmented parts of such ancient units.

In some places the boundaries as they are described in a charter may still be traced on the ground. An estate about 9 km north west of Exeter was granted by Athelstan to the church at Exeter between 925 and 939. Its eastern boundary is still represented by the sunken lane known as Armourwood Lane near Thorverton, which was originally a specially dug double-ditch, the earth heaped upon either side to form hedge banks.[17]

Cemeteries

During the fifth century interest focuses upon a number of cemetery sites, which have enough features in common to be discussed together although they do not form a rigidly defined group. Often they are very large, like that at Cannington, which had several thousand graves. The burials were usually on an east–west alignment. Grave goods are sparse, but at Cannington and Brean Down in Somerset some of the men had been buried with small knives, and at Camerton there were a few trinkets. Sometimes, as at Henley Wood (Congresbury) or Cannington, the cemetery included small buildings, perhaps enclosing special graves.

A conspicuous number of these graveyards, like those at Lamyatt, Brean Down and Henley Wood, all in Somerset, were established amid the ruins of disused temples. Most of them were clearly intended to serve neighbouring communities, like the hillfort settlers at Cannington and Congresbury. At Exeter, a graveyard developed in the ruins of the demolished basilica building in the present Cathedral Close and at Tean on Scilly, a group of graves was dug into a refuse midden, dated by sherds of imported wares. Other sites undoubtedly await discovery, some perhaps near the villa buildings of Somerset and Dorset, like that already discovered dug into the villa on Wint Hill, Banwell.

The religious significance of this varied group is hard to estimate. The graveyards all lie in an area where there was a long gap between the breakdown of central Rome authority about 400 and the earliest known West Saxon military success in Somerset in 577. The burial customs they show are those normal in the late Roman world, and none has produced proof of Christian practices, so they would seem to represent a mixed range of cultural loyalties.

In contrast to these sites are the enclosed graveyards which are most common in the western part of the peninsula. Characteristically, these consist of a round or oval area enclosed by a substantial wall of rough stone and earth. Since many have been in use as parish graveyards for many centuries, the enclosed area is generally several feet above the surrounding level. The original outside quarry ditch has frequently become a lane running round the perimeter of the site. The whole complex seems to have been described by the Old Cornish word meaning 'enclosed cemetery'. This occurs in the form *lan* as the first part of many Cornish placenames, as the comparable *llan* does in Wales, followed by a personal name or a descriptive word. These sites are often easy to recognize; but since we do not know how long they continued to be constructed, the identification of early ones, established around 500 to 600, depends upon datable finds. In practice, only a small number of sites can definitely be dated so early and yet many of the rest are likely to be as old.

At Phillack in Cornwall a scrap of imported ware appeared when the entrance to the graveyard was rebuilt, and built into the church wall above the south porch is a small slab (*fig 5·9*) carved with an early *chi-rho* form (see p. 162). Two of the early horizontally inscribed stones were set up in the important site at Beacon Hill, Lundy, where a little later the worshippers built a shrine grave. At Lewannick (re-

Fig 5·9 Chi-rho symbols. Left to right, from a coin of Magnentius *c*. 350 found at Nor'nour, a piece of pottery from Exeter, a memorial stone from Penmachno in north Wales, a mosaic pavement at the Frampton villa, Dorset, a slab at Cape Cornwall, a slab at Phillack Church, Cornwall, and inscribed stones at St Just, St Endellion, and South Hill, all Cornwall (*source: Pearce 1978, figs 1, 2*).

corded as *Lanwenuc* about 1120) one of the two bilingual stones seems to read INGENUI MEMORIA. This can be translated as 'The memorial shrine of Ingenuus', and it implies a grave which was the focus of pious observance. The view of Lewannick churchyard from the road in front of the public house gives one of the best impressions of the type anywhere in Cornwall.

By no means all the potential sixth-century graveyards have this characteristic enclosed form. East Ogwell churchyard in Devon seems to have had an inscribed stone, but the shape of the graveyard is not at first sight significant. At a large number of sites, especially in western Cornwall, or in north-east Cornwall, like Egloskerry, St Clether, or St Teath, estimate of age depends on the fact that sites with a *unique* dedication name seem likely, on balance, to have acquired that name no later than 600.

The first church buildings, probably of wood, may have been erected at these sites during the sixth or seventh centuries, to be replaced during the ninth or tenth by stone structures, an example of which was excavated at the chapel site on St Helen's, Scilly. Sacred sites, like the well chapels at Madron Baptistry or Fenton-Ia near Camborne,[18] or various seashore chapels like that at Chapel Jane, were added as secondary sites throughout the medieval period.

Undoubtedly these graveyards were primarily intended to serve the local lay Christian community, and they show how a Christian society was developing in the decades after 500. We know very little about the people who are commemorated on the memorial stones, or whose names are linked with the graveyards. Nevertheless, they seem to have been intimately connected with the early history of the sites, and their buried bones often acted as the spiritual focus of a developing cemetery during an age when the cult of the relics was enormously important. The shrine graves from Lundy and Lewannick would fit in here. Evidence from other parts of Britain enables us to guess that sometimes they may have been local clergymen, sometimes local land-holders, and sometimes members of the local monastic communities which were coming into existence during the sixth century.

Monasteries

No agreed set of features discernible in the archaeological record has so far emerged by which a British monastic site, defined here as the cemetery, church, and domestic buildings of a religious community, can be recognized, probably because a limited number of sites has been examined. The problem of distinguishing early monastery sites from those which have later been *claimed* as monastic is complicated by the fact that west of the Tamar many monasteries look exactly the same as the enclosed cemeteries. St Kew, for example, is an enclosed graveyard of much the same size and shape as Lewannick, and like

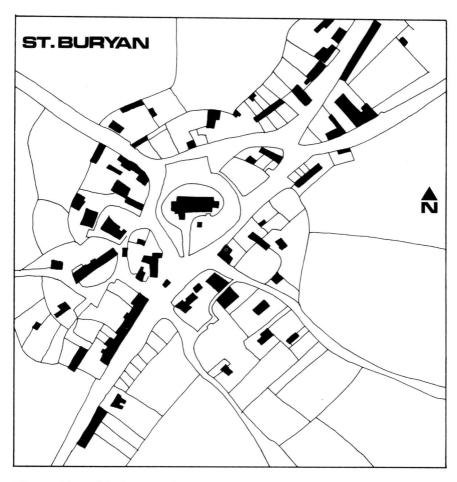

Fig 5·10 Plan of St Buryan, showing church and churchyard in centre of village (*source: Ordnance Survey*).

Lewannick it possesses a sixth-century bilingual inscription. The distinction hinges on the two-fold fact that monastery churches owned landed endowments necessary to support the community, which have left their trace in the later administrative record, and (less certainly) that a tradition enshrining a probable nucleus of truth was developed at the monastery about the founding figure whose relics normally lay in the monastery church. To him, also, the church normally will be dedicated, and his name will be part of the place name.

On this basis, St Kew, Padstow, whence the monastery moved to

Plate 38 Glastonbury, Somerset, looking east. The abbey complex is in the centre, with the Church of St John on the opposite side of High Street. The Tor shows clearly beyond.

Bodmin during the Scandinavian troubles, and Perranzabuloe, where the original site is probably represented by the tenth-century 'Oratory of St Piran' in the sands, can be singled out as monastic sites. Crantock, Probus, St Buryan where the enclosed graveyard is a classic of its kind (*fig 5·10*), St Keverne where a nearby placename, Lesneage, first recorded in 967 means 'the court of the monks' land',[19] and St Germans are all likely places. In north Devon there are St Nectan's

Plate 39 The headland and mainland, Tintagel, north Cornwall, looking south west, and showing the series of building sites, from which came imported wares, set on artificial terraces. The cemetery complex is in the centre, above the rocky bluff. Remains of the later medieval castle can be seen either side of the narrow neck.

monastery at Stoke St Nectan, and Brannoc's at Braunton, recorded as an estate called *Brancminstre* ('Brannoc's monastery') in 973.

Much further east, the great house at Sherborne, Dorset, seems to have had British origins since its early name appears to have been *Lanprobi*, although we know nothing of Probus. Congresbury is another possibility, with its traditions of St Congar. Glastonbury housed a monastic community in about 700 when King Ine of Wessex visited its holy Old Church. Excavations at the Abbey have revealed details of the early cemetery and boundary bank, and occupation on Glastonbury Tor, dated to the sixth century by its imported pottery, must be a part of the whole picture.[20]

There remains the important but enigmatic site at Tintagel, which has produced a quantity of A and B wares. Excavation has shown a range of rectangular stone buildings scattered over the headland, and what seems to have been an early cemetery with a slate headstone incised with a cross very like those sometimes stamped inside A ware bowls.[21] The classic academic interpretation of the site is as a major sixth-century monastery, but this has been challenged on the grounds of its dissimilarity to other south western sites, and its small impact on the written record.[22]

The monastic inspiration seems to have come along the trade routes from the Mediterranean with the imported wares, and from Gaul. Documentary evidence suggests that the British monasteries were founded in the decades after 500. The landed endowments must have been provided by local rulers, and in south Wales, at least, this transaction seems to have been recorded in a written form. It is even possible that some of these estates were like those which appear in the later Anglo-Saxon charters. The monks must have been actively converting the people to Christianity, and helping to establish the graveyards.

The West Saxon Church

In 635 King Cynegils of the West Saxons was baptized. Thereafter the kings of Wessex were responsible for the Church within their kingdom, and this included sensible dealings with the British monasteries which they found as they extended their power westwards. In fact, even in the eastern part of the region, some British establishments, like Glastonbury and Sherborne, seem to have survived the period of pagan rule. The policy was evidently a broad one of integration, together with the foundation where necessary of new minster churches in line with English and Gaulish practices. The minster clergy were responsible for the pastoral care of the lay population within their district, just as were the British monks within theirs, so that similarities were greater than differences in spite of various divergences in custom. By 710 both Sherborne and Glastonbury were major West Saxon monasteries, with Sherborne as the episcopal seat for the western part of the kingdom.

By about 670 a minster church had been founded at Exeter. Excavation has shown that a second phase of burials, which included one with a probably eighth-century gold ring, succeeded the fifth-century cemetery. No early minster church building attached to this graveyard has so far appeared, and it is possible that a surviving Roman building continued to be used for some time. The religious site apart, however, evidence of settlement within the Roman walls of Exeter during the fifth to ninth centuries is equivocal. Pottery is virtually non-existent; but then people may have managed without it, just as they may have used old Roman structures instead of building afresh. In all, however, it seems that the minster establishment dominated early Saxon Exeter, and provided the main link between the Roman city and the late Saxon town. The same may be true at Ilchester, where the minster church of St Andrew at Northover may

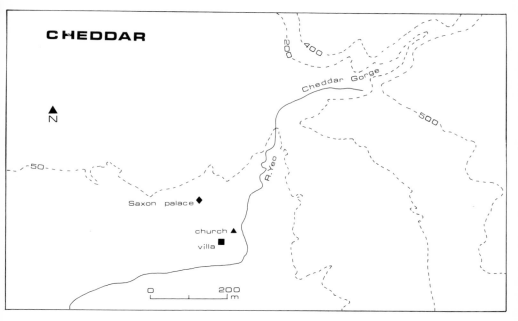

Fig 5·11 Plan of Cheddar showing relationship of villa, church, and palace (*source: Rahtz 1963, fig 17*).

be as old as the seventh/eighth century, and may even occupy the site of an earlier graveyard.

More than thirty minster churches were founded in Dorset, west Somerset and Devon. Little Saxon work survives at these sites, although traces have been found at Wimborne Minster church in Dorset, and part of the apsed east end of the late Saxon church at Muchelney in Somerset may be seen within the ground plan of the post-Conquest abbey. Some minster churches were built on, or near, fourth-century villa sites, suggesting that their landed endowments may even have been the original villa estates. This is true in Somerset of Keynsham and Cheddar (*fig 5·11*) where the ninth-century kings established a royal palace, and in Dorset of Wimborne and Whit-church Canonicorum (probably) and Halstock. Conceivably, these link up with the idea of the pre-English multiple estates, and the whole picture could have far-reaching implications for the legal and econ-omic structure of the post-Roman period.

1. *Miles, Miles 1973*
2. *Thomas 1976* and references there
3. *Hayes 1972*
4. *Thomas 1972*
5. *Pearce 1978*
6. *Thomas 1972*
7. *Hoskins 1960*
8. *Gelling 1978*
9. *Sawyer 1976a*
10. *Aston, Rowley 1974*
11. *Thomas 1976a*
12. *Bowen 1961*
13. *Fox, H. 1972*
14. *Shorter, Ravenhill, Gregory 1969*
15. *Wood 1963*
16. *Jones 1976*
17. *Hoskins 1955*
18. *Thomas 1968*
19. *Henderson 1964, 21*
20. *Radford 1971*
21. *Radford 1962*
22. *Pearce 1978*

CHAPTER SIX

Medieval Farmers
and Townsmen

The burhs

The decades either side of 900 witnessed a significant growth of town life throughout northern Europe. In this, the Scandinavian raiders and settlers seem to have acted as important catalysts. They stimulated the need for local defensive centres, and encouraged markets through which might be dispersed the goods coming along trading and raiding routes that extended from Iceland to Kiev. Nevertheless, this cannot be the complete reason, and the developing towns must have sprung from a general quickening of confidence and ambition, probably linked with a growth in population.

Many definitions, of varying degrees of sophistication, have been offered to describe the essential nature of urban settlements. In practical terms, towns are places where the inhabitants spend much of their time in the manufacture of goods and in the provision of specialized services, rather than in the production of food. Towns have regular markets, where goods can be bought and sold. The prosperous development of urban communities is often bound up with the organization of a generally accepted currency, sometimes in the form of metal coinage. In northern Europe, town development has usually been accompanied by the creation of legal and administrative forms granting varying degrees of self-government to the townsmen under the central authority, and establishing self-conscious corporate identities with their potentially important implications of morale and civic pride.

For southern England, the group of documents known as the *Burghal Hidage* offers the earliest insight into the evolution of medieval urban settlement.[1] The earliest version seems to have been drawn up late in the reign of Alfred's son, Edward the Elder, between about 915

195

and 919. It described the defensive system organized by Alfred against the Scandinavian threat, which centred upon fortified places, or *burhs*, each defended, usually by a ditch and a bank topped by a palisade (perhaps later replaced by stone work), and each manned by a garrison drawn from the local countryside. The documents do give some assessment of the men required to defend each burh, from which it may be possible to calculate the lengths of their defences, but the accuracy of these paper estimates remains doubtful.

There are no entries in the *Burghal Hidage* for Cornwall. Exeter is listed with a medium-sized assessment which seems inadequate to defend the whole circuit of the ancient Roman wall, suggesting perhaps that only certain sections required to be actually manned.[2] Later tradition credited Athelstan (924–39) with substantial reconstruction of the defences. This has never been demonstrated archaeologically, although he may have undertaken a certain amount of refurbishing.

Halwell follows with a very modest assessment. The site of this burh is lost, although its place in the list shows that it must have been somewhere in south Devon. Two possible candidates in the parish of Halwell are the earthworks at Stanborough and Halwell. Both have circuits of the right order of length, but only excavation could show if either of them was occupied during the period. Next comes a burh on the River Lyd with the second smallest assessment of the whole list. Usually this has been taken to mean Lydford, where, conceivably, there may have been pre-Saxon settlement.[3] The Lydford defences were certainly fully functioning in 997, when the *Anglo-Saxon Chronicle* tells us that the town resisted a Danish attack. The rampart and ditch of these defences can still be seen cutting off the neck of the promontory, and perhaps originally the bank ran all round the town (*fig 6·1*).

From the River Lyd the list turns to the burh described in one early version as 'Pilton' and in another as 'Pilton with Barnstaple'. The site of this burh has not yet been resolved. Traditionally, it has been assumed that the variant versions mean that the original burh was at or near the village of Pilton, just north of Barnstaple across the River Yeo, and that its function was rapidly superseded by Barnstaple itself. The Pilton burh would therefore be the fort referred to by the *Chronicle* under the year 894 (correctly 893) as the 'fort in Devonshire on the Bristol Channel' which was beseiged by forty Danish ships.

No visible earthworks survive within Pilton village, and small-scale excavation yielded no evidence of dating or planned layout which might support the suggestion that this is the site of the burh.[4] A better candidate in the Pilton area might be the earthwork usually

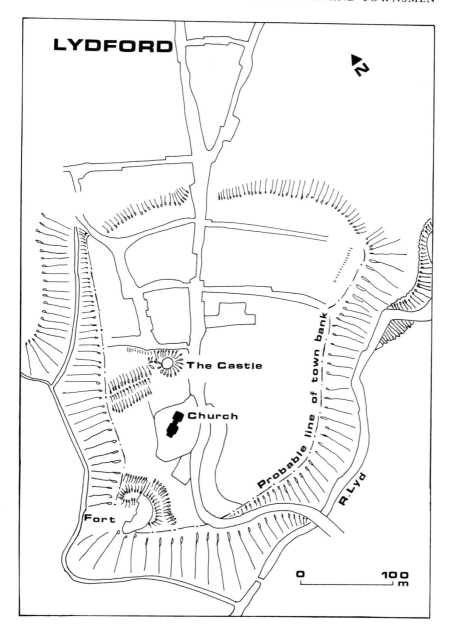

Fig. 6·1 Plan of Lydford showing burh defences, site of post-conquest fort and later castle, with early street plan (*source: Radford 1970, fig 35*).

known as Roborough Camp (or Burridge Camp) where the actual length of the (undated) defences roughly agrees with the *Burghal Hidage* assessment. It is possible, however, that a quite different site is intended, with a name comparable or similar to Pilton, and several such are known in the Barnstaple area. A further possibility is that the original burh was situated within the site of historic Barnstaple, where a topographically suitable site is offered by the spur between the Rivers Taw and Yeo. Excavation has revealed traces of Saxon settlement in the town area but this need not be as early as about 900, and any identification of Barnstaple as the original site would need to show why Pilton appears at all in the *Burghal Hidage* lists.

The next entry describes Watchet, where the burh seems to have been raided four times between 918 and 997. It is unclear whether the site is represented by the defences at Daws Castle to the west of modern Watchet, whether it is under the present town, or elsewhere. If it were under the modern town site, then Swain Street may have formed the axis of the defended area with a stream on the west, the sea on the north, and marsh on the east.[5] Then follows Axbridge. The place name cannot refer to a bridge over the Axe, which is more than 1.5 km away from the town, and probably simply indicates the burh in the vicinity of the river. The site suggests that it was chosen as a convenient outer defence for the royal palace at Cheddar. Recent fieldwork has suggested that the burh may have been sited on the lower land close to the Somerset Levels.

Next comes Lyng with the smallest assessment of all (*fig 6·2*). This formed part of an important complex developed by Alfred in the Somerset Levels at Athelney. Early in AD 879 Alfred withdrew to the

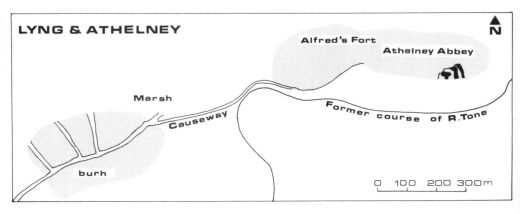

Fig 6·2 Plan of Lyng and Athelney (*source: Aston, Leech 1977, map 35*).

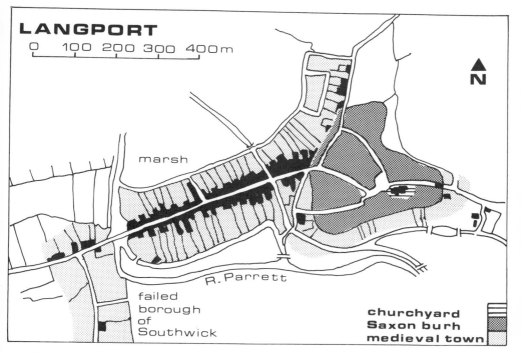

Fig 6·3 Plan of Langport, showing pattern of settlement development (*source: Aston, Leech 1977, map 32*).

marsh island of Athelney where he constructed a stronghold; and in 893, after his victory over the Danish King Guthrum, he founded a new monastery there so that the island became a defended and monastic centre. At the same time or a little later a causeway was built running westwards from the island across marshland to the spur of Lyng or East Lyng, where a second fort, that listed in the *Burghal Hidage*, was constructed.

Langport follows, and the burh there seems to have been sited on the hill at the east end of the town. The former defences are marked by a break in the slope on the west, by earthworks to the north and south west, and perhaps by the fifteenth-century Hanging Chapel which may mark the site of the east gate. The burh was probably intended to protect the royal estate of Somerton and, like Lydford, Langport may have been the site of a pre-Saxon settlement (*fig 6·3*).

It is clear that the south-western *Burghal Hidage* forts raise some problems. A number of considerations seem to have decided their sitings, among which were the strategic control of coasts and river valleys, the tactical defence of important royal centres, and the protection of urban settlements. These factors help to explain their mixed backgrounds. Exeter was the obvious centre for east Devon; Halwell, Pilton-Barnstaple, and Watchet were clearly intended to control the southern and northern coasts and Lydford was fortified to control the Tamar Valley.

Equally interesting are the omissions in the burghal list. Ilchester certainly, and Taunton probably, had fortifications of a kind by 900, and both were beginning to develop as urban centres. At both the influence of a minster church was probably important.

Late Saxon towns

Evidence including coins, excavation, the study of town plans, and documentary sources demonstrates the growth of towns through the tenth and eleventh centuries. Ecclesiastical arrangements made in about 880 established Alfred's friend, Asser, as an assistant bishop at Exeter, and perhaps Esne as another at Taunton. In or about 909 the old diocese at Sherborne was formally divided, and new bishoprics were established on a county basis at Wells, Crediton, and, ultimately, in Cornwall. At Exeter, excavation in the graveyard site west of the present cathedral has revealed a church with a semi-circular apse, probably built fairly early in the tenth century. This is surely the church of the ancient minster, built on a new site to replace an older building. It would have served as the cathedral church after the united see of Devon and Cornwall was moved to Exeter in 1050, until it was itself replaced by the building of the Norman cathedral in the early twelfth century on the present site. However, the ancient graveyard continued to be used.

Archaeological information about prosperous late Saxon Exeter is scanty, but we do know that its street plan (and so that of the modern city) differed from the Roman layout in a number of important respects. The High Street follows the Roman line, but the main Roman street serving the south-western quarter of the town ran at an angle to present Fore Street, while medieval South Street has a different line from its Roman predecessor. This implies some important re-alignments of property boundaries within the ancient walls.

Businesses were springing up, and foreign contacts formed. A range of wheel-thrown cooking pots, including some made in north-west France, were available in late Saxon Exeter, and a kiln near the present Princesshay was producing good quality pots, some of them glazed, which may have been the work of an immigrant French potter. Coins were minted in the city from Alfred's reign, although the existing Mint Lane has no proven connection with the Saxon mint.

Tenth-century Guild Statutes bear witness to a corporate organization, which could provide money and prayer on behalf of a distressed member. A letter from Bishop Eadnoth of Crediton dated 1018 mentions a *burhwitan* at Exeter, which is clearly a corporate and responsible body, and the ultimate ancestor of the present City Council. Similar bodies existed at Lydford, Totnes, and Barnstaple. By the time of the Domesday record there were in Exeter over 450 houses, many of them burgage tenements, that is properties held by tradesmen who payed a fixed rent to their landlord instead of the agricultural services which peasants owed.

Halwell declined in importance to be replaced by Totnes, where coins were minted possibly as early as Athelstan's reign, and certainly by that of Edgar (959–75). Study of the town may reveal elements of the early street plan and fortifications. Lydford maintained its status in west Devon, and coins were being minted there by about 973. The surviving town plan seems to show elements of a late Saxon layout.

Plate 40 Obverse and reverse of silver pennies of Athelred II (978–1016) (A) and Cnut (1016–1035) (B), minted at Lydford, Devon.

By the mid tenth century Barnstaple had definitely emerged as the urban centre of north Devon (*fig 6·4*). Its earliest coins may date from the reign of Eadwig (955–9) and they were certainly being minted by that of Aethelred II (979–1016). Excavation on the Castle Bailey site has revealed traces of two periods of possible Saxon occupation. A large burial ground has been discovered in the Castle area, and the relationship of this to the parish church of St Peter, first documented in the early twelfth century, remains uncertain. It is likely that elements of a planned late Saxon street layout survive in the town.[6] The line of the defences has been traced running inside Boutport Street, but it is uncertain whether any existed along the river front between the South Gate and the North Gate. Exeter, Totnes, Lydford, and Barnstaple make up the Devon main group of late Saxon towns. The only other

Plate 41 Barnstaple, Devon, taken in 1946 and looking north east, showing the historic town on the spur between the Taw and the Yeo, with the street pattern and castle site. See figure 6·4.

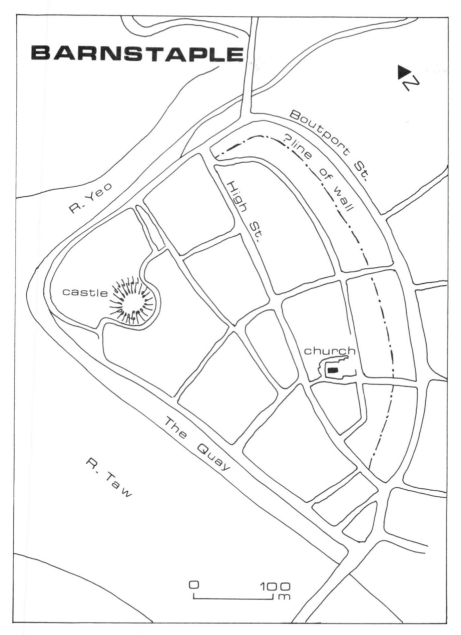

Fig 6·4 Plan of Barnstaple showing street plan, line of defences, and castle site (*source: Timms 1976*).

settlement recorded with any urban features in *Domesday Book* is that at Otterton, which possessed a market and salt workings. However, other possibilities like Plympton or Axminster cannot be ruled out.

In Somerset west of the Mendip edge Axbridge, Langport, and Watchet all possessed mints during the tenth century. Lyng never developed this facility. In 1066 Axbridge had a market and 32 burgesses, while Langport had 34 burgesses. Watchet, however, appears as a simple agricultural estate and no burgesses are recorded until 1242, when there are twelve. At South Cadbury a mortared stone wall was added to the existing defences on the line of the inner prehistoric rampart. This has been connected with the existence of a mint at the site from about 1010 to 1020. However, the late Saxon occupation seems to have been brief and insubstantial.[7] By 1086 the most substantial towns were the two which had not been listed as burhs. Ilchester had a mint, a substantial market, and 108 burgesses and its medieval wall encompassed a greater area than had its Roman wall. Taunton had 64 burgesses and a thriving market.

Other Somerset centres were developing urban characteristics during the tenth/eleventh centuries. Bruton had a mint and probably 16 burgesses, Crewkerne a mint and a market, and Frome and Ilminster both had markets: at all these the ancient minster was probably important. No trading facility is recorded for Wells in spite of its episcopal importance. Milborne Port, although without an early minster background, had a mint and, by 1086, a market and 56 burgesses, which made it a substantial town. Milverton also had a market.

In Cornwall the importance of a religious community in stimulating urban developments is obvious. From about 950 the canons of St Stephen's-by-Launceston had a mint (although for a time coining seems to have been transferred to Castle Gotha), and a market. St Petrock's monastery at Bodmin had a market and burgesses in 1086, and St German's monastery, which had been the seat of the fully established Cornish bishopric between 994 and 1050, had a market by 1066. The Bishop of Exeter had a market on his estate at Methleigh, and the monks of St Michael's Mount almost certainly had one probably at Marazion. Robert, Count of Mortain, had a market at Liskeard. The record of *cervisarii* (brewers or those who paid an ale render), at Helston, and of ten salt pans at Stratton, an important administrative centre under Alfred, point to communities which were not purely agricultural.

Urban development had taken great strides by 1066 (*fig 6·5*). The mixed backgrounds of the towns, which included Roman cities, fortified burhs, minster churches, and agricultural settlements, demonstrate the importance of geographical position and personal enterprise. No two individual histories are quite alike, a characteristic of organic growth, but the twenty or so towns, large and very small, in existence in the south west by 1066 all reflect the new spirit.

Castles

Politically, the Norman victory of 1066 represented a major break with the Saxon past. The character of Norman rule is best demonstrated in the archaeological record by the construction of castles intended to serve as military strong points, and as administrative centres from which law and order might be maintained. Castles were built in most of the substantial late Saxon towns in order to dominate these key urban settlements, but they were also constructed in rural areas to control strategic routes, and to serve as the headquarters of landed estates.

Plate 42 Okehampton Castle, Devon, from the north east. The castle, founded before 1086, lies on a spur above the West Okement River, with its artificially heightened motte crowned by a keep, and its domestic buildings in the bailey below. These buildings seem to have been laid out originally in the late thirteenth and fourteenth centuries.

205

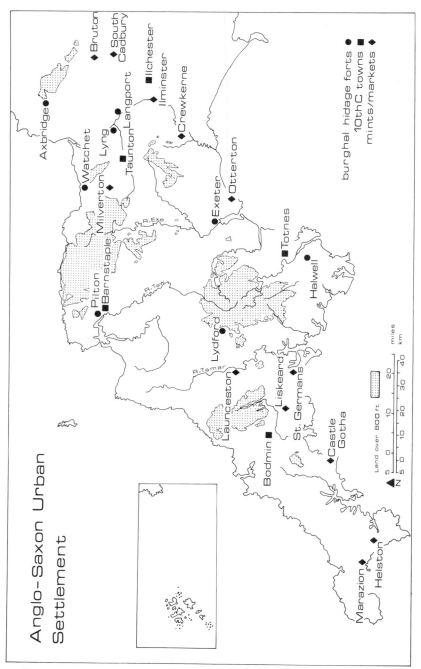

Anglo-Saxon Urban
Settlement

burghal hidage forts ●
10thC towns ■
mints/markets ◆

Bruton
South
Cadbury
Ilchester
Ilminster
Crewkerne
Axbridge
Watchet
Lyng
Taunton
Langport
Milverton
Otterton
Exeter
R.Exe
Pilton
Barnstaple
R.Taw
Totnes
Halwell
Lydford
R.Tamar
Launceston
Liskeard
St. Germans
Bodmin
Castle
Gotha
Marazion
Helston

Land over 800 ft.
N
miles
km

Fig 6·5 Anglo-Saxon urban settlement.

A number of problems surround the study of early castles, whether urban or rural, and precise dating is difficult. The first documentary reference to a site may be much later than its origin, and substantial programmes of excavation like those at Launceston[8] and Okehampton[9] are required to elucidate complex castle sites. Two common types of fortification seem to have been employed during the earliest years. A 'motte' consisted of a steep earth mound, surmounted by a stone or timber tower, and an enclosure bailey at its foot. A 'ringwork' or 'enclosed castle' had a circular bank protecting central buildings. Both were cheap quick methods of creating a useful base, which could be easily built by local, unskilled pressed labour.

The Domesday survey shows us a series of south-western castles in existence by 1086, many of them perhaps built as a result of the south-western rebellion of 1067-8. At Exeter 48 houses had been demolished on Rougement to make space for the castle, the gate tower of which still stands. The record of destroyed houses at Barnstaple, Lydford, and Totnes suggests castles in these towns also. By 1086 Okehampton had a town settlement, although the exact site of the houses is uncertain. Here Baldwin the Sheriff had erected the earliest phase of Okehampton Castle by cutting off the end of a natural spur with a bank and ditch.

Count Robert of Mortain, William I's half-brother, held *Dunhevet*, near the house of canons at old Launceston or St Stephen's-by-Launceston, where he built a castle, to which the canons' market (and

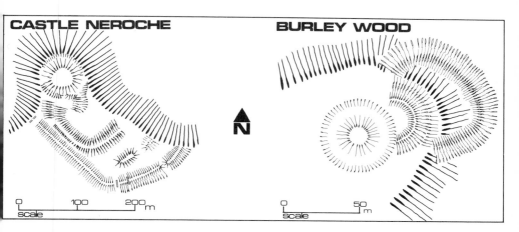

Fig 6·6 Plans of castle defences at Castle Neroche, Somerset, and Burley Wood, Devon (*source: Castle Neroche, Davidson 1972, fig 2; Burley, Shorter, Ravenhill, Gregory 1969, fig 20*).

207

ultimately their priory and its name) was transferred. Robert also possessed a castle at Trematon, to which the market of the canons of St German's was transferred, and in Somerset a castle at Montacute, the 'mons acutus', or steep hill, on which it was built ultimately giving a new name to the settlement.

Fieldwork, and other documents, suggest that many more castles existed in 1100 (fig 6·6). At Castle Neroche in Somerset, a site chosen to command the approaches to the peninsula, the Normans built an enclosure on an existing site, and this was later converted by the building of a motte.[10] A ring-ditch has been examined at Dunkerswell, Devon; a ring-ditch formed the earliest phase at Penhallam;[11] and the original work at Restormel involved a ring-work about 38 m in diameter. In Devon further rural sites are known at Burley Wood, and at 'The Rings', Loddiswell. These seem to have been only temporarily occupied, in contrast to the castles established at sites like Dunster, Plympton, and Stogumber.

Rural settlement, 900–1250

In the older view the period around 1250 saw the high tide of medieval rural colonization, which had been mounting steadily during the preceding centuries. It is likely that people were forming new settlements from the wood and waste, both by striking out into fresh areas, and by breaking new ground within the territories of existing settlements. However, we should not be tempted to over-simplify the economic and social picture because we do not understand its detail.

Some of the most interesting evidence comes from a series of upland settlement sites including Garrow Tor on Bodmin Moor, and Hound Tor near Manaton[12] and the area south of Okehampton,[13] on Dartmoor. Garrow Tor revealed nine rectangular houses, each with the living quarters separated from the byre by a paved passage. Beside the hamlet was an arable field with strips running up the hillside. Thirteenth-century pottery was found at this site.[14] Hound Tor appears in the Domesday record as *Hundatorra*, a manor held by the Abbot of Tavistock (fig 6·7). During the early period of occupation, from the tenth century or before to about 1200, there were overlying sequences of turf and wattle houses. These were divided into a southern living area with a hearth, and a northern area doubtless for cattle, and seem to represent an early form of the later medieval Dartmoor longhouse.

About 1200 these dwellings were replaced by stone structures.

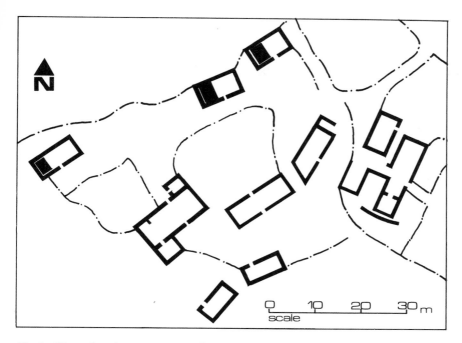

Fig 6·7 Plan of settlement at Houndtor, Dartmoor (*source: Minter 1973*).

There were three small single-roomed houses, several two-roomed longhouses equipped with hearths at the living end and central drains at the byre end, three substantial corn-drying barns on the northern side of the village, and on the eastern side a large two-roomed manor house equipped with a relatively sophisticated hearth and cooking pit. During the thirteenth century the longhouses were improved, the byres were extended, suggesting that the cattle became more important, and the manor house was reorganized internally.

In Okehampton Park, one of several apparently similar sites in the neighbourhood discernible on the aerial photograph has been excavated (*fig 6·8*) and was found to begin with a timber house and timber outbuildings, perhaps around 1130. The timber house was replaced by a stone longhouse and, between around 1180–1280, the farmstead grew to include two principal longhouses and four or five smaller buildings. The longhouses were fitted with internal timber furnishings. A complex of trackways, fields, and cattle pens related to the settlement, which documentary evidence has shown was part of Okehampton manor.[15]

o

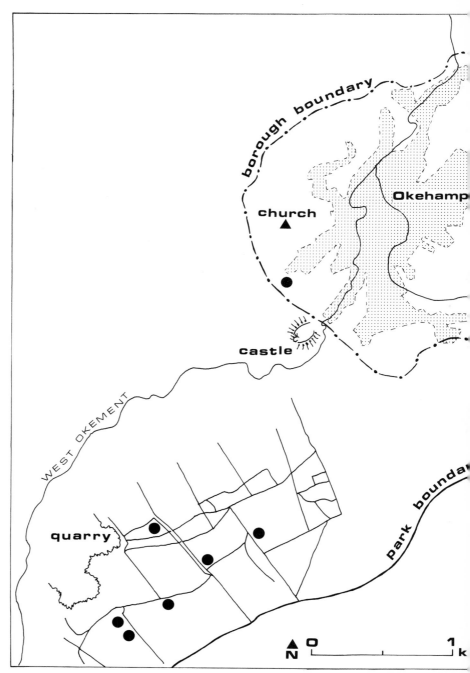

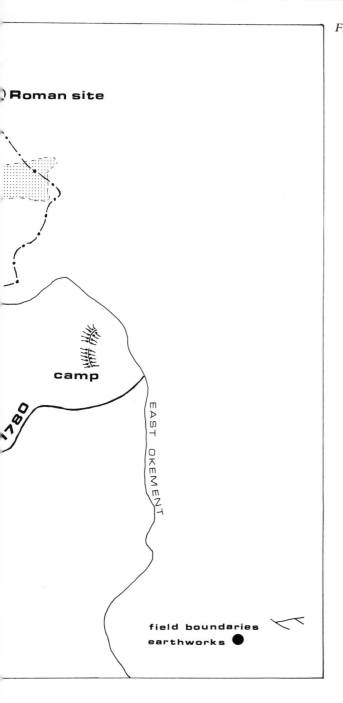

) **Roman site**

camp

1780

EAST OKEMENT

field boundaries

earthworks ●

Fig 6·8 Plan of Oke-
hampton area.
Successive land
use represented
by the Iron Age
camp, the Ro-
man site and pos-
sibly contempor-
ary earthworks,
the church, cas-
tle, and town set-
tlement area, the
medieval settle-
ment sites in
O k e h a m p t o n
Park, and the va-
rious boundaries
*(sources: Austin
1978; Balkwill
1976; Ordnance
Survey).*

Plate 43 Deserted medieval farmsteads in Okehampton Park, on the northern edge of Dartmoor, looking north-west. The excavated settlement lies at the north west of the main field boundary. From it, a track runs south to another farmstead and other settlements, tracks, and field lynchets may be spotted. Compare figure 6·8.

The field pattern at Willsworthy, on the south-western edge of Dartmoor, suggests that some of the pasture recorded there in *Domesday Book* was converted into small irregular fields at about this time. Nattor Farm on the further edge of the Willsworthy fields is first recorded in 1242. Cholwichtown on Dartmoor, the name of which means 'coldest farm', is first recorded about 1200–50 and the farmstead dating around 1500 replaced an earlier building, the remains of which survive in the yard. The name Fernacre ('bracken land') in the

De Lank Valley on Bodmin Moor may suggest similar intake from the open moor, and other names on the fringes of the same moorland point to contemporary settlement.[16]

The overall picture given by this upland evidence suggests that from about 1000 onwards people needed new land and risked settling in marginal areas. They depended upon the usual earlier medieval mixed farming, but by the thirteenth century they had progressed from turf dwellings to fairly substantial stone homes of longhouse type. The attached arable is likely to have been managed on the infield–outfield principle, and the open moor would have provided abundant grazing.

Expanding settlement within the existing pattern is more difficult to prove. Colyton, in east Devon, for example, appears in the Domesday survey as a substantial royal estate with a mill and a church. Within Colyton parish, and in neighbouring parishes also, are a conspicuous number of farms whose names include the element *hayne*, which derives from Middle English *hay*, Old English *(ge) haeg*, 'enclosure'.[17] Some of these probably represent farms newly established in the post-conquest period, but some could be new names given to existing holdings in order to reflect new tenurial arrangements.

The farmers at these new settlements seem to have organized their fields in whatever way best suited local conditions, so that their areas of intake are difficult to recognize. At many old-established sites the peasants continued to exploit the landscape of field strips, woodland, and common grazing, and perhaps new areas of subdivided fields were created. Elsewhere the fields attached to an individual holding, old and new, provided a living.

Within the villages there seem to have been occasional distinct periods of reorganization, during the early medieval period or later. These helped to create what are recognized by geographers and historians as the classic varieties of village plan. There are three main types: the linear settlement, the 'green village' with its central open space, and the irregular agglomeration. Detailed examination of a village's street pattern, its layout of individual house and garden plots, and its open spaces, can suggest to which of the three main types it belongs.

There are villages with all three general plans in southern Somerset, and probably a similar range exists in Devon.[18] Once-open greens have now been more or less completely infilled, as at Curry Mallet and Kingbury Episcopi in Somerset. Some central Devon villages, like Silverton and Thorverton, seem to have been built compactly around a central space, and Ugborough in south Devon is

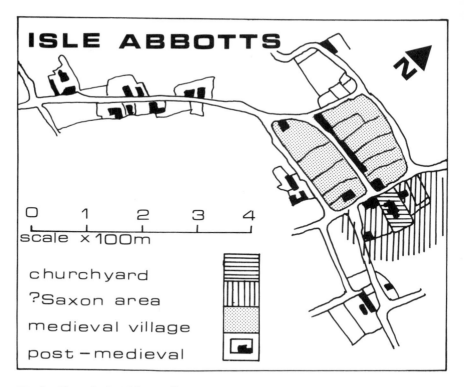

Fig 6·9 Plan of Isle Abbots village, Somerset (*source: Ellison 1976, fig 2a*).

similar. By contrast, Combe Martin in north Devon straggles down a long village street. Some linear villages show so regular a pattern as to suggest deliberate planning, perhaps in the later medieval period. Isle Abbots in Somerset, for example, shows two rows of rectangular properties stretching back from the main street to a pair of parallel back lanes, which survive as hollow ways (*fig 6·9*). At all these settlements, material goods seem to have been rather poor, and the villagers would have supplied most of their own needs, by working leather, wood, and horn. However, they were in touch with the trade of the towns and acquired some small metal objects, and pots which were being manufactured in Exeter and elsewhere.

An important aspect of the developing pattern is the network of parish churches, which had emerged by about 1150. Many of these were the ancient graveyard sites belonging to the earliest centuries of the Church in the south west, while others had been provided more recently by estate lords. Gradually they began to usurp the functions of the older minsters, and to acquire the rights which were associated with full parish churches in later medieval times. The parish boundary often followed the boundary of the estate, and so it may sometimes enshrine a land division which is very old indeed. At the same time, the functions of many ancient minsters shrank to a level much like that of parish churches, which explains why the churches of Wimborne Minster, Cullompton, or Ilminster serve a parish function today.

In areas where villages existed, parish churches were naturally built as parts of the village, and the position occupied by the church can be an important clue to the history of that village (see p. 179). In parts of Devon, and Cornwall, where dispersed settlement was more

Plate 44 Morwenstow, north east Cornwall, looking north west, showing the church, the Rectory in the trees, and Rectory Farm. There has been a Christian cemetery here since at least 950, which served as the ecclesiastical centre of a large area, finally a parish, of scattered farms and hamlets.

Plate 45 (*Left*) Cross now at Lanherne Convent, originally at the well chapel of St Gwinear, Cornwall. It is richly decorated on all sides. The lower front carries an inscription to the blessed Eid and Imah, and the back, one to Runhol, probably the sculptor. Probably late tenth century.

Plate 46 Cross in churchyard, Cardinham, Cornwall. It is carved with interlace and spiral ornament. Probably eleventh century.

usual, the graveyard was sited in a convenient gathering place. This difference helps to explain why in these areas it is the church, as at St Just-in-Roseland in Cornwall, Morwenstow in Cornwall, or Instow in Devon (meaning 'Holy place of John'), which often gives the parish its name.

Little survives of early church buildings in the south west, although probable tenth-century structures have been excavated at Fenton-Ia and Merther Uny in Cornwall.[19] Many Cornish burial grounds acquired fine standing crosses like those at Sancreed and Cardinham; Colyton in east Devon still possesses the shaft of its cross, carved with Tree of Life designs. Lodbere in Dorset and Rowberrow in Somerset both have fragments of what were once important monuments. At Copplestone in Devon, stands the tenth-century cross shaft which gave the place its name, and another, probably from the same workshop, is now set up at St Nicholas Priory in Exeter.

The early buildings, often of wood, did not survive the confident outburst of stone building during the twelfth to fifteenth centuries which gave the country most of its splendid medieval parish churches. It was the erection of these which set the seal upon each self-conscious local community.

Changing patterns in the countryside

Between 1250 and 1400 pressures for change affected medieval society. By 1400 the climate seems to have deteriorated, bringing colder wetter winters, for which, however, further local evidence would be welcome. The dreadful Black Death of 1349, followed by various lesser plagues, seems to have hit the south west as badly as other areas. These troubles, coupled with new economic opportunities for some people in an increasingly complex society, form the background to the changing pattern of settlement.

Abundant evidence from Dartmoor parishes like Widecombe[20] suggests that shrinking settlement on the upland was resulting in deserted settlements and homesteads. At Houndtor by about 1400 all but one of the longhouses were being used as barns, and perhaps the manor house was converted into a farmhouse by the addition of a byre drain. The village ceased to have a resident lord of the manor about 1250, and was finally deserted probably early in the fourteenth century. The settlement in Okehampton Park was abandoned around 1300. At first sight, this would seem like a retreat from land becoming increasingly marginal as the climate grew harsher. Nevertheless, other local elements were also important. The late medieval Dartmoor tin boom may have offered better pickings to some of the Widecombe farmers,[21] and the abandonment of the settlement near Okehampton probably relates to the creation of the Okehampton Deer Park about 1292–1306, as a hunting preserve for the earls of Devon.

At Tresmorn, on the coastal upland of north Cornwall, a hamlet of fifteen crofts, three of which revealed a long sequence of turf, cob, and finally stone houses dating probably from the tenth century to the fourteenth, had shrunk to only two substantial farmsteads by about 1350. A similar shrunken settlement has been located nearby, but the actual reasons for the depopulation remain unclear.[22]

In the lowland areas, changes in settlement patterns are even more difficult to assess, largely because the necessary field-walking and study of aerial photographs still remains to be undertaken. An analysis of the Somerset parish of Mudford near Yeovil has shown that of at least seven original hamlets two—Nether Adber and Mudford Sock—have totally disappeared, and two—Hinton and West Mudford—are much depleted. These hamlets seem to have had their own field systems. Several possible reasons can be suggested for the desertion of settlements in this area of Somerset, with its implications for other parts of the south west. The survey of the manor of Mudford and Hinton in 1554 implies that there are common arable fields but no common grazing lands or wastes, so that food production was cramped. Documentary evidence for Hinton and Nether Adber suggests that enclosure in the sixteenth century, bringing the change from arable to pasture, may be an explanation, and soil poverty may also have played a part. [23]

Over large areas of Cornwall and Devon the long-established pattern of scattered settlements with their fields remained essentially unaltered, apart, perhaps, from the enclosure of the small areas of subdivided arable farmed by some of the hamlets. Elsewhere, however, the farming landscape underwent a fundamental change. The process known as enclosure, by which large fields of subdivided arable—the strips of earlier medieval cultivation—were transformed into separate hedged closes or enclosed fields, was inevitably complex. In practical terms, enclosure usually involved a series of agreements between the lord of the manor and his tenants, who possessed customary rights over arable strips for which they paid in labour on the lord's land or, increasingly, in a money rent. These agreements involved the exchange or purchase of strips so that the lord's share could be conveniently concentrated in one parcel. They generally resulted also in the formation of some more compact tenant holdings, creating the kind of land arrangements for which 'farms' would be our natural description. The new field pattern was to dominate the life and the appearance of the countryside well into the twentieth century.

During the thirteenth and fourteenth centuries at Axminster, for example, successive Abbots of Newenham who held land in the parish were consolidating the home farm at Newenham itself, and granting in exchange arable strips which had belonged to the Abbey within the more distant subdivided arable. [24] The consolidated holdings could then be hedged, partly as a boundary mark, and partly as provision for firewood and poles. At Borcombe in east Devon in the late fourteenth century we learn of the creation of a new hedge which divided the lord's land from the tenants'. If a large area, like a lord's farm, were itself to be sublet by a separate arrangement, more divid-

Plate 47 Combe Martin, north Devon, looking south east. A linear or street village which originated a little inland, and has since grown down the valley, perhaps encouraged by becoming a borough by 1249. The field pattern, especially top left, makes it plain that the village once had large fields divided into strips.

ing hedges might be planted and the modern landscape take further shape.

Careful study of maps and documents has suggested that enclosure took a variety of forms in different parts of the south west, creating a variety of farming landscapes. In east Devon, where the conversion was substantially complete by 1450, the tenant holdings remained fragmented and mixed to a certain degree, and the enclosing process tended to take in bundles of strips to make small strip-shaped closes, giving the richly hedged appearance familiar today in these eastern parishes. At Combe Martin in north Devon the pattern of the medieval fields can still be seen, the boundaries of the strips preserved by lanes and hedges.

In the South Hams, consolidation went considerably further and involved far-reaching changes which produced large square closes with comparatively few trees, particularly in the areas immediately around farmhouses. Here, completion of the process may have been prolonged until the beginning of the seventeenth century. In Somerset too, enclosure seems to have been progressing throughout the sixteenth century. Everywhere, however, peasant farmers tended to lose the common pasturing rights on the stubble of the subdivided arable during the winter which had been customary. Many parishes retained some open waste, which was available for common grazing, but even this was over-exploited as a result of enclosing encroachments and the increased demand for pasture.

Pasture, in fact, lay at the heart of the new arrangements. Broad market forces operating in north-west Europe encouraged the production of wool, and higher wages may have helped to promote the change to stock-rearing, which is less labour intensive. In 1250 the rural economy of Axminster relied upon the mixed farming which had been traditional in the area for more than two and a half millennia but by 1550 the economy was almost entirely pastoral. Hedged fields which had been part of the common arable now provided grazing for sheep and cattle—the hedges were necessary to prevent the livestock straying, and better grass helped to improve the quality of the beasts. This development turned Devon into a county famous for its wool and its dairy produce.

Boroughs

Another facet of change is the great outburst of borough creation which characterizes the thirteenth and fourteenth centuries, when Exeter was consolidating its commercial leadership of the region. This

Plate 48 Fourteenth-century jugs from Exeter. These are wheel thrown, richly glazed, and decorated with the stripes characteristic of the Exeter potters. Heights 320–265 mm.

trend was general in England but especially marked in the south west. By around 1400 about seventy settlements in Devon, in addition to the original Saxon four, had acquired the technical privileges which made their inhabitants burgesses rather than simple peasants, a total far in excess of any other county. Somerset, which comes next, had thirty-one, and Cornwall thirty.[25] The achievement of borough status is recorded in a variety of documents, usually including a charter, and there are also some settlements which do not seem ever to have become boroughs although they acquired markets. These impressive numbers, however, conceal a mixed picture of diverse origins, and of success and failure.

Boroughs were deliberate creations brought into being by a landlord who might be the King, or an ecclesiastic, or a layman. The lord hoped that the issue of privileges, the creation of burgage tenements, and the recognition or creation of a weekly market and an annual fair, would stimulate urban growth, which would be profitable in terms of rents and dues. At its most responsible, borough creation brought into being the legal framework within which a nascent urban settlement might prosper. At its crudest, it was a form of financial speculation.

In a number of cases a borough was created from the settlement

Plate 49 Dunster, Somerset, looking north. The castle complex, founded by 1086, is in the foreground. North of it, High Street, with its regular properties and wide market place, probably represents a planned borough laid out by about 1220, and further planned blocks can be seen along West Street and Water Street, west of the castle.

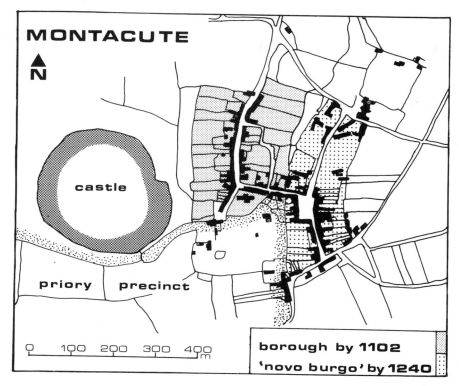

Fig 6·10 Plan of Montacute, Somerset, showing site of Domesday castle, features of Priory, and borough development (*source: Aston, Leech 1977, map 43*).

which clustered around the foot of a castle. At Montacute, for example, a borough had been established by 1102, when it was given by the Count of Mortain to the Abbey of Cluny for the establishment of a priory (*fig 6·10*). At Bridgwater, Downend, Dunster, and Nether Stowey, all in Somerset, boroughs had been established adjacent to castles by about 1200. In Devon the same is true of Plympton, the foundation charter of which was given by the Earl of Devon, and dated about 1194. Others, like those at Wellington, Wincanton, Wiveliscombe and Wells were founded by their ecclesiastical lord, the Bishop of Wells, as those at Paignton in Devon, or Penryn in Cornwall, were founded by the Bishop of Exeter.

In the south west generally, and in Devon in particular, the principle borough creation boom seems to have taken place between about 1240 and 1340. In Somerset, the distribution is fairly evenly spread

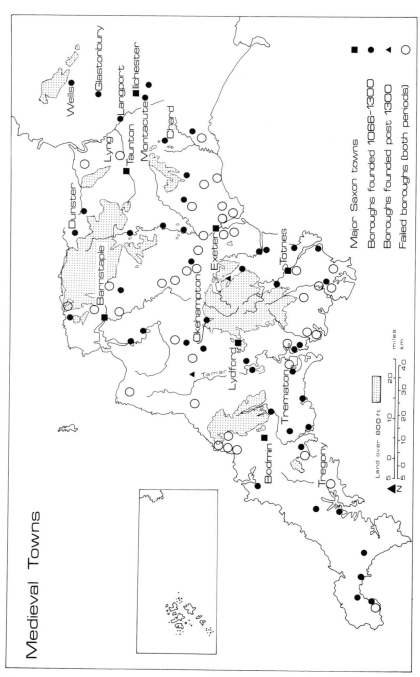

Medieval Towns

Major Saxon towns ■

Boroughs founded 1066–1300 ●

Boroughs founded post 1300 ◀

Failed boroughs (both periods) ○

Land over 800 ft

miles
km

Wells
Glastonbury
Lyng
Langport
Taunton
Montacute
Ilchester
Chard
Dunster
Barnstaple
Exeter
Totnes
Okehampton
Lydford
Tamar
Trematon
Bodmin
Tregony
N

Fig 6·11 Medieval towns.

throughout the county; but in Devon and Cornwall, the later boroughs especially showed a marked tendency to cluster along the coast, particularly the south coast, reflecting the increasing importance of maritime trade (*fig 6·11*).

The number of boroughs probably owes a good deal to the broken nature of the country, which made travel difficult. A further reason why so many were founded in Devon, and indeed also in Cornwall, may be connected with the fact that here field enclosure was under way at much the same time as the borough boom. The movement towards sheep-rearing, especially early and evident in east Devon, needed small urban centres where the wool might be processed and sold. In 1209, for example, William Brewer acquired a charter creating a free borough at Axminster with a Sunday market and an eight-day yearly fair. The economic basis of this is likely to have been the developing local wool trade, even though this is better recorded later, in the sixteenth-century records of racks, a dye house, and fulling mill, and in the seventeenth-century leases issued to dyers, tuckers and weavers.

The archaeology of urban settlements shows that boroughs differed considerably in their physical organization. The majority retained the layout of the villages from which they had sprung, with the addition perhaps of an improved market or fair site. At others, however, the enterprise of the lord created a planned town, sometimes on a new site but more often, perhaps, immediately adjacent to an existing village. These planned boroughs may still be perceived in the existing layout of some towns, with their spinal central street from which run equal-sized burgage plots, giving each tenant premises with access to the main road from which to do business, and a yard behind for vegetables and outhouses. The new plan usually incorporated a central market area.

At Chard in Somerset, the new borough established between 1206 and 1234 was laid out to the north of the existing village (*fig 6·12*). It consisted of fifty-two narrow burgage plots, each of one hectare, (about 2.5 acres) arranged on both sides of High Street and Fore Street. At Montacute the original planned borough proved too small, and a second planned area, described in 1240 as the '*novo burgo*', was created with its own market place. In Devon, 17 planned new towns have been recognized[26]—Newton Abbot, for example, was originally two adjacent new planned towns established either side of the River Lemon, that to the south being Newton Abbot, founded about 1269 by the Abbot of Tor, and that to the north Newton Bushel, founded by Theobald de Englishville about 1246.

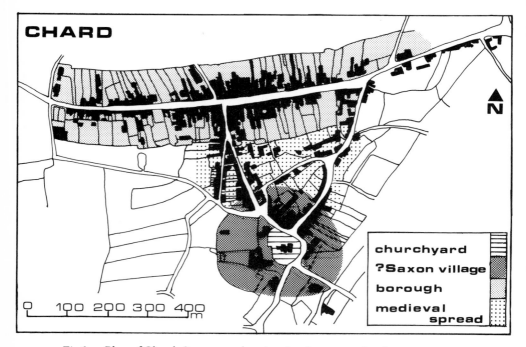

Fig 6·12 Plan of Chard, Somerset, showing development of settlement (*source: Aston, Leech 1977, map 12*).

Not all boroughs thrived. Some, like Noss Mayo or Little Totnes, in south Devon, did not even start: for neither of these boroughs is there any record of a fair or a market following their foundation, and their very sites are now in doubt. Rackley in Somerset seems to have been founded in 1189 in the hope that it would compete with Axbridge and Lower Weare for the trade passing along the River Axe. This hope was not realized, and Rackley is today a collection of farms and cottages in the parish of Compton Bishop.[27] The failure rate in Devon, where competition was greatest, was particularly high. Of the original optimistic seventy privileged settlements, less than forty had succeeded in maintaining and developing urban facilities by about 1600. Most of these successful communities, like Torrington or Tiverton, are still market towns today.

Traditional building

The changes on the land, and growth of the market towns, helped to stimulate the development of innumerable small tenant farmers. The most prosperous of these were often the men who had emerged successfully from enclosure with compact leased holdings. Their affluence is shown by the substantial farmhouses which they began to build, and which are still so conspicuous a feature of the south-western scene.

The study of regional building styles, often known as traditional or vernacular architecture, has expanded considerably over the last decade.[28] Essentially it is concerned with the domestic buildings of the farming community and their town-dwelling equivalents. The great houses like Saltram, erected by a socially superior class, belong within national architectural styles; while at the other end of the scale, the description by Vancouver about 1800 of labourers' cottages at Chilworthy in Devon, as consisting only of 'three mud walls and a hedge bank' gives a vivid insight into the poorest dwellings and their chances of survival. The vernacular tradition made use of a wide range of locally available stone, and of cob, the speciality of east and north Devon (bricks being uncommon until the mid nineteenth century) and roofs were of thatch or slate.

The sites at Hound Tor and elsewhere on Dartmoor suggest that the longhouse, with its single room crossed by a passage which divided the living area from the byre or shippon with its central drain, had developed by around 1200 at the latest. At the original longhouse of Sanders in the Dartmoor hamlet of Lettaford, built around 1530, the hall and the shippon were separated only by a low partition. Various improvements were carried out later.[29] Longhouses can be difficult to recognize, and the extent to which they were built off the moorland is still not clear.

The most common form of medieval farmhouse was that known as the 'cross-passage type'. This involved a basic three-room unit with two rooms on one side of a cross passage and one on the other, clearly shown in the plan of the house at Lower Lye, Stockland in Devon (*fig 6·13*). The hall, conventionally described as being 'above' the passage, was the principal room of the house, perhaps the only one originally with a hearth. In many cases it served as the dining-room, where food was cooked as well as eaten. The inner room beyond the hall may have been used as a sleeping chamber, until perhaps more bedrooms were added on the upper floor. The room 'below' the passage filled a variety of service needs. Naturally, the functions of rooms might alter considerably from time to time and from house to house.

The evolution of the cross-passage type farmhouse has been charted in a number of studies. It reflects the increasing desire for privacy, cleanliness, and domestic comfort. Originally such houses were single-storeyed, although often of a height equivalent to two storeys. In many cases the rooms were divided only by short partitions so that the smoke from the open hearth circulated freely, staining the underside of the thatch and the trusses.

Gradually more rooms were created by more substantial subdivisions. Around 1550–70 upper floors began to be inserted within the old open hall structure: in Devon these were often carried on internal jetties like that recognized at Sanders, Lettaford. Floors, of course, involved the building of a staircase, and of a chimney-stack and fireplaces. Stacks were sometimes placed as a dominating feature in one outside wall of the house. In the course of time, porches and wings were usually added to older buildings. The study of a group of medieval houses in the parish of Stocklinch, north-east of Ilminster, has shown an interesting series of developments from the basic cross-passage plan.[30] Traditional houses certainly continued to be built into the seventeenth century, but by the eighteenth century new dwellings of any pretensions more commonly followed the national rather than

Plate 50 Lower Lye, Stockland, Devon, looking west. The range on the right is the original cross-passage house (with minor modifications), and the position of the chimney stack is typical of rural Devon. On the left is a later addition.

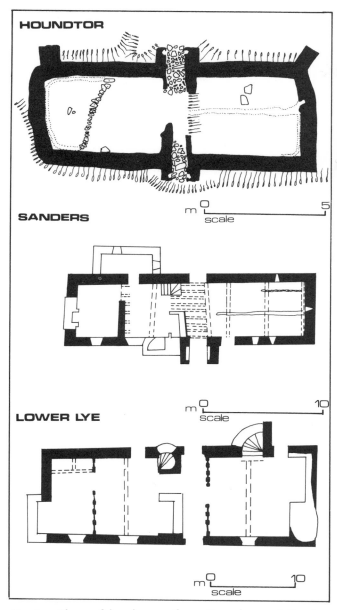

Fig 6·13 Plans of longhouses from Houndtor and Sanders Lettaford, and cross-passage house at Lower Lye, all Devon. Original parts in solid black (*source: Child 1978, figs 2, 3, 4*).

the regional style, dominated by symmetrical 'Georgian' plans and frontages.

Surrounding the farmhouse would be a more or less elaborate range of outbuildings. These might include the open-fronted cattle shed or linhay where the upper floor, designed to hold fodder, would be supported on pillars. There would be the barn, the shippon where the milk cows had individual stalls, the stable, the pigsty, and buildings to house dairy equipment and cider presses.[31] Like the farmhouses themselves, and contemporary buildings within towns, much of great interest waits to be recorded often in inconspicuous or recent-seeming structures.

1. *Hill 1969*
2. *Shorter, Ravenhill, Gregory 1969, 113*
3. *Addyman 1966*
4. *Miles, Miles 1975*
5. *Aston, Leech 1977*
6. *Timms 1976*
7. *Alcock 1972*
8. *Saunders 1977*
9. *Higham 1977*
10. *Davidson 1972*
11. *Beresford 1974*
12. *Minter 1973; Beresford 1979*
13. *Austin 1978*
14. *Dudley, Minter 1963*
15. *Austin 1978*
16. *Hoskins 1955*
17. *Gower, Mawer, Stenton 1931*
18. *Ellison 1976*
19. *Thomas 1968, 1968a*
20. *French, Linehan 1963*
21. *Gawne 1970*
22. *Beresford 1971*
23. *Aston 1977*
24. *Fox, H. 1972*
25. *Beresford, Finberg 1973*
26. *Beresford 1967*
27. *Aston, Leech 1977*
28. *Child 1978 and references there*
29. *Alcock, Child, Laithwaite 1972; Laithwaite 1977*
30. *Austin, Hall 1972*
31. *Coutin 1978; Robertson, Gilbert 1979*

CHAPTER SEVEN

Wealth from the Land

The woolmen

The demand for wool lay behind the conversion of arable to pasture, and, to an extent, behind the growth of the market towns, especially in Devon and west Somerset. Wool-processing dominated the centuries between 1300 and 1800. During the early part of the period, the industry was organized on a domestic basis. Farmers sold their own wool, often the produce of quite small flocks, to wool carders, who sold it to spinners, from whom the weavers bought their supplies of yarn. These operations were carried out in farm cottages, and often as a part-time occupation.

The cottagers produced the cloths known as Barnstaple bays, Tavistock friezes, Totnes pin whites, and Exeter kerseys, all from the local coarse long wool. Production was substantial: somewhere around 2500 bales were woven each year during the 1340s to 1390s.[1] Fulling mills were being built to speed up the cleansing and felting of wool, previously carried out by human muscle. Records tell us of mills at Dunkeswell in 1238, at Honiton and Tiverton in 1244, and over a dozen by the 1320s, but of all of these virtually nothing survives.

The wool was carried by trains of pack horses, which, together with coastal shipping, formed the usual heavy transport during the later Middle Ages. Numerous tracks, some of them famous like that across Dartmoor between the abbeys of Tavistock and Buckfast, may still be traced by the walker. The clapper bridges of Dartmoor, like that at Postbridge, built of huge natural rock slabs, were probably constructed to carry this traffic in the years after 1400, and the elaborate slab bridge on Exmoor at Tarr Steps seems to have been built for the same purpose. Throughout the Middle Ages fine stone bridges gradually replaced fords or simple constructions over the major rivers and the important bridges over the Rivers Tamar, Dart, and Exe

Plate 51 Helland Bridge, over the River Camel, Cornwall, erected in the early fifteenth century. It is 5 m in span.

probably date from the thirteenth century, although they were later rebuilt.[2]

By the fifteenth century the royal customs accounts show that the hitherto locally-orientated cloth merchants had seized the opportunity to develop markets in southern Europe. Cloths went through the port of Exeter at the rate of over 10,000 a year around 1500. On and around Exe Island, south-west of the city wall, there grew up an industrial suburb of fulling mills, dyeing vats, drying racks, and all the installations necessary for the finishing of cloth. Details of later mills erected on the sites of earlier industrial buildings can still be traced.[3]

The wealth of the Exeter merchants found expression in the city's parish churches and late medieval timbered houses, and above all in the fine roof of the Guildhall, built in 1468–9, and the Hall of the Guild of Weavers, Tuckers, and Shearsmen, begun in 1471. During the sixteenth century, Peter Blundell amassed a cloth fortune large enough to found Blundell's School at Tiverton, while the Hawkins family and Sir Francis Drake were master-minding the development of Plymouth, and the Atlantic trade.

The cloth trade reached its peak about 1720, when production in the rural hinterland and finishing on Exe Island were still in full swing. By 1850 the end of the industry was in sight, killed by competition and by inability to modernize production. Now only a few mills, like that at Dartington, still continue an ancient tradition.

The early tinners

The mineral wealth of the south west, especially of tin, has always been one of the natural factors which give the peninsula its character. Although tin has been a basic raw material since the Bronze Age, it is a fairly rare metal. In Europe, outside south-west Britain, there are only the deposits in Brittany and northern and southern Spain, and the substantial deposits of the Erzgebirge which straddle the modern frontier between East Germany and Czechoslovakia. Outside Europe, there are sizable deposits in Malaya and Bolivia, but these have only been available during the twentieth century.

The importance of the south-western tin is obvious. The ore takes the form of cassiterite, a tin oxide, which occurs in a broad belt about 150 km long and up to 30 km wide. This belt, known as the zone of mineralization, came about as a result of the massive granite intrusion which is now exposed in Penwith, Carnmenellis, Hensbarrow, Bodmin Moor, Dartmoor and Scilly, together with several much smaller bosses. As the molten granite forced its way upwards from deep in the earth's crust, minerals associated with the granite itself and with the surrounding rocks seem to have been heated and changed, and eventually they condensed to form the lodes of tin, copper, and other metallic ores.

The area is, however, not uniformly mineralized. The tin ores are usually restricted to specific areas near the centre of a granite boss or some distance away in the surrounding rocks. In the south west, cassiterite occurs as lodes like those at Levant, Penwith; it occurs as veins distributed through barren rock, as at Hemerdon Ball south west of the main Dartmoor mass; and elsewhere it occurs as alluvial deposits. These were created by the weathering of tin-rich veins during the Ice Ages and after, which deposited considerable quantities of the mineral in streams and on lower ground. In 1930, for example, the alluvial deposits at Birch Tor around the headwaters of the River Bovey in north-east Dartmoor were sampled and found to be up to 10 m deep.

Plate 52 The Plym Valley, south west Dartmoor, showing the broken landscape and heaps of debris left by early tin streaming.

These alluvial deposits create the famous 'tin streams' like those of
Dartmoor, or of the Carnon Valley and the area around Redruth in
Cornwall, from which black cassiterite pebbles could be collected
with no more equipment than a knowledgeable eye and a pair of
willing hands. These deposits were exploited by the Bronze Age
smiths, and by the traders and administrators of the Iron Age (perhaps), and the Roman period. The smelting of tin ingots from the ore
in these early times seems to have been done very simply, and has left
virtually no traces in the archaeological record.

Vital though the tin resources are, the mining industry has always
had a chequered history with bursts of activity succeeded by slumps.
The chief periods of activity since Roman times were between about
1150 and 1360, between about 1450 and 1650, and during the reign of
Victoria and into the present century. The primitive methods used by
the earliest medieval tinners make it difficult to distinguish the re-

mains of their activities from those of later workings in the moorland valleys. Alluvial cassiterite pebbles, or tinstones, were dug out from among the lighter, stream-carried sand and gravel in the valley bottoms, and the waste was thrown up in heaps along the banks of the streams. These dumps, grown often to substantial mounds, can sometimes still be distinguished, now overgrown with grass and heather, on Dartmoor and beside Cornish streams.

By the late twelfth century, however, the obvious and easily worked alluvial deposits were beginning to run out, and the tinners were forced to start working the actual lodes, a much more laborious process which involved greater mechanical ingenuity. The tinners dug into the hillside lode outcrops with picks, and made the extraction easier by diverting streams to the working places so that the force of water could wash away the lighter unwanted debris. If no natural spring was available, an elaborate system of rainwater collection had to be devised. A small reservoir like a pear or crescent-shaped pond would be dug out above the workings, and hillside channels arranged so that the pool could be fed. Further channels or leats led from the pond to the working area, through which the flow could be directed at the right time.

Some of the Dartmoor leat systems still survive, so overgrown that they can sometimes be mistaken for natural features of the moorland. On the south side of Hookney Tor, for example, a number of leats of different levels lead into the old Headland gullies from Grim's Lake. There is a crescent-shaped pond above a large area of workings on Challacombe Down in Manaton parish, and another pear-shaped one not very far away on Hameldown (Widecombe) at the head of a gully.[4]

Most of these early tin workings were 'open-air' sites involving quarry pits and trenches, some of them deep enough to create the cuttings and gullies which are characteristic of the Dartmoor scene. True shaft-mining does not seem to have been practised in any real sense in the medieval period. By the seventeenth century, however, the shafts could be dug deeper because the underground water could be removed by simple pumps. Later, the mining engineers developed horse-powered whims, wooden winch systems built on circular platforms. A nineteenth-century example of the platform survives at Wheal Florence on Crownhill Down on Dartmoor.

'Black tin' won from the earth had to be converted into 'white tin' by smelting. The early medieval tinners used the same method as their prehistoric forerunners, placing the lumps of ore in a fire and afterwards collecting tin from the ashes. However, by the early fourteenth century the invention of the blowing-house offered a more efficient process. Blowing-houses were built of stone and turf on the edges of streams, where the fall was sufficient to allow the construction of a leat taking enough water to the site to turn a small water wheel. Inside the building there would be a stone-built furnace with a fire fanned by bellows worked by the water wheel. The furnace was filled with layers of crushed ore and peat charcoal, and once the operation was underway the molten tin would drip through a grid in its base into a stone basin from which it was ladled into moulds. Each mould produced an ingot of some 200–300 lbs in weight.

The ore had to be prepared first by being crushed to a sufficiently fine state. The tinners pounded it on a mortar of hard stone, using as a pestle a stone ball or perhaps a metal-bound piece of wood. Discarded mortars, with hollows left by the crushing process, are one sign of a tin-working site. Sometimes the arrangement of mortar hollows, with two or three in a row on the same stone, indicates that a primitive mechanical stamp-like device was used for ore-crushing. Sometimes, also, the workers used a crazing-mill, formed by two mill-stones between which partly prepared ore might be ground. A pair of crazing-mill stones has been found near an old blowing-house at Gobbet on the River Swincombe on Dartmoor.[5] Improved stamping machines, consisting of a set of timber posts worked up and down by water to crush ore placed beneath them, continued to be developed throughout the late medieval period and in the following centuries.

There are many remains of blowing-houses, often known, for no clear reason, as Jews' Houses. On Dartmoor they cluster especially in the southern river valleys of the Erme, the Plym and the Meavy, where over forty are known. They are difficult to date, but it seems unlikely that any were constructed after 1740 and many are likely to be older than this. At Week Ford by the West Dart stand the remains of two buildings. In the higher of the two the remains of a possible furnace and of the wheel installations and leat can be seen, and mortar stones lie nearby. The same water supply was taken down the hill to the second blowing-house, near which are more mortars and a mould-stone. Similar groups of remains are visible at Black Tor Falls on the River Meavy, and beside the River Walkham above Merrivale Bridge. In Cornwall it is difficult to trace the sites of the early blowing-houses, although occasionally a name survives, like Blowing-House in St Austell. Documents show that a considerable number existed: two each at Calstock, St Austell and Redruth, three at Wendron and Kenwyn, and many more.

The tinners would smelt the accumulated tin ore two or four times a year. Their output required a special administrative framework organized by the Crown, and this took the form of the stannary establishment. In 1305 the towns of Tavistock, Ashburton and Chagford, with Plympton added in 1328, were recognized as the stannary towns of Devon. The designated stannary towns in medieval Cornwall were Bodmin, Lostwithiel, Liskeard, Truro, and Helston, but as the centre of the industry gradually moved west, Bodmin and Lostwithiel were replaced by Penzance. Stannary Law, which grew eventually into an elaborate system, gave the miner exemption from military service and market tolls, and allowed him to search for tin on unenclosed common land.

Two or four times a year at 'coinage times' the royal officials and receivers visited the stannary towns. Each tin ingot was stamped with its owner's name, weighed, and 'coigned', which has nothing to do with minting coins, but means that a corner of the ingot was removed so that the metal could be assayed. Little now survives of the halls in which this took place, although in a number of the Cornish towns the name Coinagehall Street survives. Coining probably took place in Bodmin in the Great Hall of the medieval priory which stood until 1837. The hall at Lostwithiel may have been in the same building as the Stannary Court, on the corner of Quay Street and Fore Street. The stannary system survived until 1838, although by then it had long been outmoded.

Dealers in tin, especially those representing the pewter manufacturers by whom the tin was chiefly bought for alloying with lead, carried on their business in the stannary towns. Most of the tin was transported to London, normally by sea from Exeter, Morwellham, Plymouth, and ports further west. Gradually, as the industry became more complex, a division developed between the miners and the smelters. The smelters, who dealt directly with the stannary officers and the metal merchants, slowly gained a financial grip on production which enabled the lucky ones to amass considerable fortunes. The tin yield was high: it has been estimated that between 1171 and 1189 average annual production of Dartmoor tin reached 343 tons, and between 1500 and 1550 it averaged 199 tons.

Canals, roads and railways

Exeter boasts one of the earliest modern canals in the country, constructed by John Trew in the 1560s to enable shipping to bypass the obstructive weir placed on the River Exe by the Countess of Devon, and so reach the open estuary of the river. In 1676 the canal was extended to Topsham, nearer the mouth of the estuary, and various improvements have been carried out since then. On the river quay stands the Custom House, completed in 1689, the Fish Market with cast-iron columns, and a row of early nineteenth-century warehouses. On the opposite side of the river is the canal basin, which can be reached by manually-operated ferry. Further along the canal is a set of important double locks. Between 1770 and 1830 a number of large-scale canal plans were considered in the south west from time to time, but the difficult nature of the terrain was discouraging, and no cross-peninsula schemes ever came to fruition.

Wheeled traffic, both coaches and carriers' waggons, increased in volume from the early eighteenth century, and this stimulated the organization of turnpike trusts who made themselves responsible for improving stated stretches of road, and financed the work by levying tolls on road users. The earliest Devon trusts were set up at Stone-house in Plymouth (1751), Exeter (1753) and Honiton (1754), all covering sections of the coaching road to London. During the early nineteenth century many more roads were constructed, and eventually some 400 toll houses, of which 83 survive, were built in Devon to house the toll collectors.

Both the Exeter Canal and the toll road system flourished until the coming of the main railway, which connected Exeter with London in 1844, Plymouth in 1849, and west Cornwall, via Brunel's bridge at Saltash, in 1859.

The development of the great mines

Copper, not tin, was king in the nineteenth-century heyday of Cornish and Devon mining, when the peninsula was among the most heavily industrialized areas of Britain, although a number of mines produced both metals. In Cornwall the copper boom lasted from roughly 1700 to 1870, and demand was heavy while the ore lasted. In 1700 production reached 2000 tons of ore, and grew steadily to achieve a maximum of 140,000 tons by about 1860, falling off steadily thereafter. Some of the profits made by great mine-owning families like the Lemons, the Pendarves and the Daveys were huge: Carn Brea Mines made £225,000 between 1834 and 1853, and Wheal Alfred £135,000 in the same period.[6] The copper was used to make a wide range of bronze (tin alloy) and brass (zinc alloy) articles and fittings, for the Army and Navy, the domestic market, the West Indies sugar refiners and the African slave traders.

In one fundamental respect copper-working in the south west

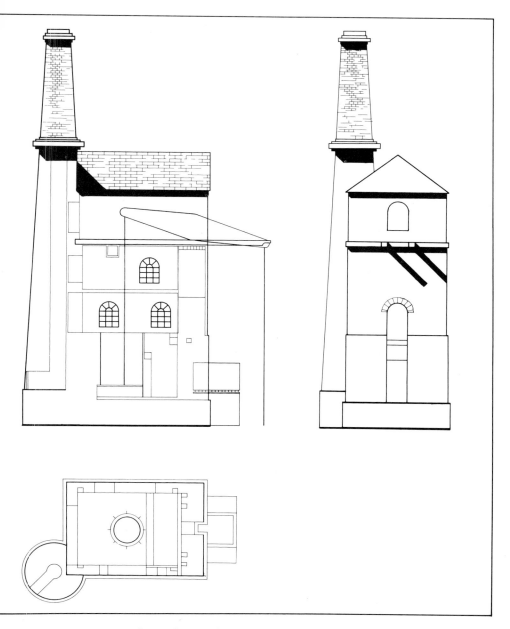

Fig 7·1 Cornish engine-house for an 80″ engine at St Day United Mines, Gwennap. Plan, side elevation and end elevation are shown (*source: Williams, undated*).

differed from that of tin. There is no coal in Cornwall or in Devon, and so the mined copper ore usually had to go to South Wales to be smelted. In about 1755 John Vivian set up a successful smelting works at Hayle, with fuel provided by imported coal, and this venture has left its traces in harbour and wharf improvements at the site which is still called Copper-House. However, in the ensuing business rivalry the Cornish entrepreneurs were forced to join the Welsh smelters. The results of their cooperation can still be seen in the Copper Bank Smelting Works at Swansea, managed by the Cornishman Pascoe Grenfell and Owen Williams, the works at Penclawdd west of Gowerton, where Vivian built a small harbour and cottages for his Cornish workmen, and the huge Vivian works at Hafod in the lower Swansea valley.

Most of the mines were infinitely more complex than the early tin workings. Frequently they involved the full range of mine shafts, underground tunnels to follow the lodes, and adits—tunnels designed to slope away to lower ground outside the mine through which water might be drained. The whole mining enterprise both encouraged and was dependent upon the development of heavy industrial machinery, of which the most important were the steam pumping engines which alone could keep the shafts free of water. The first true forerunner of the modern steam engine, designed by a Devon man, Thomas Newcomen, was successfully installed in a Staffordshire colliery in 1712. Essentially, it consisted of a cylinder connected by a piston to the massive overhead beam, the other end of which was connected to a bucket pump which dropped down the mine shaft. The cylinder was alternately filled with steam, and then turned into a vacuum chamber by condensing the steam with a water jet. This caused atmospheric pressure to force down the piston, and so transfer power via the beam to the pump.

By 1727 at least five, and probably more, of these atmospheric engines had been installed at Cornish mines, and their numbers grew steadily through the century, but a limiting factor was their heavy consumption of coal, which had to be imported from South Wales. The improved machines of James Watt, true steam engines where steam and not atmospheric pressure provided the power, did not use so much coal, and by 1783 Watt engines had virtually replaced the older Newcomen machines throughout Cornwall.[7]

The engine houses required to enclose these engines remain the most impressive monuments of past industrial activity (*fig 7·1*). Today these derelict stone buildings scattered so thickly across Cornwall may be the only mark of mines which once employed hundreds of men, and involved miles of underground workings to depths of a thousand feet. The design of engine houses changed little over two centuries. They had to anchor the engine against its heaviest possible load, and this explains their massive construction and so their survival. The design incorporated a boiler house and chimney stack, and the engine house was frequently built as a part of the general mine building.

The major sources of copper were grouped in a number of clearly defined areas: West Penwith around St Just, the region around Redruth, further east on the Hensbarrow and Bodmin Moors, in the Tamar Valley, and around North Molton on the flank of Exmoor. Tin was found in West Penwith and Dartmoor, and many other metals were produced from time to time throughout the peninsula.

The mines around St Just

The deserted engine house of Ding Dong which dominates the heathery moorland of St Just symbolizes the rise and fall of what was once one of the greatest mining areas in the world. The coast from Portheras Cove to Whitesand Bay, deeply cut by narrow coves known locally as zawns, is crossed by series of mineralized lodes, generally running in a north-west/south-east direction, running under the land, outcropping in the cliffs, and continuing under the sea. Most of the lodes contain both tin and copper ores at varying points.

These ores had been exploited spasmodically since prehistoric times, but the erection of the first steam engine in the area, at Carnyorth in 1807, sparked off a tremendous development of deep mining which lasted until the early 1870s. In the quarter ending July 1821, St Just produced 80 tons of tin, nearly an eighth of the entire Cornish yield. Between 1820 and 1927 Levant Mine alone had a recorded production of nearly 130,000 tons.[8]

The most famous mines are those whose workings ran far out under the sea. The prospectus for Levant Mine issued in July 1836 enthused 'the deepest level, only 180 fathoms, is the richest part . . . the ores of copper and tin are of the richest description'. Eventually the Levant workings ran at levels over 1500 ft beneath the sea floor, and the tin and copper ore was taken to the shore line by pit ponies. By about 1842 the Rev. John Buller, vicar of St Just, could describe how, especially in stormy weather, the miners heard 'the awful grandeur of the rounded boulders rolling overhead as they are driven backwards and forwards by the force of the waves'. In 1919 Levant was the tragic scene of the worst Cornish mining disaster when the man engine, installed to take miners up and down because of the mine's great depth, broke and thirty-one men were killed.

South from Levant lay Botallack, with its cliff-edge engine houses at the Crowns, from which the Boscawen Diagonal Shaft ran far out under the Atlantic Ocean. The principal lode outcropped in the rocks below the mine buildings, showing grey, yellow and purple copper ores. In the early days tin was the principal metal, but the mine was on the point of closing when the sudden discovery in 1841 of rich copper lodes made it overnight one of the most profitable investments in the county. The sentiment which surrounded the visit of the Prince and Princess of Wales to Botallack in 1865 is in sharp contrast to the grimmer realities represented by the great strike of 1853, when the price of metals was dropping and the mine's future was uncertain. Desolation now hangs over the interesting remains on the Crown Cliffs, finally abandoned after a sequence of hopes and depressions in 1914.

On Kenidjack Cliffs stood Boswedden Mine, positioned to exploit the numerous tin and copper lodes which run across country and off-shore. In its heyday Boswedden included a series of workings like Wheal Castle, Williams and Praze, and Yankee Boy Mine. Wheal Castle was working by 1822, producing both copper and tin, and by the 1860s its shafts ran for 0.8 km under the sea (*fig 7·2*). Like many Cornish mines, however, its financial position was always shaky, and it seems to have been abandoned by 1873.

The town of St Just is itself a monument to the miners and their families, who built the granite cottages, and the mine owners and captains who organized financial backing through the Capital and Counties Bank in Bank Square. When the great mining depression of the 1870s set in many families were forced to emigrate from the area to the mines of the Rand and Australia. At the St Just Post Office, which stood near the Clock Tower, it was possible to buy a through ticket to Johannesburg or Hancock in Michigan.

Redruth, and further east

The slopes of the valley through which the road between Redruth and Portreath runs are strewn with engine houses, buildings, and workings—all that remains of the Tolgus group of mines, which, between 1825 and 1883, produced nearly 150,000 tons of copper ore. Beside the road between Truro and Redruth, just beyond Chacewater, stood the engine houses of one of the oldest of the copper mines, Great Wheal Busy, where the earlier Newcomen engine was replaced by a new Watt engine in 1777.

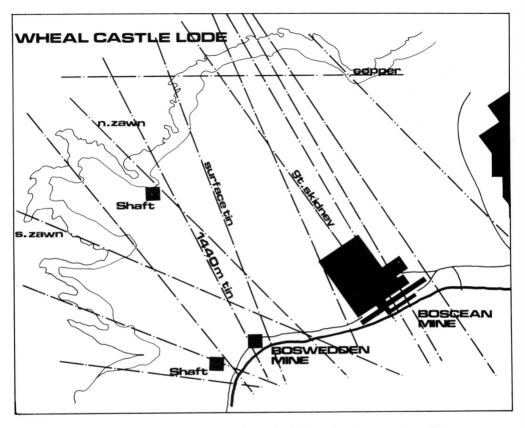

Fig 7·2 Plan made in 1882 of Wheal Castle Lode, St Just, showing mine installations and lodes running into the sea (*source: Noall 1973, 76*).

To transport the ore from these mines to South Wales, a tramline was built in 1812 linking Scorrier with the harbour at Portreath—much of its course can still be traced. A second railway line, completed in 1824 and using horse traction, linked Redruth with the south coast at Penpol. A third great line, worked by locomotives from the start, was opened in 1838, and connected the mines of Camborne, Dolcoath and Carn Brea with Hayle, where the railway ended in Foundry Square (*fig 7·3*).

Further east beyond Portreath was a series of mines along the edge of the coast, including the engine house of Wheal Lushington on Porthtowan beach (now converted into a private house). Nearby lay the Charlotte United Mines, whose engine house survives on the west

243

side of Chapel Porth Valley, and just south of St Agnes Head is the Towanwroath shaft engine house of Wheal Coates.

A series of mines including Par Consols, Fowey Consols and St Austell Consols was created near the coast south and south east of Hensbarrow Moor, and to serve the mines Rashleigh developed the port of Charlestown, and Treffry that of Par, which is entirely artificial and was completed between 1829 and 1840.

On Caradon Hill on the south-east flank of Bodmin Moor stand the remains of twenty-five mines and their network of tramways, all that is now left of the great copper mines based on rich lodes luckily discovered about 1837, when the mines further west were beginning to be exhausted. One of the most impressive areas is now the South Phoenix site with its mill, tram road beds, count house, drilled granite blocks and grass-grown depression which was once the pond.

The Tamar Valley

The River Tamar winds through some of the most metalliferous

Fig. 7·3 Cornish smelters' house marks used on bar and block tin, impressed on semi-molten metal by dies. Shown approx. 0.25 full size (*source: Barton 1967*).

country in the south west. Long before the great days of the nineteenth century, the lodes of the Bere Alston peninsula were producing silver and lead: in 1294 370 lbs of silver ore were sent to King Edward I from the quays of the River Tavy.[9] The workings were revived in the nineteenth century and probably more than a million ounces of silver produced before they were abandoned. A little further east, on the slope of Gibbet Hill north of Mary Tavy, stands the deserted engine house of Wheal Betsy Mine, which from 1806 onwards annually produced about 4000 oz of silver until about 1877.

By 1798 it was clear that the existing transport routes to the Tamar from the mines around Tavistock like Wheal Betsy, Wheal Friendship and Wheal Crowndale, which relied upon teams of horses and mules, had become inadequate. The answer was the Tavistock Canal, the brain-child of John Taylor, to link the Tavy with the ancient Tamar port of Morwellham. The canal ran across country for over 7 km and the work involved the cutting of a tunnel about 2.4 km long under Morwell Down. At its southern end a double-track incline to carry wagons connected the canal with the Morwellham quays. The canal was officially opened in June 1817, and much of it can still be easily traced, including the early nineteenth-century warehouses and cot-

Plate 53 Wheal Coates, just south of St Agnes head, looking west, showing engine house and mine buildings probably dating from 1861–89. Towanwroath Shaft is nearby.

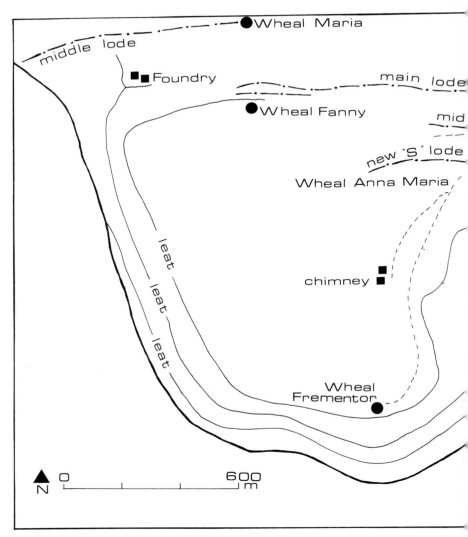

Fig 7·4 Plan of Devon Great Consols showing lodes and mines (*source: Booker 1967, 148*).

tages at the old Tavistock Canal Wharf, and the canal aqueduct over the River Lumburn near Crowndale.

A number of small mines developed in the area, but these were completely overshadowed by the discovery of fabulously wealthy copper deposits in a pheasant covert at Blanchdown, owned by the seventh Duke of Bedford. The first workings in 1844 created a sensa-

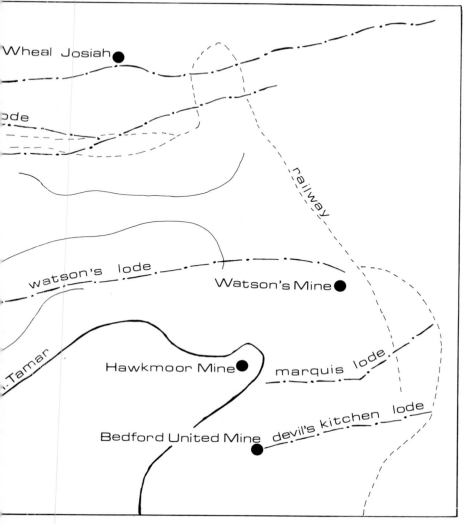

Wheal Josiah

lode

railway

watson's lode

Watson's Mine

Tamar

Hawkmoor Mine

marquis lode

Bedford United Mine

devil's kitchen lode

tion. They dispelled the belief that no really rich mine would ever be found west of Truro, but they were also the last great copper strike to be made in the west country. By 1864 the workings were organized as the Devonshire Great Consolidated Copper Mining Company, or Devon Great Consols.

Eventually, a complicated sequence of lodes was discovered, and exploited by a series of shafts and tunnels (*fig 7·4*). The workings covered an area of nearly 70 hectares (30 acres) in the bend of the Tamar. Water for operating pumping machinery was run from the

Tamar in 'the Great Leat', completed in 1849, and in two further leats. The urgently needed railway, worked by locomotives and opened in 1859, ran from the mines to a point above Morwellham, from which an incline ran to connect it with the quays. By 1857 the Duke of Bedford had received over £100,000 in dues, and individual shareholders were correspondingly enriched. From his profits, the Duke built a new central square, market hall, and town hall at Tavistock, and miners' cottages at Tavistock and Morwellham.

The managers of Devon Great Consols hoped that as the copper ore ran out, other metalliferous lodes would be discovered. By 1885 tin stone had failed to appear, and although sales of arsenic from the workings helped to keep the mine alive, financial storm clouds began to gather. In June 1902 the mine finally closed. By order of the Duke, the shafts were filled and the buildings tumbled so that little now remains of what had been the largest copper mine in Europe.

Mines were also being developed on the western side of the Tamar

Plate 54 Morwellham, Devon, looking across the Tamar, as it was about 1900. The canal can be seen in the dark line running across the background hill beside the cottage. The Devon Great Consols Incline can be seen down the hill, running, by way of a tunnel to the raised gantries of the great Dock. Compare figure 7·5.

in the area between Gunnislake and <u>Callington</u>, now a deserted and tumbled landscape of derelict engine houses and abandoned dumps. Here there were once at least eighty mines, of which the best known are Drakewalls at the top of Gunnislake Hill, Hingston Down Consols, and Kit Hill, the stack of which survives on the crown of the hill. To serve this area, the East Cornwall Mineral Railway was built by 1872 to run from Kelly Bray just west of Kit Hill to Calstock Quay.

Morwellham, now developed as a vistors' centre, gives a fascinating insight into the life of the Tamar Valley as it used to be a century ago, when these quays were the most important copper ore exporters in Europe (*fig 7·5*). Here can be seen the southern entrance to the Tavistock Canal Tunnel and remains of the rails of the canal incline, together with the quays for shipping Great Consols copper ore, lime kilns, and the Bedford cottages, all now quiet beside the reedy river.

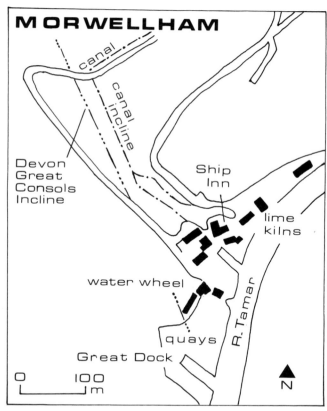

Fig 7·5 Plan of Morwellham port (*Booker 1976*).

249

Dartmoor

The Industrial Revolution created a rising need for the raw materials which the granite mass of Dartmoor and its surrounding country could help to supply. Demand stimulated fresh interest in the reserves of tin and copper ore, and in the products of the granite itself.

Well over a hundred mines are known to have existed on the moor since 1800, although records are often imperfect. The naturally hilly terrain meant that lodes could sometimes be reached by horizontal tunnels or adits driven into the hillside, and if these were used in conjunction with vertical shafts the water could be drained through the lowest adit and a difficult problem cheaply solved. Sometimes engine houses and pumping equipment were necessary, but little survives on the moor itself.

Old mining areas, with their overgrown scars and dumps, are still highly dangerous. In an area like Vitifer, where old surface workings are obvious, much remains below ground, and apparently solid earth may be only the top of a choked shaft plunging many metres below. The area around Birch Tor and Vitifer, together with Golden Dagger and East Vitifer, and several smaller mines, carries the most extensive range of tin-mining remains on Dartmoor, although little survives of the mine buildings. Working at Vitifer and Golden Dagger continued off and on from about 1780 to 1930.

An interesting group of remains, all now on private ground, which formed Wheal Cumpston mine near Dartmeet has recently been plotted.[10] Wheal Cumpston was worked for tin intermittently during the early nineteenth century and substantial remains survive of the solidly built structure of granite blocks which was the mine Captain's house. A well preserved ore-dressing floor had been terraced into the hillside, and its wheel pit shows that here a wheel powered crushing stamps. Below this is a lower dressing floor. Sixty metres below the wheel pit, the water-flooded adit runs into the hillside (*fig 7·6*). Wheal Cumpston has all the typical elements of a nineteenth-century Dartmoor tin mine: workings, buildings, and dressing floors. Many other sites can be found on the open moor.

Surface granite, or moorstone, has been used since the Middle Ages for the cutting of domestic quern stones, cheese and cider presses, and feeding troughs. Quarrying did not begin until about 1780, and among the best known quarries were those at Haytor, which produced the granite for London Bridge. A remarkable tramway was built in 1820 to carry stone from the quarry to the Stover Canal at Teigngrace. The track was built of granite blocks carved with

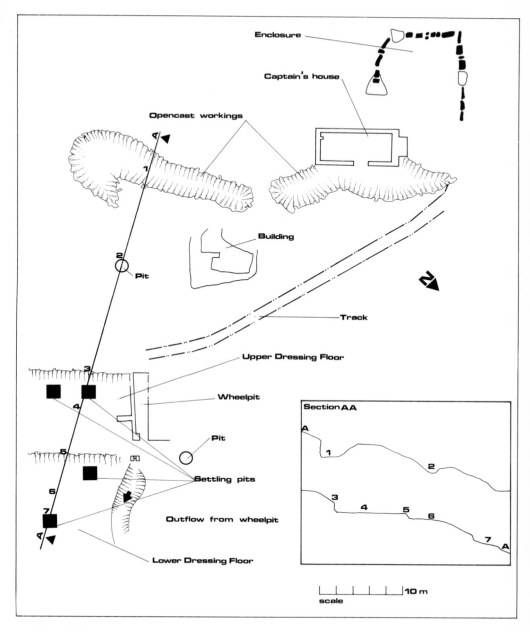

Fig 7·6 Plan of Wheal Cumpston tin mine, Holne (*source: Greeves 1978, fig 2*).

rails, and large lengths complete with branch lines and points can still be traced on Haytor Down.

In the background of much of the Dartmoor industry from very early times was the right of turbary, that is the right of the Dartmoor settlers to cut peat for fuel. Peat must have fuelled the earliest blow-ing-houses, and served domestic needs until about 1900 or a little later. It was cut from the ground in long strips or 'journeys' about 40 m long, using a special turf-iron. Many overgrown peat-ties, as the cutting areas were called, can still be spotted on the moor.

Greater Exmoor

The mineral deposits on and around the upland of Exmoor have always attracted adventurers. Silver lead deposits at Combe Martin were worked as early as the thirteenth century and 270 lbs of Combe Martin silver were provided for the dowry of Edward I's daughter Eleanor. A new and profitable lode was found and worked in Queen Elizabeth I's reign, and mining continued into the nineteenth century.

The area around North and South Molton was an important centre for the mining of copper and iron ore during the eighteenth and nineteenth centuries,[11] and a series of mines straddled the Exmoor border parishes. Substantial remains of standing mine buildings sur-vive at Stowford and Bampfylde, North Molton. Small but exciting quantities of gold have been found in the area.

The Quantock Hills were also the scene of much nineteenth-century mining activity. Among the most productive enterprises were the copper mines at Dodington, where the red sandstone engine house still stands. Another similar building nearby marks the original site of the engine. In their day these north Devon and west Somerset mines yielded valuable ores and made money for their owners, but gradually they became uneconomical and ceased production.

Clay working

China clay, or kaolin, and ball clay both derive from decomposed granite. Their extraction has created the extraordinary bleached lunar landscapes which are so striking a feature of parts of the moorland areas. The Chinese method of using kaolin to manufacture high quality porcelain was a closely guarded secret until 1718, when a search began for European deposits. The Quaker chemist William Cookworthy discovered the china clay in the St Austell area in 1746

Plate 55 Peat cutting and stacking near Bridestowe on Dartmoor in the early 1950s.

and this became the basis of his famous porcelain production. The deposits have been exploited ever since.

China clay working started on the Lee Moor area of Dartmoor in 1830, and other pits in the neighbourhood have been developed in this century by English China Clays Ltd, and their subsidiaries, who also manage the St Austell workings, like that at Blackpool. The kaolin is used in a huge range of manufacturing processes.

Ball clay has been transported by water to be laid down as sediments in natural basins, like that formed by the valleys of the Teign and the Bovey, where the ball clay is of very high quality. The clay has been used on a small scale since the late sixteenth century, chiefly for the manufacture of tobacco pipes. From the eighteenth century to the present day, the industry has grown in response to the need for ceramics, and major workings are operated in the Bovey Tracey area.

The monuments of industry

The mineral wealth which poured from the earth of the peninsula during the nineteenth century created a series of foundries and factories, the remains of which are now of great interest. Every year more people become fascinated with industrial archaeology, for which a substantial literature now exists. At Exeter the malthouses and leats at and near Exe Island are worth a visit[12] and the Bridgwater port installations and the harbours of Plymouth are equally rewarding.[13]

Pottery manufacture was in an important class of its own, although little now survives apart from some installations at the Litchdon Pottery in Barnstaple, and some important museum collections. The earliest record of north Devon manufacture in 1689 mentions the sale of pottery in Crock Street in Barnstaple, but the name alone suggests that this had already been going on for some time. The local clay deposits were exploited, and during the seventeenth and eighteenth centuries the potters built up a substantial trade with Ireland and north America.

The tablewares were of slipware, decorated by scratching through the white outer slip so that the deep red body made a bright contrast. Among the most famous pieces are the harvest jugs, which seem to have been commissioned sometimes by local farmers to hold cider and beer at harvest suppers. Many had inscriptions: one made at Bideford in 1766 reads

> Come fill me full and Drink about,
> and Never Leave till all is out,
> and if that will not make you merry,
> fill me again and Sing Down Derry!

The present scene

The south west is still the source of precious resources without which our complicated society cannot function. The clay companies annually extract hundreds of thousands of tons from the 26 or so pits in operation, mainly on the St Austell moorland and the southern flanks of Dartmoor. Peat extraction is a major operation in the Somerset Levels. Mining ventures, like Geevor near St Just, where operations have been successfully extended into the old below-sea workings of Levant, or South Crofty mine near Redruth, are attracting serious attention. Farming, equally, is an extraction industry in its own way. New methods which involve the ploughing of upland areas left unploughed for centuries or perhaps never ploughed at all, deep ploughing, and the creation of large fields by the removal of hedge-rows and boundaries, alter our landscape in order to produce more food. All this industrial activity necessarily implies the building of roads, reservoirs, and a wide range of services.

The south west is also one of the most beautiful and varied areas of Britain. It is the home of rare wild species like the otter, and the red deer of Exmoor. It is especially rich in the physical remains of our past, and Dartmoor holds one of the most important reserves of archaeological monuments in Europe. Its coasts and moors annually attract thousands of visitors who have a right to expect fresh air and the enjoyment of their historical and natural heritage. All these things are under threat from development and its consequences. The fact that this interesting and lovely countryside is created by geological forma-tions and potential farming land of outstanding economic and social importance is a fundamental dilemma which can be neither solved nor ignored, but must be coped with as well as possible in the interests of the public as a whole.

Archaeologists have an important part to play in the effort to find a reasonable balance so that the heritage may be conserved. Many archaeological organizations, mostly created since 1950, are working hard to survey and record sites so that informed advice can be given on, say, the archaeological consequences of a road or reservoir con-struction. If the destruction of a site is necessary, then it is to be hoped that it can be recorded before it disappears. Needless to say, the task of trying to reconcile the conflicting interests of development and protection is never easy.

1. *Youings 1969*, 169
2. *Hoskins 1972*
3. *Chitty 1971*
4. *French, Linehan 1963*
5. *Harris 1972*, 28
6. *Todd, Laws 1972*, 201
7. *Barton 1967*
8. *Noall 1973*
9. *Booker 1967*
10. *Greeves 1978*
11. *Slader 1964*.
12. *Chitty 1971*
13. *Porter 1971; Gaskell Brown 1973*

RETROSPECT

Many patterns can emerge in a long view of the past. Some of these may appear only in the eye of the archaeologist, shifting as different explanations of social change find favour. But others must be genuine, truly reflecting the experience of our ancestors. By and large, these patterns are common to southern Britain, and indeed north-western Europe as a whole. Within this wide area, however, the south-western peninsula of Britain has a distinct regional character.

Three broad phases seem to emerge. During the earliest phase, men lived in shifting human bands which, as the Palaeolithic and then the Mesolithic passed into the Neolithic, increasingly learned to bring food resources more and more directly under their own control. Elaborate communications, through which goods and ideas could be exchanged, were important to these people. They built up networks which ran the length of the peninsula, and exploited its characteristic resources. In the later part of this long phase, they built impressive gathering places like the great tombs of the Dartmoor fringes, but many or most of them do not seem to have acquired settled homes. The Late Neolithic and Early Bronze Age may have been a transitional period, during which an elite appears plainly for the first time.

Then, around 1500 BC, we see an abrupt change. Farmers parcelled out the land, and built substantial homes and outbuildings with attached corn fields, grazing rights, and cemeteries. Closely defined territories like those on Dartmoor suggest the gradual emergence of a small, aggressive, land-owning class supported by the peasants. This social system persisted throughout late prehistoric, Roman, and post-Roman Dumnonia. Indeed, in some places in the south west it survived, with important modifications in the arrangement of fields and settlements, well into the twentieth century.

Meanwhile, from around AD 1000, townsmen were developing

small urban communities, and these increased as the later Middle Ages progressed. Their activities stimulated the industrial revolution of the late eighteenth century, which, with its greedy demand for metals, transformed large areas of the south west into the mining camps of the new age.

Throughout much of the archaeological record, hilltops are conspicuous. They have the haunting quality which clings to high places that have been important to many generations. Carn Brea was a Neolithic fortified settlement, then an Iron Age hillfort, and finally the site of mines. Worlebury Hill and many more saw occupation in the Neolithic, the Iron Age, and the Roman and post-Roman centuries. Above all, to stand on South Cadbury hilltop, with its Neolithic and Bronze Age traces, its Iron Age defences, its probable Roman temple, its post-Roman fortifications, and its Saxon burh, is to feel history beneath the feet. The hills are mostly deserted now; their place was taken by Exeter, the principal Roman foundation within the peninsula, and by the monasteries and the new towns of the Middle Ages. Hilltops, and then towns, were part of the flow of exchange and trade. As time passed, they became the homes of craftsmen, and of ceremony and prestige, all at the service of war-like aristocrats, who controlled the land and its resources.

The visible remains of tree clearance and land use, plain upon the face of the peninsula, show the effort which has always supported this superstructure. Here lies the solid continuity of society, running back perhaps 5000 years. This is clear in areas of Dartmoor like Sherril or Horridge Common where prehistoric field systems merge into medieval and then modern fields, and very ancient walls still control the pattern of cultivation. Broadsands tomb, first built around 3000 BC, is now part of the hedge bank which once marked the boundary between the parishes of Paignton and Churston Ferrers. Was an ancient tomb used as a convenient landmark whenever the division was first set out, or was the tomb first built on a boundary which has remained important ever since? Many Bronze Age barrows pose exactly the same question, like Setta Barrow which stands on the county boundary between Devon and Somerset. Some estates, like those belonging to minster churches, which do not appear in the written record until an Anglo-Saxon charter, could even have originated in the prehistoric period. Some institutions, like the peat-cutters' rights in the Somerset Levels, or the grazing rights possessed by the Dartmoor commoners, may be equally ancient.

Religious customs seem to be a basic part of this fundamental continuity. The coming of Christianity created monasteries, which were soon integrated into the land-holding class within the peninsula, and stimulated the formation of local graveyards. Nevertheless, the intellectual impact of the new faith is likely to have been generally slight. The cult of the dead was essentially much the same, whether it focused upon a chambered tomb, a barrow cemetery or a medieval shrine grave. Archetypal impulses prompted worshippers to build circular sacred places, like the henges of the Neolithic, the stone circles and ring cairns of the Bronze Age, and the western circular enclosed cemeteries of the Early Christian period, many of which are still in use today as parish graveyards.

Continuity and change are abiding elements in the past. Archaeology itself is changing, in the south west as elsewhere in Britain. What we can now see and say is the result of work carried out in the past hundred years. What we may be able to say in the future will probably be different, but will certainly be equally fascinating.

GLOSSARY

Artefact	Man-made article, often used for tools of stone or metal.
Barrow	Earth mound erected over a ritual site, often a burial. Barrows were built by many pre-Christian communities in Britain, but the term arises most frequently in the south west in connection with Neolithic and Bronze Age sites. Alternative name often used on Ordnance Survey maps is *tumulus*.
Cairn	Mound of stones, often the stone equivalent of a barrow.
Chert	A glassy, hard mineral, occurs as layers or nodules usually in limestones.
Cist	Sometimes spelt 'kist', or used in the form 'kistvaen'. Grave lined with stone slabs to form a box shape, and covered with stone slabs. Generally of Beaker/Early Bronze Age date (but sometimes post-Roman).
Clitter	Debris resulting from tor formation.
Flint	Variety of chert, occurs in chalk.
Highland or Upland	The areas of northern and western Britain largely composed of older, harder rocks giving mountainous or rugged countryside. Dartmoor and most of Cornwall lie within it.
Lowland zone	The area of southern Britain largely composed of newer rocks giving soft countryside. The lower Exe Valley and east Devon lie within it.
Menhir	From two British words meaning 'long stone'. Sometimes used in place of the English 'standing stone'.
Petrological anaylsis	Technique by which samples from stone artefacts, often axes, or from pottery, may be compared with samples

collected in the field, so that the origin of the stone or pot clay can be indicated.

Pollen analysis Technique by which samples of ancient pollen from an archaeological site may be assigned to plant species, and so the ancient vegetation cover assessed.

Pound Stone-walled enclosure, might be of any date but often prehistoric.

Quoit Local term, used particularly in Cornwall, to describe a megalithic tomb, or the remains of one.

Spindle-whorl Pierced circular disc of stone or clay, needed to weight the end of a wooden spindle shaft used in the twisting of thread from loose wool.

Wheal Term for mine used in Devon and Cornwall, especially in the nineteenth century.

SELECTED
RADIO CARBON DATES

The technical problems which surround radio carbon dating are difficult, and have important implications. Radio active carbon, or Carbon 14, exists in the atmosphere in a known proportion to ordinary carbon, Carbon 12. Both are absorbed, in relative proportions, by all living plants and animals, and cease to be absorbed once the plant or animal is dead. Unlike C12, C14 decays, so the proportion of C14 against C12 left in a dead organic sample, usually charcoal, wood, or bone, can be measured and the age of the sample calculated.

However, the C14 in the sample may not have decayed at the average rate, and errors in sampling and processing must be allowed for. Therefore a radio carbon date is only an expression of probability and not an accurate fix. For this reason radio carbon dates are expressed as, for example, 2000 bc ± (plus or minus) 150. 2000 represents the central point in a band of 300 years in which there is a two to one probability that the date actually falls. It will be seen that one date is of little use, and valid conclusions can only be based upon groups of dates.

The time during which a given quantity of C14 decays by half is called its 'half-life', and the original calculation upon which early C14 dates were based reckoned this half-life as 5568 years. More accurate calculations now reckon it as about 5730 years. To save confusion, C14 dates are still generally worked out and quoted (as they are in this book) on the basis of the old half-life, but the difference between these dates and revised dates can sometimes be significant.

Originally, it was assumed that the amount of C14 in the atmosphere, and so its proportion to C12, has always been the same. However, checks like the building up of tree-ring sequences by counting back annual rings from the present in specimens of the long-lived American Bristlecone Pine tree, and producing C14 dates for these at intervals, have shown that this is not the case. It seems that at some periods there was more C14 in the atmosphere than at some others, and so for these periods the C14 dates turn out to be too recent. Radio carbon dates, therefore, are not true year dates. For this reason it has become the accepted convention to quote a C14 date as bc or ad,

261

reserving BC and AD for true year dates. Sometimes dates are expressed as bp (before present). For calculating purposes the 'present' is reckoned as AD 1950 so, for example, 2000 bc might be represented as 3950 bp.

Radio carbon dates can be calibrated and so converted into true year dates. Unfortunately, however, there is as yet no general agreement on how this should be done. Various tables, with full discussions, have been published in the volumes edited by Renfrew (1974) and Watkins (1975), where it will be seen that possible calibrations can differ significantly. As a broad rule-of-thumb guide, dates around 3000 bc are probably about 800 years too recent, those around 2000 bc about 500 years too recent, and those around 900 bc about 100 years too recent. It is also very important to remember that in the case of charcoal it is the date of the tree that is being measured, not the date of its use. Oak heartwood, for example, might be several centuries old before it was made into a Neolithic house or a Bronze Age coffin.

Radio carbon dates are published in various journals from time to time, but also in the journal *Radiocarbon*. The Council for British Archaeology publishes at intervals abstracts of C14 dates in its *Archaeological Site Index to Radiocarbon Dates for Great Britain and Ireland*. A selected, short list of radio carbon dates of relevance to the south west is given below, but many interesting dates are necessarily omitted. The dates are normally arranged in chronological order, but this strict order has not been maintained where the same broad occupation at a single site has yielded a range of dates which it would be unhelpful to break up. For each entry is given some details of the sample and its context, the radio carbon date calculated on the 5568 half-life and presented as bc or ad, the laboratory reference number (for details of which see CBA *Archaeological Site Index*), and the published reference (*Radiocarbon* is abbreviated as *RC*).

Kent's Cavern, Devon.
   Early upper Palaeolithic 'leaf-point' level.
   Gr N 6202. Mellars 1974, 93.
26,770 bc ± 450

Kent's Cavern, Devon.
   Later upper Palaeolithic level associated
     with single-sided harpoon.
   Gr N 6203. Mellars 1974, 93.
12,325 bc ± 120

Sun Hole, Cheddar, Somerset.
   Upper Palaeolithic layer with bones of *Ursus Arctos*
     (brown bear).
   BM-524. Mellars 1974, 93.
10,428 bc ± 150

Westward Ho!, Devon.
   Peat above Mesolithic midden.
   Q-672. RC 6, 1964, 126.
4635 bc ± 130

Ballynagilly, Tyrone.   3675 bc ± 150
   Charcoal from pit with sherds.
   UB-197. *RC* 12, 1970, 288–9.

Hembury Neolithic enclosure, Devon.   3330 bc ± 150
   Burnt layer in ditch with Neolithic pot.
   BM-138. *RC* 5, 1963, 106.

Hembury Neolithic enclosure, Devon.   3150 bc ± 150
   Charcoal from ditch bottom.
   BM-130. *RC* 10, 1968, 2.

Fussell's Lodge, earthen long barrow, Wiltshire.   3230 bc ± 150
   Charcoal with burnt stones and flints over primary
     burials.
   BM-134. *RC* 10, 1968, 2.

Sweet Track, Somerset.   3190 bc ± 100
   Peat immediately under track rails.
   Q-1102. *RC* 17, 1975, 43.

Carn Brea, Cornwall.   3049 bc ± 64
   Charcoal from Neolithic structural complex.
   BM-825. *RC* 18, 1976, 37.

Carn Brea, Cornwall.   2747 bc ± 60
   Charcoal from beneath collapsed stones.
   BM-824. *RC* 18, 1976, 37.

High Peak, Devon.   2860 bc ± 150
   Charcoal from Neolithic occupation.
   BM-214. *RC* 11, 1969, 287.

South Cadbury, Somerset.   2825 bc ± 115
   Pit on hill summit, hazel shells.
   I-5927. *RC* 18, 1976, 186.

South Cadbury, Somerset.   2501 bc ± 120
   Pit on hill summit with Neolithic pot, bones,
     flint.
   I-5928. *RC* 18, 1976, 186.

Honeygore (West) Track, Somerset.   2807 bc ± 60
   Hazel from track.
   Q-999. *RC* 15, 1973, 163.

Ascott-under-Wychwood, chambered tomb, Oxfordshire.   2785 bc ± 70
   Charcoal from buried soil surface, dates mound
     construction.
   BM-429. *RC* 18, 1976, 19.

Hazard Hill, Devon.   2750 bc ± 150
   Charcoal from occupation.
   BM-150. *RC* 11, 1969, 287.

Three Holes Caves, Torbryan, Devon.   2500 bc ± 200
   Layer 5, microliths with some Neolithic elements.
   I-549. Rosenfeld 1964, 3–26.

Mount Pleasant, Class 2 henge, Dorset.   2098 bc ± 54
   Charcoal from base of enclosure ditch, N entrance.
   BM-793. *RC* 18, 1976, 24.

Abbot's Way Track, Westhay, Somerset.   2068 bc ± 80
   Wooden peg from track.
   Q-926. *RC* 12, 1970, 549, 596.

Amesbury, bell barrow, Wiltshire.   1788 bc ± 55
   Burial with early-style beaker under crown of barrow.
   BM-287. *RC* 18, 1976, 17.

Crig-a-Mennis barrow, Perranzabuloe, Cornwall.   1565 bc ± 90
   Barrow with two ribbon handled urns.
   NPL-193. Christie 1960.

Tregiffian entrance grave, Cornwall.   1539 bc ± 59
   Charcoal from collared urn in pit in tomb floor.
   BM-935. *RC* 18, 1976, 39.

Watch Hill, Cornwall.   1520 bc ± 70
   Pit dug in base of barrow ditch in primary use of site.
   HAR-654. Miles 1975a.

Shaugh Moor, Devon.   1480 bc ± 90
   Charcoal from pit inside ring cairn with faience beads.
   HAR-2220. Wainwright *et al.* 1979.

Upton Pyne, round barrow, Devon.   1386 bc ± 53
   Material from Urn 4.
   BM-402. Pollard, Russell 1976.

Shaugh Moor, settlement, Devon.   1210 bc ± 70
   Charcoal associated with enclosure wall.
   HAR-2475. Smith, Wainwright 1978.

Gwithian, Cornwall.   1120 bc ± 103
   Charcoal from cremation, Layer 5.
   NPL-21. *RC* 5, 1963, 36.

Trevisker, Cornwall.   1110 bc ± 95
   Charcoal from House A floor.
   NPL-134. *RC* 12, 1970, 183–4.

South Cadbury, Somerset. 925 bc ± 90
    Ox bone from ditch beside SW entrance through
      later defences.
    I-5971. *RC* 18, 1976, 186.

Bratton Fleming, Devon. 882 bc ± 42
    Late 'Trevisker' pot, cremation beneath barrow.
    BM-1148. King, Miles 1976.

Westhay Track, Somerset. 850 bc ± 110
    Birch timber marked with axe cuts of LBA type.
    Q-308. *RC* 1, 1959, 69–72.

Trevisker, Cornwall. 185 bc ± 90
    Charcoal, floor of Hut 2, Glastonbury style pot.
    HAR-135. *RC* 12, 1970, 183–4.

Carn Euny, settlement, Cornwall. ad 90 ± 100
    Storage pit in courtyard house IV.
    HAR-335. Christie 1978.

Exeter, Mary Major cemetery, Devon. ad 420 ± 80
    Burial.
    HAR-1613. Bidwell 1979, 111.

Cannington, cemetery, Somerset. ad 730 ± 110
    Skeleton from grave shrine.
    Birm-70. *RC* 11, 1969, 268.

PLACES TO VISIT

Short details have been given of some of the most important archaeological sites in the region, although this list is selective and many have been omitted. Further information can be found in standard guides, like those by Grinsell (1970, 1970a). Churches, stately homes, and domestic buildings generally have been omitted, since details of these can easily be found elsewhere. Inclusion in this list does not mean that a site is necessarily freely accessible to visitors. Accessibility and opening hours should be checked locally.

Palaeolithic and Mesolithic
Kent's Cavern, Torquay, Dev. SX 934641
In Ilsham Road, signposted off Babbacombe Road, car park.

Cheddar Caves, Som. ST 466539
By the B3135 through Cheddar.

Wookey Hole Caves, Som. ST 533478
Off A371 W. of Wells to N. end of Wookey Hole village.

Westward Ho! submerged forest, Dev. SS 4330
By Pebble Ridge on beach.

Early Neolithic
Carn Brea hill top, Cor. SW 685407
By footpath from road SW. of Redruth.

Lanyon Quoit, Madron, Cor. SW 430337
N. of road between Madron and Morvah.

Men-an-Tol, Madron, Cor. SW 427349
Along path leading NE. from road across Bosullow Common.

Trethevy Quoit, Cor. SX 259688
Signposted. Turn W. off B3254 between Liskeard and St Cleer.

Zennor Quoit, Cor. SW 469380
On hill S. of B3306, 1.5 km SE. of Zennor.

Mulfra Quoit, Cor. SW 452353
By footpath off road between Penzance and Porthmeor, about 450 m up hill.

Corringdon Ball, chambered barrow, Dev. SX 670614
Through South Brent to footpath at SX 683603.

Spinster's Rock, denuded chambered barrow, Dev. SX 700908
Beside A382, 1.6 km S. of Whiddon Down.

Hembury hill top, Dev. ST 113031
W. of A373, about 6 km from Honiton.

South Cadbury hill top, Som. ST 628252
By footpath from South Cadbury village.

Treen, entrance graves, Cor. SW 438371
By footpath on W. side of Penzance–Gurnard's Head road.

Brane, entrance grave, also known as Chapel Euny, Cor. SW 401282
From A30 to Brane Farm, permission to view to be obtained from the farm.

Tregiffian, entrance grave, Cor. SW 431244
On verge of B3315, original cup-marked stone now in RIC.

Later Neolithic and Early Bronze Age

Trippet Stones, stone circle, Cor. SX 131750
N. of A30, 11 km from Bodmin.

Stripple Stones, henge, Cor. SX 144752
1.6 km E. of Trippet Stones.

Boscawen-Un, stone circle, Cor. SW 412274
By footpath S. from Land's End road.

Nine Maidens, stone row, Cor. SX 937676
Footpath from A39 at SX 934676.

West Taphouse, round barrows, Cor. SX 143633
N. of A390, 8 km NE. of Lostwithiel.

Bant's Carn, entrance grave, St Mary's, Scilly. SV 911123
Near N. end of golf course.

Innisidgen and Lower Innisidgen, entrance graves, St Mary's, Scilly. SV 921127
Road over Helvear Down passes near.

Old Man, standing stone, Gugh, Scilly. SV 891084
On slope of Kittern Hill, Gugh.

Butterdon Hill stone row and barrows, Harford, Dev. SX 657594
By footpath from Harford Moor Gate.

Drizzlecombe stone rows and cairns, Sheepstor, Dev. SX 592670
By footpath from Ditsworthy Warren House, sites between path and River Plym.

Merrivale stone settings, Dev. SX 553746
Just S. of A384 on bend of road E. of Merrivale village.

Scorhill stone circle, Gidleigh, Dev. SX 655874
From Gidleigh, climb of 0.8 km.

Lakehead Hill, stone cists, Lydford, Dev. SX 644774
Footpath from Bellever Youth Hostel west uphill.

Five Barrows, North Molton, Dev. SS 732368
Parking place at Comerslade on the ridgeway. The barrows are on the summit to the S.

Hameldown Barrows, Widecombe, Dev. SX 706795
Approach from B3212 by road from Shapley Common southwards, footpath up to Hameldown Tor and along ridgeway.

Setta Barrow, High Bray, Dev. SS 726381
E. of ridgeway from Mole's Chamber to Kinsford Gate. The county boundary crosses the barrow.

Withypool, stone circle, Som. SS 838343
By footpath from road between Withypool and Sandyway Cross.

Alderman's Barrow, Som. SS 837423
S. of road going NW. from Exford to Lucott Cross.

Joaney How and Robin How, cairns, Som. SS 908426
Walk of 0.4 km from road running N. over Dunkery Hill.

Later Bronze Age
Rough Tor, hut circles and field system, Cor. SX 141815
By Rough Tor on Bodmin Moor.

Samson Flats, field system, Scilly. SV 881129
Visible at low tide.

Shovel Down, reave, Chagford, Dev. SX 660856
From Batworthy, climb of about 0.8 km.

Foales Arrishes, huts and field system, Dev. SX 737758
On hill, 0.4 km SW. of road at Hemsworthy Gate.

Grimspound, enclosure with hut circles, Dev. SX 701809
S. off B3212 between Moretonhampstead and Warren House Inn at Shapley Common, site is E. off road.

Legis Tor, enclosure, Sheepstor, Dev. SX 570654
Footpath beside N. bank of River Plym.

Valley of the Rocks settlement, Lynton, Som. SS 706497
Footpath from Lynton.

Iron Age

Carn Brea, hillfort, Cor. SW 685407
By footpath from road SW. of Redruth.

Chun Castle, hillfort, Cor. SW 405339
SW. from road off B3306 at Bosullow Common, then walk uphill.

Castle Dor, hill slope enclosure, Cor. SX 103548
E. of B3269 between Lostwithiel and Fowey.

The Rumps, Pentire Head, cliff castle, Cor. SW 934810
Off B3314 at St Minver W. to Pentire Farm, and walk 0.5 km.

Trevelgue Head, cliff castle, Cor. SX 827630
By footpath W. of B3276, N. of St Columb Porth.

Carn Euny, courtyard houses, fogou, Sancreed, Cor. SW 403288
By lane N. from Brane.

Harlyn Bay, cemetery and museum, Cor. SX 877758
S. of road through Harlyn, W. of Harlyn Bridge.

Giants Castle, cliff castle, St Mary's, Scilly, SV 925100
On SE. point of island.

Hembury, hillfort, Dev. ST 113031
N. of A313, about 6 km from Honiton.

Woodbury, hillfort, Dev. SY 032874
B13180 runs through hillfort.

Countisbury, hillfort, Lynton, Dev. SS 741493
On Wind Hill, S. of A39, above Lynmouth Bay.

Milber Down Camp, hill slope enclosure, Haccombe, Dev. SX 884699
Road from Newton Abbot via Watcombe to Torquay crosses site.

Clovelly Dykes, hill slope enclosure, Dev. SS 311235
N. of A39(T) and W. of B3237 turning into Clovelly opposite garage.
Permission to visit from East Dyke Farm.

Kestor, settlement, Dev. SX 665867
From A382 to W. of Chagford, road to Batworthy crosses site.

Ham Hill, hillfort, Som. ST 480168
S. of Stoke-sub-Hamdon on A3088.

Brent Knoll, hillfort, Som. ST 341510
Approach from M5 or A38(T).

South Cadbury, hillfort, Som. ST 628252
By footpath from South Cadbury village.

Worlebury, promontory hillfort, Som. ST 315625
By road from Weston-super-Mare.

Roman

Chysauster, courtyard houses, Madron, Cor. SW 472350
By B3311 and NW. from Badger's Cross.

Halangy Down, courtyard village, St Mary's, Scilly. SV 910124
On Halangy Down.

City Wall, Exeter (much rebuilt during medieval period), Dev. SX
917924
S. end of South Street, Post Office Street, Trinity Green.

Martinhoe, fortlet, Dev. SS 663493
Track from Martinhoe village.

Charterhouse-on-Mendip, mining settlement, Som. ST 500565
S. of B3134 between Burrington Combe and Castle of Comfort Inn.

Post Roman and Early Medieval

Men Scryfa, Madron, inscribed stone, Cor. SW 427353
Path NE. across Bosullow Common, from road.

St Just churchyard, inscribed stone in church, Cor. SW 372315
St Just-in-Penwith village.

Lewannick church and churchyard, inscribed stones, Cor. SX 808276
Lewannick village.

Tintagel Headland, Cor. SX 049891
Path through valley from Tintagel village.

Doniert's Stone, St Cleer, Cor. SX 237688
In enclosure on S. side of B3360 N. of Liskeard.

Lanherne cross, Cor. SX 872660
By footpath to nunnery from Lanherne.

Lustleigh church, inscribed stone, Dev. SX 785813
In centre of village.

Graveyard, inscribed stones, Beacon Hill, Lundy. SS 133443
Beside Beacon Hill or Old Lighthouse.

Lydford, town rampart (and castle), Dev. SX 510847
W. off A386.

Colyton cross, Dev. SY 246940
In church.

Copplestone cross, Dev. SS 771026
Beside A377 at village crossroads.

Winsford Hill, inscribed stone, Som. SS 889335
SE. end of Winsford Hill, E. of B3223, under modern shelter.

Glastonbury Abbey, Som. ST 501387
In Glastonbury town.

Cheddar Palaces, Som. ST 457532
In grounds of Kings of Wessex School, marked by concrete blocks.

Muchelney Abbey, Som. ST 428248
In village.

Later Medieval

Restormel Castle, Cor. SX 104614
1.6 km N. of Lostwithiel.

Launceston Castle, Cor. SX 330846
In town centre.

Plen an gwary, playing place for dramas, St Just, Cor. SW 372315
St Just town.

Totnes Castle, Dev. SX 800605
Within Totnes town.

Okehampton Castle, Dev. SX 584943
Beside Castle Lane, SW. from Okehampton.

Clapper Bridge, Postbridge, Dev. SX 789649
Over East Dart River, Postbridge.

Dunster Castle, Som. SS 991434
In village, off Taunton–Minehead road.

Nunney Castle, Som. ST 737457
5.6 km SW. of Frome.

Tarr Steps Bridge, clapper type, Som. SS 868323
Across River Barle.

Industrial Archaeology

Wheal Grey engine house and stacks, Cor. SW 595291
On slope of Tregoning Hill, Ashton.

Wheal Martyn clay works, Cor. SX 004555
At Wheal Martyn.

South Wheal Francis buildings, ore stamps, etc. Cor. SW 680395
At Carnkie, Camborne.

Copperhouse Docks and Hayle installations, Cor. SW 586380 (approx.)
Around mouth of Hayle River.

Ding Dong engine house, Cor. SW 434345
Across Bosullow Common, St. Just.

Botallack mine, Cor. SW 364333
On and near cliff, between sea and Botallack village.

Levant mine, Cor. SW 360340
On and near cliff by road W. from Trewelland.

Exeter Canal, Quays, Warehouses, etc. Dev. ST 921918 (approx.)
By foot from Exe Bridge.

Litchdon Pottery, Barnstaple, Dev. SS 560329
Litchdon Street.

Cheriton Cross Tollhouse, Dev. SS 773930
S. side of A30 Exeter to Okehampton in village.

Eylesbarrow, various tin working remains, Dev. SX 592676
Approached by tracks E. of Sheepstor village.

Week Ford blowing houses, Dev. SX 663723
Reached from Hexworthy–Holne road.

Birch Tor—Vitifer tin mining remains, Dev. SX 680810 (approx)
Reached from Warren House Inn on B3212.

Wheal Betsy Engine House, old workings, Dev. SX 510812
E. of A386, across Bleakdown.

Haytor Granite Tramway, Dev. SX 751778
On Haytor Down, off Widecombe–Manaton road.

Morwellham Port, Dev. SX 446697
From A390, 3.3 km W. of Tavistock.

Museums

The principal collections of material from the south west are listed below, but much of importance is also held elsewhere.
Royal Institution of Cornwall, River Street, Truro
Wayside Folk Museum, Zennor
Penlee House Museum, Penzance
City Museum, Drake Circus, Plymouth
Rougemont House Museum, Castle Street, Exeter
The Museum, Babbacome Road, Torquay
County Museum, The Castle, Taunton
County Museum, High Street West, Dorchester
The British Museum
The Ashmolean Museum, Beaumont Street, Oxford

BIBLIOGRAPHY

ABBREVIATIONS

Ant. J.	*Antiquaries Journal*
Arch.	*Archaeologia*
Arch. Camb.	*Archaeologia Cambrensis*
Arch. J.	*Archaeological Journal*
BAR	*British Archaeological Reports*
CBA	*Council for British Archaeology*
Cornish Arch.	*Cornish Archaeology*
CRAAGS	*Committee for Rescue Archaeology in Avon, Gloucester and Somerset*
Current Arch.	*Current Archaeology*
DAS	*Devon Archaeological Society*
DCRA	*Devon Committee for Rescue Archaeology*
HMSO	*Her Majesty's Stationery Office*
J. Brit. Arch. Ass.	*Journal of the British Archaeological Association*
JRIC	*Journal of the Royal Institution of Cornwall*
J. Roy. Soc. Antiq. of Ireland	*Journal of the Royal Society of Antiquaries of Ireland*
Med. Arch.	*Medieval Archaeology*
PDA(E)S	*Proceedings of the Devon Archaeological (Exploration) Society*
PDNHAS	*Proceedings of the Dorset Natural History and Archaeological Society*
Phil. Trans. Roy. Soc.	*Philosophical Transactions of the Royal Society*
PPS	*Proceedings of the Prehistoric Society*
Proc. U. Bris. Spel. Soc.	*Proceedings of the University of Bristol Spelaeological Society*
PSANHS	*Proceedings of the Somerset Archaeological and Natural History Society*
TDA	*Transactions of the Devonshire Association*
TNHSTP	*Torquay Natural History Society Transactions and Proceedings*

S

ADDYMAN, P. V. 1966. Lydford, Devon. *Med. Arch.* 10, 168–9.
ALCOCK, L. 1971. *Arthur's Britain.*
—— 1972. *By South Cadbury is that Camelot.*
—— 1980. The Cadbury Castle sequence in the First millennium BC. *Bulletin Board of Celtic Studies* 28, 654–718.
ALCOCK, N. W., Child, P. and Laithwaite, M. 1972. Sanders, Lettaford. A. Devon longhouse. *PDAS* 30, 227–33.
APSIMON, A. 1965. The Roman Temple on Brean Down, Somerset. *Proc. U. Bris. Spel. Soc.,* 1964–5, 10, 195–258.
—— 1968. The Bronze Age Pottery from Ash Hole, Brixham, Devon. *PDAS* 26, 21–30.
—— 1969. An early Neolithic House in Co. Tyrone. *J. Roy. Soc. Antiq. of Ireland* 99, 165–8.
APSIMON, A. and Greenfield, E. 1972. The Excavation of Bronze Age and Iron Age Settlements at Trevisker, St Eval, Cornwall. *PPS* 38, 302–381.
ASHBEE, P. 1958. The Excavation of Tregulland Barrow. *Ant. J.* 38. 174–196.
—— 1974. *Ancient Scilly.* Newton Abbot.
—— 1976. Bant's Carn, St Mary's, Isles of Scilly: An Entrance Grave Restored and Reconsidered. *Cornish Arch* 15, 11–26.
ASHE, G. 1971. ed. *The Quest for Arthur's Britain.*
ASTON, M. 1977. Deserted Settlements in Mudford Parish, Yeovil. *PSANHS* 121, 41–53.
ASTON, M. and Leech, R. 1977. *Historic Towns in Somerset,* CRAAGS.
ASTON, M. and Rowley, R. T. 1974. *Landscape Archaeology.*
AUSTIN, C. and Hall, R. 1972. The Medieval Houses of Stocklinch. *PSANHS* 116, 86–100.
AUSTIN, D. 1978. Excavations in Okehampton Deer Park, Devon, 1976–1978. *PDAS* 36, 191–239.
AVERY, M. 1976. Hillforts of the British Isles: A Student's Introduction in *Hillforts: Later Prehistoric Earthworks in Britain and Ireland* ed. D. Harding, 1–58.
BALKWILL, C. J. 1976. *Archaeology and Development in Rural Devon.* DAS/DCRA Publications No. 2.
BALKWILL, C. J. and Silvester, R. J. 1976. Earthworks on Sourton Down, near Okehampton. *PDAS* 34, 86–9.
BARKER, G. and Webley, D. 1978. Causewayed Camps and Early Neolithic Economies in Central Southern England. *PPS* 44, 161–186.
BARTON, D. B. 1967. *A History of Tin Mining and Smelting in Cornwall.* Truro.
BECKETT, S. C. and Hibbert, F. A. 1978. The Influence of Man on the Vegetation of the Somerset Levels. *Somerset Levels Papers* No. 4, ed. J. Coles, 86–90.
BERESFORD, G. 1971. Tresmorn, St Gennys. *Cornish Arch.* 10, 55–72.

274

—— 1974. The Medieval Manor of Penhallam, Jacobstow, Cornwall. *Med. Arch.* 18, 90–145.

—— 1979. Three described medieval settlements on Dartmoor. *Med. Arch.* 23, 98–158.

BERESFORD, M. 1967. *The New Towns of the Middle Ages.*

BERESFORD, M. W. and Finberg, H. P. R. 1973. *English Medieval Boroughs.* Newton Abbot.

BIDWELL, P. 1979. *The Legionary Bath-House and Basilica and Forum at Exeter.* Exeter Archaeological Reports; Vol 1.

—— 1980. *Roman Exeter: Fortress and Town.* Exeter.

BOOKER, F. 1967. *The Industrial Archaeology of the Tamar Valley.* Newton Abbot.

—— 1976. *Morwellham in the Tamar Valley.* Dartington Amenity Research Trust.

BOWEN, H. C. 1961. *Ancient Fields.* British Association for the Advancement of Science, Research Committee on Ancient Fields.

BOWEN, H. C. and Fowler, P. J. ed. 1978. *Early Land Allotment. BAR* 48.

BRADLEY, R. 1978. *The Prehistoric Settlement of Britain.*

BRANIGAN, K. 1976. Villa Settlement in the West Country, in Branigan, Fowler 1976, 99–119.

BRANIGAN, K. and Fowler, P. J. ed. 1976. *The Roman West Country.* Newton Abbot.

BROOKS, R. T. 1974. The Excavation of the Rumps Cliff Castle, St Minver, Cornwall. *Cornish Arch.* 13, 5–50.

BROWN, A. P. 1977. Late Devensian and Flandrian Vegetational History of Bodmin Moor, Cornwall. *Phil. Trans. Roy. Soc.* B, 276, 251–320.

BROWN, P. D. C. 1970. A Roman Pewter Mould from St Just in Penwith, Cornwall. *Cornish Arch.* 9, 107–10.

BURGESS, C. and Miket, R. ed. 1976. *Settlement and Economy in the Third and Second Millennia BC. BAR* 33.

BURGESS, C. and Shennan, S. 1976. The Beaker Phenomenon: Some Suggestions, in Burgess, Miket 1976, 309–23.

BURL, A. 1979. *Prehistoric Stone Circles.* Princes Risborough.

CAMPBELL, J. 1977. *The Upper Palaeolithic of Britain.* Vols. 1, 2. Oxford.

CAMPBELL, J. A., Baxter, M. S. and Alcock, L. 1979. Radio carbon Dates for the Cadbury Massacre. *Antiquity* 53, 31–8.

CHILD. P. 1978. Farmhouse Building Traditions, in *Devon's Traditional Buildings,* 7–17.

CHITTY, M. 1971. *A Guide to Industrial Archaeology in Exeter.* Exeter Industrial Archaeology Group.

CHRISTIE, P. M. L. 1960. Crig-a-mennis: A Bronze Age Barrow at Liskey, Perranzabuloe, Cornwall, *PPS* 26, 76–97.

—— 1978. The Excavation of an Iron Age Souterrain and Settlement at Carn Euny, Sancreed, Cornwall. *PPS* 44, 309–433.

CLARK, G. 1966. The Invasion Hypothesis in British Archaeology. *Antiquity* 40, 172–89.

CLARK, J. G. D. 1952. *Prehistoric Europe: The Economic Basis.*
—— 1972. *Star Carr: A Case study in Bio-Archaeology.* Addison-Wesley Modular Publications 10, 1–42.
CLARKE, D. 1970. *Beaker Pottery of Great Britain and Ireland.* 2 Vols.
CLARKE, P. J. 1971. The Neolithic, Bronze and Iron Age, and Romano-British finds from Mount Batten, Plymouth, 1832–1939. *PDAS* 29, 137–61.
COLES, J. 1976. Archaeology in the Somerset Levels, 1975, in *Somerset Levels Papers* ed. J. Coles, No. 2, 4–6.
—— 1977. Archaeology in the Somerset Levels, 1976, in *Somerset Levels Papers* ed. J. Coles, No. 3, 4–6.
—— 1978. The Somerset Levels: A Concave Landscape, in Bowen, Fowler 1978, 147–8.
COLES, J. and Orme, B. 1976. The Sweet Track, Railway Site, in *Somerset Levels Papers* ed. J. Coles, No. 2, 34–65.
COUTIN, K. 1978. Farm Buildings, in *Devon's Traditional Buildings*, 18–26.
CUNLIFFE, B. 1978. *Iron Age Communities in Britain.* 2nd. edition.
DAVIDSON, B. K. 1972. Castle Neroche: An Abandoned Norman Fortress in South Somerset. *PSAHNS* 116, 16–58.
Devon's Traditional Buildings 1978. Devon County Council.
DIMBLEBY, G. W. 1963. Pollen Analyses from Two Cornish Barrows. *JRIC* N.S. 4, 364–75.
DREWETT, P. 1977. The Excavation of a Neolithic Causewayed Enclosure on Offham Hill, East Sussex, 1976. *PPS* 43, 201–42.
DUDLEY, D. 1957. Excavations at Bodrifty, Mulfra Hill, near Penzance, Cornwall. *Arch. J.* 113, 1–32.
DUDLEY, D. and Minter, E. M. 1963. The Medieval Village at Garrow Tor, Bodmin Moor, Cornwall. *Med. Arch.* 7, 272–94.
DYMOND, C. W. 1902. *Worlebury.* 2nd. edition, Bristol.
EARL BRYAN, 1968. *Cornish Mining.* Truro.
ELKINGTON, H. D. H. 1976. The Mendip Lead Industry, in Branigan, Fowler, 1976, 183–97.
ELLISON, A. 1976. *Villages Survey: An Interim Report.* CRAAGS Occasional Papers No. 1.
EVANS, J. G., Limbrey, S. and Cleere, H. 1975. ed. *The Effect of Man on the Landscape: the Highland Zone.* CBA Research Report No. 11, 1975.
EVANS, P. 1975. The Intimate Relationship: An Hypothesis Concerning Pre-Neolithic Land Use, in Evans, Limbrey, Cleere, 43–8.
FARLEY, M. E. and Little, R. I. 1968. Oldaport, Modbury: A Re-Assessment of the Fort and Harbour. *PDAS* 26, 31–6.
FIELD, J. and Miles, H. 1975. An Upper Palaeolithic Site at Honiton. *PDAS* 33, 177–82.
FLEMING, A. 1978. The Prehistoric Landscape of Dartmoor, Part 1: South Dartmoor. *PPS* 44, 97–123.
FLETCHER, M. J., Grinsell, L. V. and Quinnell, N. 1974. A Long Cairn on Butterdon Hill, Ugborough. *PDAS*, 32, 163–5.

276

FOWLER, P. J. 1962. A Native Homestead of the Roman Period at Porth Godrevy, Gwithian. *Cornish Arch.* 1, 17–60.

—— 1972. ed. *Archaeology and the Landscape.*

FOWLER, P. J. and Evans, J. G. 1967. Plough-marks, Lynchets and Early Fields. *Antiquity* 41, 289–301.

FOX. A. 1948. The Broad Down (Farway) Necropolis and the Wessex Culture in Devon. *PDAES* 4, 1–19.

—— 1952a. The Castlewich Ringwork: A New Henge Monument in S.E. Cornwall. *Ant. J.* 32, 67–70.

—— 1952b. Roman Objects from Cadbury Castle. *TDA* 84, 105–14.

—— 1954. Excavations at Kestor. *TDA* 86, 21–62.

—— 1957. Excavations on Dean Moor, 1954–6. *TDA* 89, 18–77.

—— 1968. Excavations at the South Gate, Exeter, 1964–5. *PDAS* 26, 1–20.

—— 1973. *South West England.* 2nd. edition, Newton Abbot.

FOX, A. and Ravenhill, W. 1959. A Roman Signal Station on Stoke Hill, Exeter. *TDA* 91, 71–82.

—— 1966. Early Roman Outposts on the North Devon Coast. *PDAS* 24, 3–39.

—— 1969. Excavation of a Rectilinear Earthwork at Trevinnick, St Kew, 1968. *Cornish Arch.* 8, 89–97.

—— 1972. The Roman Fort at Nanstallon, Cornwall. *Britannia* 3, 56–111.

FOX, A., Radford, C. A. R., Rogers, E. H. and Shorter, A. H. 1950. Report on the Excavations at Milber Down, 1937–8. *PDAES* 4, 1949–50, 27–66.

FOX, H. 1972. Field Systems of East and South Devon, Part I: East Devon. *TDA* 104, 81–135.

FRENCH, H. and Linehan, C. D. 1963. Abandoned Medieval Sites in Widecombe-in-the-Moor. *TDA* 95, 168–79.

GASKELL BROWN, C. 1973. *Industrial Archaeology of Plymouth.* Workers Education Association.

GAWNE, E. 1970. Field Patterns in Widecombe Parish and the Forest of Dartmoor. *TDA* 102, 49–69.

GELLING, M. 1978. *Signposts to the Past.*

GORDON, A. S. R. 1941. The Excavation of Gurnard's Head, an Iron Age Cliff Castle in Western Cornwall. *Arch. J.* 97, 96–111.

GOVER, J., Mawer, A. and Stenton, F. 1931. *The Place-Names of Devon* Part I. Cambridge.

—— 1932. *The Place-Names of Devon* Part 2. Cambridge.

GREEVES, T. A. P. 1978. Wheal Cumpston Tin Mine, Holne, Devon. *TDA* 110, 161–71.

GRINSELL, L. V. 1970. *The Archaeology of Exmoor.* Newton Abbot.

—— 1970a. *Discovering Regional Archaeology: South Western England.* Princes Risborough.

HARRIS, HELEN. 1972. *The Industrial Archaeology of Dartmoor.* Newton Abbot.

HAWKINS, A. B. 1973. Sea Level Changes in South-West England, in *Marine Archaeology* ed. D. J. Blackman, Colston Papers 23.

HAYES, J. 1972. *Late Roman Pottery.* British School at Rome, London.

HAYWARD, L. C. 1972. The Roman Villa at Lufton near Yeovil. *PSAHNS* 116, 59–77.

HENCKEN, H. O'N. 1932. *The Archaeology of Cornwall and Scilly*.

—— 1933. Excavation at Chysauster, 1931. *Arch.* 83, 237–84.

HENDERSON, CHARLES. 1964. *Cornish Church Guide*, reprinted, Truro.

HIGGINBOTHAM, E. 1977. Excavations at Woolley Barrows, Morwenstow. *Cornish Arch.* 16, 10–16.

HIGHAM, R. A. 1977. Excavations at Okehampton Castle, Devon. Part I: The Motte and Keep. *PDAS* 35, 3–42.

HILL, D. 1969. The Burghal Hidage: The Establishment of a Text. *Med. Arch.* 13, 84–92.

HIRST, F. C. 1936. Excavations at Porthmeor, Cornwall. *JRIC* 24, 1–81.

HOGG, A. H. A. 1975. *Hillforts of Britain*.

HOSKINS, W. G. 1955. *The Making of the English Landscape*.

—— 1960. *The Early Expansion of Wessex*. Leicester University, Dept. of Local History, Occasional Papers No. 13.

—— 1972. *Devon*. Newton Abbot.

JACOBI, R. 1979. Early Flandrian Hunters in the South West. *PDAS* 37, 48–93.

JARVIS, K. 1976. The M5 Motorway and the Peamore/Pocombe Link. *PDAS* 34, 41–72.

JARVIS, K. and Maxfield, V. 1975. The Excavation of a First-Century Roman Farmstead and a Late Neolithic Settlement, Topsham, Devon. *PDAS* 33, 209–65.

JEFFERIES, J. S. 1974. An Excavation at the Coastal Promontory Fort of Embury Beacon, Devon. *PPS* 40, 136–52.

JERMY, D. E. 1969. A Possible Roman Road Aligned on Stratton, Cornwall. *Cornish Arch.* 8, 81–3.

JONES, G. R. 1976. Multiple Estates and Early Settlement, in Sawyer 1976, 15–40.

KING, G., Miles, H. 1976. A Bronze Age Cist Burial at Trebartha, Northill. *Cornish Arch.* 15, 27–30.

LAITHWAITE, M. 1977. Sanders, Lettaford *PDAS* 33, 84.

LANGMAID, N. 1971. Norton Fitzwarren. *Current Arch.* 28, 116–20.

LEACH, P. J. 1975. *Ilchester 1975: Interim Report*. CRAAGS.

LEECH, R. 1976. Larger Agricultural Settlements in the West Country, in Branigan, Fowler 1976, 142–61.

LIDELL, D. M. 1930. Excavations at Hembury Fort, Devon, 1930. *PDAES* 1, 40–63.

—— 1931. Excavations at Hembury Fort, Devon, 1931. *PDAES* 1, 90–120.

—— 1932. Excavations at Hembury Fort, Devon, 1932. *PDAES* 1, 162–90.

—— 1935. Excavations at Hembury Fort, Devon (1934 and 1935). *PDAES* 2, 135–75.

MACALISTER, R. A. S. 1945, 1949. *Corpus Inscriptionum Insularum Celticarum* Vols. 1, 2.

MANNING, W. 1976. 'The Conquest of the West Country', in Branigan, Fowler 15–41.

MEGAW, J. V. S. 1976. Gwithian, Cornwall: Some Notes on the Evidence for Neolithic and Bronze Age Settlement, in Burgess, Miket 1976, 51–79.

MELLARS, P. 1974. The Palaeolithic and Mesolithic, in Renfrew 1974, 41–99.

—— 1975. Ungulate Populations, Economic Patterns, and the Mesolithic Landscape, in Evans, Limbrey, Cleere 1975, 49–56.

MERCER, R. J. 1970. The Excavation of a Bronze Age Hut-Circle Settlement, Stannon Down. *Cornish Arch.* 9, 17–46.

—— 1974. Carn Brea. *Current Arch.* 47, 360–5.

MERRYFIELD, D. L. and Moore, P. D. 1974. Prehistoric Human Activity and Blanket Peat Initiation on Exmoor. *Nature*, 250, 439–41.

MILES, H. 1975a. Barrows on the St Austell Granite, Cornwall. *Cornish Arch.* 14, 5–81.

—— 1975b. Excavations at Woodbury Castle, East Devon, 1971. *PDAS* 33, 183–208.

—— 1977. The A38 Roadworks 1970–3. *PDAS* 35, 43–52.

—— 1977a. The Honeyditches Roman Villa, Seaton, Devon. *Britannia* 8, 107–48.

—— 1977b. Excavations at Killibury Hillfort, Egloshayle 1975–6. *Cornish Arch.* 16, 89–121.

MILES, H. and Miles T. J. 1969. Settlement Sites of the Late Pre-Roman Iron Age in the Somerset Levels. *PSANHS* 113, 17–55.

—— 1973. Trethurgy. *Current Arch.* 40, 142–7.

—— 1975. Pilton, North Devon. Excavations within a Medieval Village. *PDAS* 33, 267–98.

MINTER, E. M. 1973. Eleven Years of Archaeological Work on Dartmoor. *TNHSTP* 16, Part 3, 1972–3, 112–20.

NOALL, CYRIL. 1973. *The St Just Mining District.* Truro.

O'NEILL, B. ST. J. 1934. The Roman Villa at Magor Farm, near Camborne, Cornwall, *J. Brit. Arch. Ass.* 39, 116–75.

—— 1952. The Excavation of Knackyboy Cairn, St Martin's, Scilly. *Ant. J.* 32, 21–34.

—— 1961. *Ancient Monuments of the Isles of Scilly.* HMSO.

PALMER, R. 1976. Interrupted Ditch Enclosures in Britain: The Use of Aerial Photography for Comparative Studies. *PPS* 42, 161–86.

PATCHETT, F. 1951. Cornish Bronze Age Pottery, Part 2. *Arch. J.* 108, 44–65.

PEACOCK. D. 1969a. Neolithic Pottery Production in Cornwall. *Antiquity* 43, 145–9.

—— 1969b. A Contribution to the Study of the Glastonbury Ware from South-Western Britain. *Ant. J.* 49, 41–61.

—— 1969c. A Romano-British Salt-Working Site at Trebarveth, St Keverne. *Cornish Arch.* 8, 47–65.

PEARCE, S. 1978. *The Kingdom of Dumnonia.* Padstow.

PEARSON, M. P. 1978. Churston Court Farm: A Multi-Period Flint Scatter. *DAS Newsletter*, 9, 1978, 3.

Piggot, S. 1938. The Early Bronze Age in Wessex. *PPS* 3, 52–106.

Pollard, S. H. M. 1965. Neolithic and Dark Ages Settlements on High Peak, Sidmouth. *PDAS* 23, 35–59.

—— 1967a. Radiocarbon Dating, Neolithic and Dark Age Settlements on High Peak. *PDAS* 25, 41.

—— 1967b. Seven Prehistoric Sites near Honiton, Devon. Part I. *PDAS* 25, 19–39.

—— 1971. Seven Prehistoric Sites near Honiton, Devon. Part II. *PDAS* 29, 162–80.

—— 1974. A Late Iron Age Settlement and a Romano-British Villa at Holcombe, Near Uplyme, Devon. *PDAS* 32, 59–161.

Pollard, S. H. M. and Russell, P. 1969. Excavation of Round Barrow 248b, Upton Pyne, Exeter. *PDAS* 27, 49–78.

—— 1976. Radio carbon Dating, Excavation of Round Barrow 248b, Upton Pyne, Exeter. *PDAS* 34, 95.

Porter, Edmund. 1971. *Bridgwater Industries, Past and Present*. Bridgwater.

Radford, C. A. R. 1952. Prehistoric Settlements on Dartmoor and the Cornish Moors. *PPS* 18, 55–84.

—— 1958. The Chambered Tomb at Broadsands, Paignton. *PDAES* 5, 147–68.

—— 1962. The Celtic Monastery in Britain. *Arch. Camb.* 111, 1–24.

—— 1970. The Later pre-Conquest Boroughs and Their Defences. *Med. Arch.* 14, 83–103.

—— 1971. Glastonbury Abbey, in Ashe, 1971, 59–78.

Radford, C. A. R. and Swanton, M. 1975. *Arthurian Sites in the West*. University of Exeter.

Rahtz, P. 1963. The Saxon and Medieval Palaces at Cheddar, Somerset, an Interim Report of Excavations in 1960–62. *Med. Arch.* 7, 53–66.

Rahtz, P. and Fowler, P. J. 1972. Somerset AD 400–700, in Fowler 1972, 187–217.

Renfrew, Colin. 1974. ed. *British Prehistory*.

Robertson, R., Gilbert, G. 1979. *Some Aspects of the Domestic Archaeology of Cornwall*. Institute of Cornish Studies and Cornwall Committee for Rescue Archaeology.

Rosenfeld, A. 1964. Excavations in the Torbryan Caves, Devonshire II. Three Holes Cave. *PDAS* 22, 3–26.

Russell, V. and Pool, P. A. S. 1964. Excavation of a Menhir at Try, Gulval. *Cornish Arch.* 3, 15–26.

St Joseph, J. K. 1977. Air Reconnaissance in Roman Britain, 1973–6. *Journal of Roman Studies* 77, 125–6.

Saunders, A. 1977. Excavations at Launceston Castle 1970–76: Interim Report. *Cornish Arch.* 16, 129–37.

Saunders, A. D. 1963. Excavations at Castle Gotha, St Austell: Second Interim Report. *Cornish Arch.* 2, 49–51.

Saunders, C. 1972. The Excavations at Grambla, Wendron, 1972: Interim Report. *Cornish Arch,* 11, 50–2.

SAWYER, P. H. 1976. ed. *Medieval Settlement*.

—— 1976a. Introduction: Early Medieval English Settlement, in Sawyer 1976, 1–7.

SHORTER, A. H., Ravenhill, W. L. D., Gregory, K. J. 1969. *Southwest England*.

SIMMONS, I. G. 1969. Environment and Early Man on Dartmoor. *PPS* 8, 203–19.

SLADER, J. M. 1964. *Days of Renown*. Stoke-on-Trent.

SLEE, A. H. 1952. The Open Fields of Braunton: Braunton Great Field and Braunton Downs. *TDA* 84, 142–9.

SMITH, K. and Wainwright, G. 1978. South Dartmoor, Devon. *PPS* 44, 446–7.

SPENCER, P. J. 1975. Habitat Change in Coastal Sand-Dune: The Molluscan Evidence, in Evans, Limbrey, Cleere, 1975, 96–103.

STAINES, S. 1979. Environmental Change on Dartmoor. *PDAS* 37, 21–47.

STRINGER, C., Andrews, P. and Currant, A. 1979. The Search for Early Man at Westbury. *Royal Anthropological Institute News,* 30, 4–7.

THOMAS, C. 1958. *Gwithian, Ten Years Work, 1949–58*. West Cornwall Field Club, Camborne.

—— 1964. The Henge at Castilly. *Cornish Arch.* 3, 3–14.

—— 1966. The Character and Origins of Roman Dumnonia, in *Rural Settlement in Roman Britain*. CBA Research Report No. 7, ed. Thomas C., 74–98.

—— 1968. *The Christian Antiquities of Camborne*. St Austell.

—— 1968a. Merther Uny, Wendron. *Cornish Arch.* 7, 81–2.

—— 1971. *The Christian Archaeology of North Britain*. Oxford.

—— 1972. The Irish Settlements in Post-Roman Western Britain: A Survey of the Evidence. *JRIC* N.S., 4, 251–74.

—— 1976. Imported Late-Roman Mediterranean Pottery in Ireland and Western Britain: Chronologies and Implications. *Proc. Royal Irish Academy* 76, Section 3, 245–55.

—— 1976a. Introduction to Part II, in Sawyer 1976, 91–3.

—— 1978. Types and Distributions of Pre-Norman Fields in Cornwall and Scilly, in Bowen, Fowler 1978, 7–15.

THOMAS, C., Fowler, P. J. and Gardner, K. 1969. Lundy 1969. *Current Arch.* 16, 138–42.

THOMAS, C. and Wailes, B. 1967. Sperris Quoit: The Excavation of a new Penwith Chamber Tomb. *Cornish Arch.* 6, 9–23.

THREIPLAND, L. M. 1956. An Excavation at St Mawgan-in-Pydar, North Cornwall. *Arch. J.* 113, 33–81.

TIMMS, S. 1976. *Urban Survey of Devon*. DAS/DCRA, unpublished.

Tin. Mineral Resource Consultative Committee. HMSO, undated.

TODD, A. C. and Laws, P. 1972. *The Industrial Archaeology of Cornwall*. Newton Abbot.

TURNER, J. 1978. Field Work on Dartmoor. *DAS Newsletter*, 9, 1978, 2–3.

WACHER, J. 1975. *The Towns of Roman Britain*.

WAINWRIGHT, G. 1960. Three Microlithic Industries from South-West England and their Affinities. *PPS* 26, 193–202.

WAINWRIGHT, G. and Longworth, I. 1971. *Durrington Walls: Excavations 1966–1968*. Reports of the Research Committee of the Society of Antiquaries of London, No. XXIX.

WAINWRIGHT, G., Fleming, A., Smith, K. 1979. The Shaugh Moor Project: First Report. *PPS* 45, 1–35.

WATKINS, T. 1975. ed. *Radiocarbon: Calibration and Prehistory*. Edinburgh.

WEBSTER, G. 1959. An Excavation at Nunnington Park, Wiveliscombe. *PSANHS* 103, 81–91.

WHITTLE, A. W. R. 1977. *The Earlier Neolithic of S. England and its Continental Background. BAR Supplementary Series* 35.

WILLIAMS, H. V. undated. *Cornwall's Old Mines*. Truro.

WILLOCK, E. H. 1936. A Neolithic Site on Haldon. *PDAES* 2, 244–63.

—— 1937. A Further Note on the Neolithic Site at Haldon. *PDAES* 3, 33–43.

WOOD, J. E. and Penny, A. 1975. A Megalithic Observatory on Dartmoor. *Nature* 257, 205–7.

WOOD, J. E. 1978. *Sun, Moon, and Standing Stones*. Oxford.

WOOD, P. D. 1963. Open Field Strips on Forrabury Common, near Boscastle. *Cornish Arch.* 2, 29–33.

WOODS, G. MacAlpine. 1929. A Stone Age Site in East Devon (Beer Head). *PDAES* 1, 10–14.

WORTH, R. H. 1935. Dartmoor Exploration Committee, Twelfth Report. *TDA* 67, 115–30.

—— 1943. The Prehistoric Rounds of Dartmoor. *TDA* 75, 273–302.

YOUINGS, J. 1969. 'The Economic History of Devon, 1300–1700' in *Exeter and its Region*, ed. F. Barlow 1969, 164–74. Exeter.

YOUNG, A. and Richardson, K. M. 1955. Report on the Excavations at Blackbury Castle. *PDAES* 5, 43–67.

INDEX

Page references at the end of each entry in italics refer to figures.

Cannington, 174, 185–6, 265
Carnanton, 157
Carn Brea, 37–8, 40, 44, 47, 56, 114,
116, 129, 238, 257, 263, 266,
269, *39*
Carn Creis, 91
Carn Euny, 110–11, 152, 265, 269, *110*
Carn Gluze (Ballowal), 79, *78*
Carnmenellis, 17, 233
Carnsew, Hayle, 169
Carvossa, 149
Carwynnen, chambered tomb, 54
Castilly, 73
Castle Dor, 103, 105, 106, 269
Castle Gotha, 108, 128, 151, 204, *107*
Castle Neroche, 208, *207*
Castlewich, 73, *74*
Catsgore, 153, 160, *154*
causewayed camps, 39–40
cereals, 33
Chagford, 86, 237
Chard, 225, *226*
Charmouth, 177
Charterhouse-on-Mendip, 140, 150,
270
Cheddar, 166, 193, 198, 262, 266, 271,
193
Chilworthy, 227
china clay, 253–4
Chi-rho monogram, 162, 186, *187*
Cholwichtown, 66, 76, 212
Chun Castle, 116, 168, 269, *174*
Chun Quoit, 53
Churston Court Farm, 40
Chysauster, 111, 152, 270, *152*
cinerary urns, 62
Clovelly Dykes, 105, 269, *105*
Cocksbarrow, 85
Colebrook, 143
Colyton, 213, 216, 270
Combe Martin, 214, 220, 252
Combwich, 149
Congresbury, 161, 168, 185–6, 191
Constantine of Dumnonia, 175
cordoned ware, 103–4, 105, 108, 110,
117, 128, *103*
Corringdon Ball, chambered tomb, 53,
56, 267, *51*
Cotleigh, 131
Crantock, 190

Crediton, 200, 201
Creechbarrow, 178
Crewkerne, 204
Crig-a-Mennis, Perranzabuloe, 65, 264
crosses, 216–17, 270
Crownhill Down, 235
Cuckoo Ball, chambered tomb, 53, 56
Cundodden, 73

daggers (Bronze Age), 85, 89, 91
Dainton Common, 100
Dartmoor, Prehistoric, 17, 26, 29, 30,
40, 53, 55, 66, 69, 70, 75–8, 80, 81,
85–6, 91, 92–9, 104, 119, 120, *51, 93,
95, 97, 98* Roman, 150, medieval and
post-medieval, 208–13, 217, 227,
231, 233–7, 241, 250, 252, 253, 255,
256–7, 272, *209, 229, 251*
Dean Moor, 93–4, 96
Denbury, 105
Deventiasteno, 149
Devon Great Consols, 246–9, *246–7*
dioceses, 162, 192, 200
Doniert's stone, 177, 270
Dorchester, 132, 133, 144, 145, 150,
158, 162
Dozemary Pool, 25
Drewsteignton, 87
Drizzlecombe, 77, 267
Dunster, 208, 223, 271

East Ogwell, 188
East Week, 44, *30*
Embury Beacon, 117–19, *117*
engine houses, 240–1, *239*
entrance graves, 54, 79
Exeter, 133–40, 143–5, 150, 155, 157,
158, 162, 166, 185–6, 192, 196,
200–1, 204, 207, 217, 220, 223,
231–3, 237–8, 254, 265, 270, 272,
134–5, 139, 146–7, 187
Exe Valley, 17, 21, 37, 40, 66, 80, 136,
140, 153
Exmoor, 17, 26, 34, 40, 54, 74, 78–9,
80, 100, 106, 172, 231, 241, 252,
255, *169*

faience, 91
Farway Down, 58, 62, 80, 83, 91, *60,
82, 84*